£13.50

AF850932

# LEGISLATION

AUSTRALIA
The Law Book Company Ltd.
Sydney : Melbourne : Brisbane

CANADA AND U.S.A.
The Carswell Company Ltd.
Agincourt, Ontario

INDIA
N. M. Tripathi Private Ltd.
Bombay
*and*
Eastern Law House Private Ltd.
Calcutta *and* Delhi
M.P.P. House
Bangalore

ISRAEL
Steimatzky's Agency Ltd.
Jerusalem : Tel Aviv : Haifa

MALAYSIA : SINGAPORE : BRUNEI
Malayan Law Journal (Pte.) Ltd.
Singapore

NEW ZEALAND
Sweet & Maxwell (N.Z.) Ltd.
Auckland

PAKISTAN
Pakistan Law House
Karachi

# LEGISLATION

By

DAVID R. MIERS, LL.M., D. Jur.

*Senior Lecturer in Law, University College, Cardiff*

*and*

ALAN C. PAGE, LL.B., Ph.D.

*Senior Lecturer in Law, University of Dundee*

LONDON
SWEET & MAXWELL
1982

*Published in 1982 by*
*Sweet and Maxwell Limited of*
*11 New Fetter Lane, London.*
*Computerset by Promenade Graphics Limited, Cheltenham*
*and printed in Great Britain*
*by T. J. Press (Padstow) Ltd.,*
*Padstow, Cornwall*

**British Library Cataloguing in Publication Data**

Miers, David R.
Legislation.
1. Legislation—Great Britain
I. Title II. Page, Alan C.
328.41'07 JF441

ISBN 0-421-27110-8
ISBN 0-421-27120-5

*All rights reserved.*
*No part of this publication may be*
*reproduced or transmitted, in any form*
*or by any means, electronic, mechanical, photocopying,*
*recording or otherwise, or stored in any retrieval*
*system of any nature, without the written permission*
*of the copyright holder and the publisher, application*
*for which shall be made to the publisher.*

©
D. R. MIERS & A. C. PAGE
1982

*To Maggie and Sheila*

# PREFACE

Legislation constitutes the single most important source of law in our society. Most central government activity is carried on within a statutory framework. The affairs of local authorities, nationalised industries, public corporations and private commerce are defined and directed by legislation. There is hardly any aspect of the education, welfare, health, employment, housing, income and public conduct of the citizen that is not regulated by statute. The preparation, enactment, interpretation and implementation of legislation are therefore matters of the first importance; not just for those whose behaviour is affected by the law, but also for those who are professionally involved in those matters. For governments, the preparation and enactment each year of a legislative programme implementing their manifesto promises and responding to the more routine requests of departments constitute vital features of their terms of office.

Yet in our experience the importance of legislation in our society is seldom fully appreciated by students; in particular they often seem insufficiently aware of, or unfamiliar with, its importance both as a source of law and as the foundation for the majority of substantive law courses studied. This is undoubtedly due in part to the overwhelming emphasis in traditional, and more seriously, in contemporary legal education, on reading and reconciling cases as the main lawyer-like skills to be acquired. Indeed, by virtue of the emphasis placed on case-handling and precedent, legal education seems to be in danger of perpetuating, consciously or unconsciously, that self-same bias in favour of the common law which earlier generations so roundly condemned when manifested by the judiciary in their approach to the interpretation of statutes.

A second reason lies in the generally fragmentary, and in some instances misleading, treatment of legislation in the available literature. Whereas the conception, formulation, enactment, interpretation and implementation of legislation are inter-related activities, they are nowhere dealt with *as a whole,* systematically and comprehensively. They are instead variously addressed, for different purposes and for different audiences, within political science and government, constitutional law, drafting, legal systems and legal method, jurisprudence and the sociology of law. This fragmentary treatment, in our view, seriously limits students' appreciation of the significance and importance of legislation.

In setting out to redress this imbalance we are conscious of the fact that our subject matter was such that everyone would have his or her own ideas about what the book should or should not contain. We were also aware of the enormous value of earlier disparate contributions to this field. These include C. K. Allen's *Law in the Making*, J. A. G. Griffith's early work culminating in his *Parliamentary Scrutiny of Government Bills* and S. A. Walkland's *The Legislative Process in Great Britain.* Where appropriate we have drawn on these contributions and acknowledge our own indebtedness to them. On the other hand, we have consciously sought to avoid the repetition of the more specialised material found in a Thornton, a Craies or a Maxwell as inappropriate for a work of this general nature. Beyond this our aim essentially has been to provide a systematic and comprehensive account of legislation applicable in the United Kingdom from its inception to its implementation. For reasons explained fully in Chapter 1 we conceive of legislation as a mainly government-inspired activity. Consequently we concentrate on public general Acts and their various non-Parliamentary equivalents, in particular, subordinate legislation and Community legislation.

The book originated in our teaching experience at University College, Cardiff, and was jointly conceived and developed. Because of Alan Page's departure for Dundee in 1979, responsibility for the initial draft of individual chapters was divided; Alan Page was responsible for Chapters 1, 3, 5, and 6, David Miers for Chapters 2, 4, 7 and 8.

In writing this work we have inevitably accumulated a great many debts. The greatest of these is owed to Bob Ferguson who, despite the pressure of other commitments, read drafts of all of the chapters and made a great many invaluable suggestions. We would also like to thank Dr. A. Mughan, Professor J. C. Wylie, Professor T. C. Daintith, T. St. J. N. Bates and Professor R. Lempert for reading and commenting on various drafts; Joyce Brunton, Christine Davies and Jennifer Dix for typing the final manuscript; and Susanna Marsh for preparing the index. Finally, our thanks go to our publishers for their assistance, encouragement and forbearance.

ACP

March 1982 DRM

CONTENTS

# TABLE OF CASES

# TABLE OF STATUTES

### AUSTRALIA



### NEW ZEALAND



### EUROPEAN ECONOMIC COMMUNITY

Chapter One

# PRELIMINARY QUESTIONS

This book is primarily about the making, interpretation and impact of legislation applicable in the United Kingdom. In this introductory chapter we examine four preliminary questions. First, what is legislation, how may it be defined and what forms does it assume; secondly, who makes it; thirdly, why is it necessary; and finally, what legal, as opposed to political or conventional, restrictions, if any, are there on those making it?

## WHAT IS LEGISLATION?

### *DEFINITION AND FORMS*

The expression "legislation" is commonly used in at least two senses. First, the expression is used to convey something of the nature of the activity involved: its use denotes the enactment of rules of law or the process of deliberate law-making or law changing. As we shall see not all legislation lays down rules, but this normally constitutes its dominant and explicit purpose. In this respect legislation differs from, for example, adjudication, the primary function of which is the settlement of disputes in accordance with pre-existing rules. To the extent that judges do make law, for example where there is no appropriate rule available, they do so only interstitially within the context of the discharge of their primary function.

The second and more obvious sense in which the expression "legislation" is used is to denote the results or products of the legislative process under discussion; in this sense it may be coterminous with Acts of Parliament in the case of the United Kingdom; Regulations, Directives and Decisions in the case of the European Economic Community and so on. Once again we may distinguish these results or decisions from other decisions including judicial decisions. There are several points of contrast here. To the extent that legislation serves as a mechanism for the settlement of disputes or the resolution of conflicts it frequently embodies compromises and trade-offs between the conflicting interests. Judicial decisions, on the other hand, normally favour one party. In legislative acts the words used are themselves the formulation of the rule; legislative rules are "rules in fixed verbal form."[1] In judicial decisions, on the other hand, the words used by the judge in stating the basis for his decision are treated as only one possible formulation or approximation of the rule, and the rule itself may be recast or reformulated for the purpose of subsequent decisions. However, we regard the most important contrast between legislative and judicial decisions as being the prospective and general qualities of legislative decisions. Legislative decisions normally look to the future and to abstractly defined categories of persons and events. By contrast judicial decisions are retrospective and specific. They are directed in the first place to the past relations and conduct of the parties and to the determination of the dispute between them.

As used in these two senses the expression presupposes a fairly high degree of political and legal differentiation. At a minimum it implies first, as we have suggested, a distinction between general rules which are intended to govern human conduct in an indeterminate number of future instances and individual rules or commands which are intended to apply in a specific instance or a limited number of instances only. Secondly, it implies the existence of some person or agency, the legislature, which is equipped and authorised to promulgate such general rules.[2] Let us examine each of these implications more fully.

Generality is frequently treated as being the hallmark of legislation. Under the EEC Treaty a distinction must be drawn between legislative acts whose validity can be impugned only in severely limited circumstances, and administrative or executive acts whose validity can be challenged more freely. In distinguishing these two categories of acts the European Court has stressed the general and abstract character of legislative acts. " . . . a regulation, being essentially of a legislative nature, is applicable not to a limited number of persons, defined or identifiable, but to categories of persons viewed abstractly and in their entirety . . . a measure which is applicable to objectively determined situations and which involves immediate legal consequences in all Member States for categories of persons viewed in a general and abstract manner cannot be considered as constituting a decision."[3] Some writers have gone so far as to insist that legislation must be general and not particular in

[1] Twinning and Miers, *How To Do Things With Rules* (2nd ed., 1982), pp. 143–144.

[2] Akzin, "Legislation: Nature and Functions", in *International Encyclopaedia of Social Sciences* (Sills ed., 1968), Vol. 9, p. 221.

[3] Cases 16, 17, 19–22/62, *Confédération nationale des producteurs de fruits et légumes* v. *Council* [1962] E.C.R. 471, 478–479.

its scope; a rule which does not fulfill this condition cannot properly be called a law.[4]

If, however, we examine any volume of statutes we immediately come across examples of statutes which do not fulfill this condition. The point was made forcefully by Maitland: " . . . the power of a statute is by no means confined within what a jurist or political philosopher would consider the domain of legislation. A vast number of statutes he would class rather as *privilegia* than as *leges*; the statute lays down no general rule, but deals only with a particular case." An Act authorising expenditure "is certainly not in the jurist's sense a law, it is no general rule, but this minute appropriation of supplies is a most important part of the work of every session, and it is effected by statute; the same formulae is used as though a general law were being made . . . "[5] Neither are these examples confined to what may be termed spending legislation. The War Damages Act 1965 lays down a general rule but it was enacted to deal with a specific case retrospectively. Immunity Acts such as the National Health Service (Invalid Direction) Act 1980 are enacted with the same purpose but make no attempt to lay down a general rule. Nevertheless, despite the fact that these statutes offend against the principle of generality, they enjoy and have the force of law.

Given our inability to reconcile the concept of legislation as general rules with the practice of legislation, we have chosen in this book to concentrate on legislation as the product of specified law-making bodies. The principal body with which we shall be concerned is the Queen in Parliament and, accordingly, we shall be concentrating to a considerable extent on Acts of Parliament, notably those in the form of public general Acts. Such Acts, as the examples above illustrate, may be both general and specific. For our purposes it is the body by which legislation is made which distinguishes legislative rules from other rules of law and from other rules which, as we shall see, may be regarded as legislative in their effect. This formal approach accords with that adopted by other writers.

> "The decisive criterion for identifying legislation as a process and laws as the result of the process is increasingly the formal criterion of the identity of the enacting agency. In a curious reversal of roles, instead of legislation being explained as the activity which aims at the enactment of laws, we tend today to

[4] See *e.g.* Fuller, *The Morality of Law* (1969), pp. 33–94.

[5] Maitland, *The Constitutional History of England* (1908), pp. 382, 385.

> hold as laws those rules which are arrived at by the process of legislation."[6]

Because it is an elected body Parliament occupies a pre-eminent position in the field of law-making in the United Kingdom. Its pre-eminence is reflected in the status of Acts of Parliament as the highest recognised form, and the most important source, of law in the United Kingdom.[7] Parliament is not the only law-making body, however, as a brief historical survey demonstrates.

To the extent that legislative decisions were distinguished from other forms of decisions, the power to make laws was exercised originally by the Crown in the person of the Sovereign. The relationship between this inherent law-making power of the Crown and the rival and supreme legislative authority claimed by Parliament formed one of the key issues in the seventeenth century constitutional struggle between the Crown and Parliament. The outcome of that struggle was to exclude the possibility of its use to create new criminal offences, to impose new obligations on individuals or in any way to alter the general law of the land.[8] Anomalous though it may appear the Crown (in the shape now of the government), therefore retains the power under the Royal Prerogative to legislate within these limits, usually in the form of Orders in Council. Until recently the exercise of that power was of considerable importance in relation to the colonies but to the extent that it has not been superseded or circumscribed by statute it is now of little domestic significance, except in relation to the civil service and the armed forces. Because of this we shall not be concerned with it further in this book, although its propensity to crop up in unexpected ways should not be overlooked. For example, the establishment of a compensation scheme for victims of crimes of violence, the money for which has been duly appropriated by Parliament, has been treated as an example of the exercise of the Crown's legislative prerogative:

> "It may be a novel development in constitutional practice to govern by public statement of intention made by the executive government instead of legislation. But this is no more than a reversion to the ancient practice of government by Royal Proclamation, although it is now subject to the limitations

[6] Akzin, *op. cit.*, p. 222.

[7] For the impact of membership of the European Communities on the status of Acts of Parliament see below, pp. 20–23.

[8] *Case of Proclamations* (1611) 12 Co. Rep. 74.

imposed upon that practice by the development of constitutional law in the seventeenth century."[9]

Although Parliament emerged during the seventeenth century as the supreme law-making body, the expansion in the functions of government from the nineteenth century onwards made it effectively impossible to decide all issues of collective choice in the form of Acts of Parliament. Accordingly the practice developed of delegating specified powers to make legislation to various bodies including government departments. As a result of this development government departments today exercise extensive law-making powers and delegated or subordinate legislation accordingly constitutes a major source of law. The final element in this brief survey is provided by the accession of the United Kingdom to the European Communities in 1973. As a result of membership Community law became part of the law applicable in the United Kingdom. One important source of Community law is legislation made by the institutions in the exercise of the law-making powers transferred to them by the Member States under the Treaties.[10] Because of their importance we shall be concerned in varying degrees with legislation made by government departments and Community institutions during the course of the book. One immediate consequence of this expansion in the number of law-making bodies which may be noted at this point is the need for some mechanism or hierarchy of rules in terms of which conflicts between the legislation made by these bodies may be resolved. We deal with this issue in the last section of this chapter.

One final point may be made. It is possible to examine legislation not as a legal phenomenon in the sense of those decisions which are recognised and enforced as legislation by the courts, but sociologically in the sense of those rules governing human conduct which are regarded as binding by the relevant individuals. Here the essential element is not the attitude of the courts but the mutual expectations and understanding of individuals. Some such rules, for example those of a club or a trade association, may exercise a substantial and pervasive influence on individual behaviour without necessarily being legally recognised and enforceable. When these rules are recognised and enforced, as in the case of custom and usage, they do of course become part of the formal law. In studying legislation it is important to bear in mind the relationship between formal rules, of

[9] *R.* v. *Criminal Injuries Compensation Board, ex. p. Lain* [1967] 2 Q.B. 864, 886, *per* Diplock L.J.. More generally, see Daintith, "Regulation by Contract: The New Prerogative" (1979) 32 C.L.P. 41; and for a recent dramatic example see the Requisitioning of Ships Order 1982.

[10] See below, pp. 167–168.

which legislation is a species, and these informal rules, and the extent to which the latter may act as a substitute for the former. Ministerial and departmental circulars which "advise" local authorities and other bodies how to exercise their powers provide a good example. They are invariably made without statutory backing and they do not assume any recognised legislative form. In the absence of statutory backing they cannot alter existing legal rights and duties. Nevertheless it seems clear that in many areas they are regarded as binding both by those who issue them and those to whom they are addressed.[11]

## *PARLIAMENTARY LEGISLATION*

We have chosen to provide a fuller exposition of the main forms of parliamentary legislation at this point, both for the sake of completeness and because an understanding of these forms constitutes an essential preliminary to the examination of other areas with which we are concerned. Readers who are familiar with this material may prefer to turn to the next section on who legislates.

In examining the forms of parliamentary legislation a clear distinction must be drawn between the form in which Bills are introduced and the forms which they assume once enacted. As regards the former, Bills are either public or private. The main significance of this division is procedural; the class to which a Bill is assigned determines the form and method of its consideration. In addition "these two classes of Bills comprise the two great directions in which the legislative action of Parliament is displayed: it may either be directed to the production of a *public general act*—that is to say, a law affecting the whole public, one which belongs to the *jus generale publicum*—or it may lay down, in the form of an act of Parliament, some special rule affecting only a special section of the nation, what may be called *jus particulare*."[12] This distinction does not correspond exactly to the classification adopted in the statute book which distinguishes three classes of Acts: Public General Acts, Local Acts, and Private and Personal Acts. Whereas Acts in the first and third categories result from public and private Bills respectively, those in the second category, which to add further confusion are commonly described as Private Acts, may result from either private or public Bills.

[11] *e.g.* Joint Circular 46 and 81/78, from the Department of the Environment and the Welsh Office on the implementation of Dir. 77/62 EEC (public supply contracts). Despite the use of the "advisory" form both the context and the attitudes of addressees suggest that circulars such as these are regarded as binding.

[12] Redlich, *The Procedure of the House of Commons* (1908), Vol. 2, pp. 256–257.

## PUBLIC GENERAL ACTS

Public general Acts constitute the predominant and characteristic form of parliamentary legislation. As we have seen they are introduced in the form of public Bills. A public Bill "which affects a particular private interest in a manner different from the private interests of other persons or bodies of the same category or class"[13] is called a hybrid Bill. The enactment of such Bills is governed by a special procedure incorporating elements of both public and private Bill procedure. When enacted they too become public general Acts.

### Classification of Public General Acts

An Act of Parliament, whether a public general Act or otherwise, is composed of a series of parts some of which are essential such as the title and enacting formula, others of which, such as the preamble, are merely optional. The main feature of this form is its extreme elasticity which enables its adoption to the infinite variety of subjects upon which legislation may be enacted. Legislation may be enacted in pursuance of major items of party policy,[14] on constitutional matters,[15] in the implementation of international or Community obligations,[16] or in pursuance of minor aspects of administration or law reform.[17] Given this variety any attempt to classify the public general Acts themselves must be tentative and susceptible to contradiction. Indeed no attempt is made in the annual volumes of *Public General Acts and Measures* to classify Acts other than that they are printed chronologically in these volumes according to their chapter number which represents the order in which they received the Royal Assent.

Nevertheless the perceived disadvantages of this system have been among the factors which have led to attempts to formulate alternative systems of classifying the statutes. These alternative classifications vary according to the purpose for which they were devised. Two broad series of purposes may be identified. First, given that one of the primary shortcomings of the traditional classificatory system of chronological arrangement is that it does not present the user of the statutes with all the relevant legislation on a subject in one place, considerable and recurrent efforts have been devoted to devising a classification which would enable the user to discover

[13] Erskine May, *Parliamentary Practice* (19th ed., 1976), p. 862.
[14] *e.g.* Social Security Act 1979; Local Government, Planning and Land Act 1980.
[15] *e.g.* Government of Ireland Act 1920; European Communities Act 1972.
[16] *e.g.* European Assembly Elections Act 1981; Companies Act 1980.
[17] *e.g.* Bees Act 1980; Charging Orders Act 1979.

quickly and accurately the statutory law on a given topic. Under this system, which is adopted in *Statutes in Force*, statutes which are considered to belong to a common category are assembled together in a group under a single title such as "agency," "agriculture," "ancient monuments and memorials," "animals" and "armed forces." There are however considerable difficulties in choosing the categories which are to be used as the organisational basis. Although there are certain well established legal categories, these do not present themselves as pre-determined or as uncontroversial; there may be genuine disagreement as to the appropriateness of choosing one category in preference to another.[17a] Moreover, individual statutes often deal with more than one subject.

Secondly, a number of classifications have been advanced with a view to reform. Areas in which reform has been sought on the basis of new or revised classifications include parliamentary procedure and statutory interpretation. As regards the former the main aim has been the development of appropriate parliamentary procedures for the consideration of different types of Bills. For example, it has been suggested that a distinction should be drawn between "policy" Bills and Bills which are of a mainly "administrative" character and which do not in themselves raise issues of policy. These administrative Bills would be dealt with more quickly than policy Bills.[18] In relation to statutory interpretation revised classifications have been advanced as the basis for the development of rational and systematic criteria for the interpretation of statutes. For example, Friedmann has argued that although "there is no magic guide to the proper interpretation of statutes, a differentiation between various types of statutes should greatly assist an intelligent and rational approach to statutory construction." In pursuance of this aim the main categories of statutes which he distinguished were, constitutional statutes, statutes implementing a specific social objective, statutes carrying out specific legal reforms, statutes implementing international conventions, penal statutes, taxation statutes and, lastly, statutes whose effects are predominantly technical.[19]

## LOCAL AND PRIVATE ACTS

Whereas public Bills are introduced for the general benefit, private Bills are introduced for the particular interest or benefit of some

[17a] *cf. Statutes in Force* and *Halsbury's Statutes*.

[18] Drewry, "Legislation" in *The Commons Today* (Walkland and Ryle ed., 1981), pp. 110–112.

[19] *Law and Social Change in Contemporary Britain* (1951), pp. 239–265. See further below, p. 207.

person or body of persons, for example, the shareholders of a company or the inhabitants of a borough, city or county. As such they constitute one among a number of forms of what may be described generically, for the sake of convenience, as private legislation. Historically private legislation represents one of the last vestiges of Parliament's judicial function. It is defined by Erskine May as "legislation of a special kind for conferring particular powers or benefits on any person or body of persons—including individuals, local authorities, statutory companies, or private corporations—in excess of or in conflict with the general law."[20]

## Classification of Private Legislation

Private legislation may take the following four forms: (1) Private Bills; (2) Bills for confirming Provisional Orders; (3) orders subject to special parliamentary procedure under the Statutory Orders (Special Procedure) Acts 1945 and 1965 and Bills presented in pursuance of those Acts; and (4) Bills for confirming Provisional Orders under the Private Legislation Procedure (Scotland) Act 1936.

### *Private Bills*

As a proportion of the annual legislative output of Parliament the significance of private Bills has declined markedly. This can be seen most clearly in relation to personal Acts which relate solely to the "estate, property, status or style, or otherwise to the personal affairs of individuals." Since 1948 only nine such Acts have been passed. Although Local Acts are of greater importance in that they represent a continuing source of powers for local authorities, they have undergone a similar decline.[21]

Two factors account for the decline in the significance of private Bills from the point of view of both individuals and local authorities. The first of these factors was the introduction of the three alternative forms of private legislation outlined below. More generally the necessity for such legislation has been reduced as a result of the enactment of public general Acts, the provisions of which may be adopted by local authorities, and more importantly, amendments to the general law allowing individuals to achieve results which previously could only be effected by private Bill procedure. Changes in status such as divorce or naturalisation can now be brought about

[20] *Op. cit.*, p. 857.

[21] See now Local Government Act 1972, s.239; Local Government (Scotland) Act 1973, s.82; Study of Parliament Group, "Private Bill Procedure: A Case for Reform" (1981) P.L. 206.

by administrative acts or judicial decree under general enabling legislation and in this respect, as in others, public general Acts now constitute a far more significant source of rights and powers for individuals than private Acts.

*Bills for confirming Provisional Orders*

Procedure by way of provisional order was introduced during the nineteenth century as a simpler means of enabling, for example, local authorities to obtain powers other than by way of private Bill procedure. The main object of this reform was to reduce the costs to the parties and the time spent by Parliament in the consideration of private Bills. This was effected by statutorily delegating to the relevant government department the task of considering any applications for increased powers. The first Act making such provision was enacted in 1845[22] and the system rapidly became widespread particularly in relation to local government. Under it Ministers are empowered, on the application of an interested party and after the necessary procedural requirements have been complied with, to make a provisional order, the order then being given legal effect or confirmed by a Provisional Order Confirmation Bill introduced for that purpose. Provisional order procedure is now virtually obsolete, having been effectively replaced by special procedure orders, and with the exception of the Private Legislation Procedure (Scotland) Act 1936, very few powers remain to make provisional orders requiring confirmation by a confirming Bill.[23]

*Orders subject to special parliamentary procedure under the Statutory Orders (Special Procedure) Acts 1945 and 1965, and Bills presented in pursuance of these acts*

If the significant contribution to private legislation in the nineteenth century was made by the introduction of provisional order procedure, the equivalent contribution in the present century has been made by the introduction of special parliamentary procedure which has effectively taken the process of rationalisation one step further by removing the need for confirming legislation save in exceptional circumstances. The acceptance by the major political parties of the necessity for increasing the amount of time available after the war for the enactment of reconstruction legislation, provoked considerable interest in alternative methods of enacting legislation and a general reassessment of existing legislative

[22] Port, *Administrative Law* (1929), p. 113.

[23] For a list see Erskine May, *op. cit.*, pp. 1024–1025; and see Local Government Act 1972, s.240.

methods. As regards private Bill procedure this reassessment led to the enactment of the Statutory Orders (Special Procedure) Act 1945. The provisions of this Act, as amended, apply to any order made or confirmed under an Act which confers a power on an authority to make or confirm such orders and which also provides that they shall be subject to special parliamentary procedure. While provision is made for the consideration of these orders by Parliament, in that they may be annulled by resolution of either House, they do not normally require further confirmation. The procedure on orders relating only to Scotland has been assimilated so far as possible to that followed under the Private Legislation Procedure (Scotland) Act 1936.

*Bills for confirming Provisional Orders under the Private Legislation Procedure (Scotland) Act 1936*

As the territorial exceptions mentioned above indicate, there are differences between the system of private legislation which applies to England and Wales and the system applicable to Scotland. In Scotland the effective result of the Private Legislation Procedure (Scotland) Act 1899 as amended was, save in respect of Estate Bills, to replace private Bill procedure by the system now set out in the consolidating enactment, the Private Legislation Procedure (Scotland) Act 1936. Parties who wish "to obtain parliamentary powers in regard to any matter affecting public or private interests in Scotland," instead of presenting a petition for a private Bill must petition the Secretary of State to make a provisional order. As with provisional order procedure that order is then given legal effect by a confirmation Bill enacted for that purpose.

## WHO LEGISLATES?

The second question which we identified was who makes legislation. It should be clear from the above analysis that the answer to this question will vary in accordance with the form of legislation under discussion. However, two basic forms of law-making may be distinguished: institutional law-making, whereby laws are made by a person or institution recognised as having the power and the authority to validly declare laws; and contractual law-making, whereby the rules governing the future conduct of the parties to the contract are made by agreement between them.[24]

Although our concern is with institutional law-making, one of the

[24] On contractual law-making see further Turpin, *Government Contracts* (1972), p. 97.

premisses upon which this work is based is that despite the analytical differences between them, both forms of law-making *may* in practice display considerable similarities. Thus contractual law-making may serve regulatory ends and be as coercive in its impact as institutional law-making. As Kessler notes in respect of standard-form contracts: "Freedom of contract enables enterprisers to legislate by contract and, what is even more important, to legislate in a substantially authoritarian manner without using the appearance of authoritarian forms."[25] Equally we would argue that institutional law-making is based upon implied notions of agreement and consent (real or imagined). The lineage of these ideas may be traced to the contract-based political theory advanced by Hobbes and Locke in terms of which consent forms the only legitimate basis for the exercise of the coercive power of government. These ideas have important consequences for our treatment of the legislative process. Not only may we regard the legislature as the institutional mechanism for the attainment and maintenance of that consensus, but we may also view the legislative process as on occasion involving the continuous making and remaking of that consensus, a process graphically described by Aneurin Bevan in the context of delegated legislation as "legislation by negotiation."[26]

Turning against this background to the primary focus of our concern—public legislation in the United Kingdom—the legally correct answer to our question is that such legislation is made by the Queen in Parliament. While legally correct, as a description of actual practice this answer is highly misleading, for, with the exception of the restricted opportunities for private Members, legislation is in practice a function of government. As Griffith observes:

> "When Parliament is called the Legislature what is meant is that no body or person can issue an order, rule, regulation, scheme or enactment having the force of law without Parliamentary authority. But it does not follow that Parliament is responsible for the whole of the legislative process or that an enactment which Parliament has not specifically examined is invalid. In other words, 'to legislate' may mean either to authorise the action which turns a legislative proposal into a law or to carry through the whole legislative process. In this

[25] "Contracts of Adhesion—Some Thoughts About Freedom of Contract" (1943) 54 Col. Law Rev. 629, 640. On the use by government of contract terms as a regulatory device see Turpin, *op. cit.*, pp. 244–259; Daintith *op.cit.*

[26] Report from the Select Committee on Delegated Legislation (1953; H.C. 310), Minutes of Evidence p. 145.

> latter sense legislation today is more a Governmental than a Parliamentary function."[27]

Or as Amery puts it:

> "Parliament is not, and never has been, a legislature, in the sense of a body specially and primarily empowered to make laws. The function of legislation, while shared between 'King, Lords and Commons in Parliament assembled' has always been predominantly exercised by Government, which, indeed, has never allowed Parliament as such to take any initiative in one of its most important fields, that of finance."[28]

The government's position as the government and its domination in practice of the legislative process are intimately connected. At one level the relationship may be treated as justified by reference to principle: without the capacity to legislate the government would not be able, in any meaningful sense of the term, to govern. This argument was clearly expressed by politicians in the mid-nineteenth century.

> "Those to whom the executive authority is entrusted, have also the duty of recommending to the legislature the measures it should adopt, and must retire if their advice is not generally followed. By this arrangement the executive government is able to act with the vigour which the assurance of having its policy supported when necessary by legislation can alone give to it. . . . Constantly the executive government of a great nation is compelled to apply to the legislature for new powers, or new laws, to meet exigencies that arise. How greatly its action would be crippled, if it could not depend upon obtaining the assistance of this kind which it requires."[29]

It is this argument which underlies the widespread recognition and acceptance of the view that the government both has the right and is under a duty to introduce legislation. At a more empirical level it is simply because the government is the government that it dominates the legislative process in practice. Consequently, its domination of the process stems from those factors which make it the government, in particular its command of a majority in the House of Commons upon which it can normally rely to vote in its favour. The control

[27] "The Place of Parliament in the Legislative Process" (1951) 14 M.L.R. 279, 290–291.

[28] *Thoughts on the Constitution* (2nd ed., 1954), pp. 11–12.

[29] Grey, *Parliamentary Government* (1858), pp. 16–17; and see Griffith, "Legislation" in *The Commons in Transition* (Hanson and Crick ed., 1970), pp. 22–23.

which this gives the government is buttressed by the exclusive possession of the initiative in relation to finance which as Campion observes, has "long given the government the chief role in legislation,"[30] and its control of the timetable.[31]

Historically this dominance was established during the course of the nineteenth century as a corollary of the expanding responsibilities of government. Before the first Reform Act of 1832 responsibility for the initiation of legislation was largely left to individual peers or members of the House of Commons.[32] During the following decades this responsibility became increasingly to be seen as a function of government.[33] Summarising the changes that took place during the course of the nineteenth century Walkland writes that this period "essentially saw a nationalisation and centralisation of legislative initiative in the hands of the government, a massive supplementation of Private Bill procedure by government-introduced Public General Acts, and a marked diminution in the opportunities for private members to legislate."[34] By the end of the century this transformation was complete. "Only in form" Parris writes, "was parliament a law-making body: in substance the law was made elsewhere."[35]

If then Parliament is no longer the "meeting ground and decision-forming organ for the national community as a whole . . . the centre which forged the general rules to prevail in the competitive game, out of the multitude of divergent individual interests,"[36] what are its functions in relation to legislation? First, by signifying its assent to legislative proposals, Parliament performs a legitimating function both in the narrow legal sense of giving them the force of law and in the wider sociological sense of investing them with democratic credentials. "The House of Commons is essentially a body in which the backbench members ratify decisions taken elsewhere. It legitimises but does not legislate."[37] Beyond this the existence of the party system makes it difficult to arrive at any universally agreed set of functions. Prior to the emergence of representative government Parliament could be viewed as an essentially homogeneous institution with a collective interest and

[30] *Parliament : A Survey* (1952), p. 26.

[31] See below, pp. 107 *et seq.*

[32] Holdsworth, *A History of English Law* (1938), Vol. XI, p. 371.

[33] Walkland, *The Legislative Process in Great Britain* (1969), pp. 14–15; Parris, *Constitutional Bureaucracy* (1969), pp. 168–170.

[34] "Government Legislation in the House of Commons" in *The House of Commons in the Twentieth Century* (Walkland ed., 1979), p. 247.

[35] *Op. cit.*, p. 184.

[36] Kircheimer, *Politics, Law, and Social Change* (1969), p. 181.

[37] Hanson and Walles, *Governing Britain* (3rd ed., 1980), p. 69.

purpose distinct from and frequently opposed to that of government. Given however that Parliament is now at one and the same time the institution from which the party element in government is drawn and the forum in which that element exercises power there is, in theory at least, an identity of purposes between the permanent element in government and the majority party for the time being. It is in this sense that Mackintosh writes: "the chief function of the House of Commons [is] to support the government of the day, to defend its policies and carry its legislation."[38]

It by no means follows from this that, as is sometimes asserted, Parliament is simply a rubber stamp. The fulfilment of a government's legislative programme requires the effective and repeated mobilisation of its majority. If the capacity to legislate depends in the first place upon the command of the support of a majority in the House of Commons, and thereafter upon the retention of its support, then anything which threatens to deprive it of that majority, such as the likelihood of defeat at a general election or of transfers of allegiance from one party to another, or which calls its existence into question on a particular issue, such as the possibility of a backbench revolt, must impose constraints upon the legislative proposals brought forward by a government. Because these constraints imposed by the parliamentary system are invisible, being reflected in what governments do not do rather than in what they do, they tend to be ignored. They are nevertheless real. Moreover, in their existing form the procedural stages which must be completed before Parliament signifies its assent to proposals provide their opponents, whether from within the governing party or from other parties, with the opportunity to make their views known and to seek their amendment. These opportunities are examined more fully in Chapter 5 below.

## THE NECESSITY FOR LEGISLATION

Attitudes to legislation vary markedly ranging from, on the one hand, the belief that everything can be "well fixt by a good law"[39] to, on the other hand, a general unwillingness to contemplate recourse to legislation except as a last resort:

> "The administrator's general practice . . . has been to shun legislation where other means can achieve his ends. He prefers to see things taking shape in the real world before he invents an

[38] Mackintosh, *The Government and Politics of Britain* (3rd ed., 1975), p. 39.
[39] Quoted in Harper, *The English Navigation Acts* (1939), p. 381.

> elaborate legal construction, because he knows with such a construction, devised *in vacuo*, nothing may ever correspond. In an obscure way, he is not unfriendly to the old conception of law as custom, and where the subject matter of the business allows he may try to stimulate a habit of behaviour and recommend legislation only where the habit is widely enough diffused to bring effective enforcement reasonably within sight."[40]

Whatever the attitude to legislation there are certain circumstances in which its enactment constitutes a necessary part of the attainment of given policy objectives. The necessity for legislation in these circumstances stems from two related sources: law and constitutional convention. As a matter of law, legislation is required, first, for effecting changes in the law. In particular it is required for effecting changes in existing legislation and in existing rights and duties derived from the common law except insofar as, in the case of the latter, the common law itself provides an alternative mechanism for their alteration, for example, by agreement.[41] Secondly parliamentary approval expressed in the form of legislation is required for the levying of taxation.[42] The general legislative expression of this requirement is the annual Finance Act, and it is similarly reflected in legislation authorising the levying of special taxes such as the Petroleum Revenue Tax Act 1980.[43]

The same requirement applies to central government expenditure, the requisite legislative authorisation being provided by the annual Appropriation Acts. However, as Daintith has pointed out, although the only formal requirement regarding legislative authority for government spending is that the amount and purpose for which it is incurred should be covered by an appropriate heading or vote in each year's Appropriation Act, governments almost invariably seek in addition long-term or permanent statutory sanction for policies involving continuing expenditure, despite the absence of any legal necessity for such legislation.[44] This is exemplified by such measures as successive Export Credit Guarantee Acts. The source of this practice is not law, but rather constitutional convention as formulated and enforced by the Treasury in conjunction with the

[40] Sisson, *Spirit of British Administration* (1959), p. 72.

[41] *Case of Proclamations* (1611) 12 Co. Rep. 74; Bill of Rights 1689, Arts. 1 and 2.

[42] Bill of Rights 1689, Art. 4.

[43] On the importance of the legislative form in this respect see *Bowles* v. *Bank of England* [1913] 1 Ch. 59.

[44] "Public and Private Enterprise in the United Kingdom" in *Public and Private Enterprises in Mixed Economics* (Friedmann ed., 1974), p. 212.

Comptroller and Auditor-General and the Public Accounts Committee of the House of Commons. It is, Turpin observes, "a convention of long standing that where continuing functions are to be exercised by a government department, particularly if these will result in commitments to expenditure beyond a given financial year, the power to incur the expenditure should be defined by statute."[45]

The great proportion of legislation enacted annually in the United Kingdom can be explained by one or a combination of these legal and conventional requirements.[46] Where they are applicable they also mean that an opportunity is afforded for parliamentary consideration of the underlying policy. Although this is not a book about the significance of law within the system of government, it may be noted by way of conclusion that it by no means follows from this that all government policies must be submitted for parliamentary consideration and approval in the form of legislation. In the United Kingdom the emphasis in legislation has always been on implementing rather than expressing policies and to the extent that alternative mechanisms are available to governments, policies need not be sanctioned by legislation. Apart from simple agreement government may rely on its economic power through, for example, the insertion of fair wages and racial discrimination clauses in government contracts. Equally it may use the threat of legislation as in the case of the securities market to induce compliance with a desired pattern of behaviour or the establishment of a scheme of self-regulation as an alternative or a complement to statutory regulation. Finally where its powers are sufficiently broad it may rely on the manipulation of the existing legal framework, and in particular on the exploitation of the opportunities afforded by it to achieve its ends, as in the enforcement of pay policy during the latter years of the Labour Governments 1974–79. Compared to legislation each of these alternatives has its deficiences in terms of scope, clarity and certainty of result. Nevertheless they exist as significant alternatives to regulation by statute which can be pressed into service as circumstances dictate.

[45] *Op. cit.*, p. 19. On the uncertainties surrounding the interpretation and application of the "normal rule" as thus expressed, see Daintith, "Public and Private Enterprise in the United Kingdom", *op. cit.*, pp. 210–213.

[46] Legislation may also be enacted to "declare" the law, or for solely political reasons. One of the best examples of the latter was the Supplies and Services (Extended Purposes) Act 1947. The legal changes which it introduced in the Government's powers under the Supplies and Services (Transitional Powers) Act 1945 were largely minor and there seems little doubt that it was enacted as an expression of the government's commitment to overcoming the economic crisis.

## RESTRICTIONS ON THE LEGISLATURE

Leaving aside for the moment the position of Community law we have seen that constitutionally legislation in the United Kingdom is made by the Queen in Parliament. The final question which we identified for discussion was whether there were any *legally* enforceable restraints on the exercise by the legislature as thus defined of its law-making powers. At one time the answer to this question would have been a categorical and unequivocal no. More recently, however, the legal consequences of the accession of the United Kingdom to the European Communities and discussions of the possibility of creating such restraints for the future, most notably in the form of a Bill of Rights, have prompted a reassessment of that answer.

As the source of that negative answer our starting point must be the doctrine of the legislative sovereignty or supremacy of Parliament as traditionally formulated and understood. For Dicey, who expounded the doctrine in its classic form, the doctrine meant legally[47] "neither more nor less than this, namely, that Parliament . . . has, under the English constitution, the right to make or unmake any law whatever; and further, that no person or body is recognised by the law of England as having a right to override or set aside the legislation of Parliament." Stated positively, Dicey continued, the doctrine meant that: "Any Act of Parliament, or any part of an Act of Parliament, which makes a new law, or repeals or modifies an existing law, will be obeyed by the courts." Stated negatively it meant that: "There is no person or body of persons who can, under the English constitution, make rules which override or derogate from an Act of Parliament, or which (to express the same thing in other words) will be enforced by the courts in contravention of an Act of Parliament."[48]

As thus formulated three features of the doctrine appear to us to merit emphasis. First, as regards the legislative competence of the Queen in Parliament, the doctrine recognises in Parliament the sole and exclusive right to enact legislation. By virtue of that monopoly only Parliament, and by definition no one else, has the right to make or change the law. Admittedly there are, on their face, exceptions to this proposition. As we have seen legislation may be made by the

[47] On the political content of the doctrine, see Wilson, *Cases and Materials on Constitutional and Administrative Law* (2nd ed., 1976), pp. 225–228.

[48] *An Introduction to the Study of the Law of the Constitution* (10th ed., 1959), pp. 39–40. On whether the doctrine as thus stated applies throughout the United Kingdom, see Mitchell, *Constitutional Law* (2nd ed., 1968), pp. 69–74; Wade and Phillips, *Constitutional and Administrative Law* (9th ed., 1977), pp. 77–80.

government alone by virtue of delegated legislative powers or the Royal Prerogative and by the courts in the exercise of their adjudicative functions. The point to note, however, about these apparent exceptions is that they are carried on either under the authority of Parliament as in the case of delegated legislation, or with its implied acquiescence as in the case of judicial law-making or the exercise of the remaining prerogative powers to legislate. In the last analysis the exercise of these law-making powers can be overridden by the express will of Parliament.[49] Secondly, and relatedly, the doctrine denies the existence of any legal limitations on the subject matter of the exercise of Parliament's law-making powers. In Sir Edward Coke's famous phrase, the power and jurisdiction of Parliament "is so transcendent and absolute, as it cannot be confined either for causes or persons within any bounds."[50] Finally, as regards the results of the legislative process, by denying the existence of any legal restraints on Parliament's legislative powers and, in particular, the competence of the courts to pass upon Acts of Parliament, the doctrine recognises them as the highest form of law in the United Kingdom to which all other forms of legislation are ultimately subordinate and by reference to which the validity of these other forms may be judicially assessed. Confronted with an Act of Parliament the competence of the courts is restricted to its interpretation and application.

As was suggested above, the reassessment to which the doctrine has been subject in the light of recent political and constitutional developments has weakened the case for its uncritical and unqualified acceptance and accordingly as formulated it should be approached with a degree of caution. Given that it represents the rationalisation of a particular pattern of constitutional development—the initially successful denial by Parliament of any rival law-making power to its own[51]—it cannot be assumed *a priori* that its content will remain unchanged no matter what constitutional realignments take place or, more materially, that because the courts have in the past eschewed any signs of willingness to review the competence of legislation they will continue to do so in the future.

[49] Given that, as we have seen, parliamentary legislation is a function of government there is, of course, no incentive for government to restrict its prerogative power to legislate.

[50] 4 Co. Inst. 36.

[51] It is arguable that some of the developments reviewed above, notably ministerial circulars, represent a weakening of Parliament's legislative monopoly.

## *THE IMPACT OF THE COMMUNITIES*

The greatest impetus to the reassessment of the doctrine has stemmed from the accession of the United Kingdom to the European Communities. According to the constant jurisprudence of the European Court the two fundamental ideas upon which Community law is based are, first, that it constitutes a separate system of law or "new legal order" and, secondly, that in cases of conflict between Community law and national law the former takes precedence over the latter. These ideas were clearly expressed by the Court in its judgment in *Costa* v. *E.N.E.L.*:

> ". . . the EEC Treaty has created its own legal system which, on the entry into force of the Treaty, became an integral part of the legal systems of the Member States and which their courts are bound to apply.
>
> By creating a Community of unlimited duration, having its own institutions, its own personality, its own legal capacity and capacity of representation on the international plane and, more particularly, real powers stemming from a limitation of sovereignty or a transfer of powers from the States to the Community, the Member States have limited their sovereign rights, albeit within limited fields, and have thus created a body of law which binds both their nationals and themselves.
>
> The integration into the laws of each Member State of provisions which derive from the Community and more generally the terms and the spirit of the Treaty, make it impossible for the States, as a corollary, to accord precedence to a unilateral and subsequent measure over a legal system accepted by them on a basis of reciprocity. Such a measure cannot therefore be inconsistent with that legal system. The executive force of Community law cannot vary from one State to another in deference to subsequent domestic laws, without jeopardising the attainment of the objectives of the Treaty. . . . "[52]

In relation to the doctrine of the legislative supremacy of Parliament three features of this separate system of law stand out. First, Regulations made by the Community institutions in the exercise of the legislative powers conferred upon them by the EEC Treaty are directly applicable, that is they form part of the law applicable within Member States without any intervening act on the part of the domestic legislature being either necessary or, indeed,

[52] Case 6/64 [1964] E.C.R. 585, 593–594.

permissible.[53] Secondly, in certain well-defined circumstances Community law, whether contained in provisions of the Treaties, Regulations or, exceptionally, Directives and Decisions, is directly effective, that is it confers rights upon individuals which national courts are obliged to uphold. Finally, as we have indicated, in cases of conflict between Community law and national law the necessity of ensuring the uniform application of Community law requires that precedence be given to the former over the latter. The consequences of this for national courts were stated unambiguously by the European Court in its judgment in the *Simmenthal case*: " . . . every national court must, in a case within its jurisdiction, apply Community law in its entirety and protect rights which the latter confers on individuals and must accordingly set aside any provision of national law which may conflict with it, whether prior or subsequent to the Community rule."[54]

The consequences of the foregoing for the doctrine, however characterised, are clearly far-reaching. First, the Queen in Parliament no longer has a monopoly of law-making power. As long as the United Kingdom remains a member of the Communities, the institutions of the Communities can enact legislation which is applicable within the United Kingdom. This consequence was recognised and allowed for by the European Communities Act 1972, section 2(1) of which provides:

> "All such rights, powers, liabilities, obligations and restrictions from time to time created or arising by or under the Treaties, and all such remedies and procedures from time to time provided for by or under the Treaties, as in accordance with the Treaties are without further enactment to be given legal effect or used in the United Kingdom shall be recognised and available in law, and be enforced, allowed and followed accordingly; and the expression 'enforceable Community right' and similar expressions shall be read as referring to one to which this subsection applies."[55]

Secondly, accession involved the acceptance of restrictions on the subject-matter of the exercise of Parliament's competence. The transfer of legislative powers to the Communities involved by necessary implication the renunciation of any parallel capacity to legislate within those areas covered by the Treaties, save to the

[53] EEC Treaty, Art. 189; Case 34/73, *Variola* v. *Italian Finance Administrative* [1973] E.C.R. 981.

[54] Case 106/77 *Italian Finance Administration* v. *Simmenthal* [1978] E.C.R. 629, 644.

[55] And see, *ibid.*, s. 3.

extent allowed for by Community law itself. Given that, as we have seen, legislation in the United Kingdom is a function of government there was no need for this consequence to be recognised by statute. All that was necessary was for the government itself to refrain from seeking the enactment of legislation inconsistent with Community law.

What is the position, however, where the government fails inadvertently or deliberately to observe this self-imposed limitation? It is in these circumstances that the most significant implications for the doctrine arise. Whereas Community law requires priority to be accorded to it over conflicting provisions of national law, in terms of the doctrine of the sovereignty of Parliament the judiciary cannot review the competence of national legislation and, moreover, are obliged to give effect to it. In recognition of this potential conflict section 2(4) of the European Communities Act 1972 provides that " . . . any enactment passed or to be passed . . . shall be construed and have effect subject to the foregoing provisions of this section . . . " namely, section 2(1) incorporating those provisions of Community law conferring "enforceable Community rights" upon individuals. The judiciary are thus enjoined to interpret and apply domestic legislation in a manner consistent with Community law. The discharge of that task in turn raises the possibility that where conflicts do arise which cannot be resolved by interpretation effect will be denied to inconsistent provisions of domestic law.

Against this it has been argued that none of the foregoing consequences materially affect the doctrine. In particular the effectiveness of section 2(4) of the European Communities Act 1972 against implied or express repeal has been questioned on the grounds, first, that in terms of the doctrine, no Parliament can bind its successors, and secondly that the related maxim of statutory interpretation, *lex posterior derogat priori*, means that effect must be given to the most recent expression of the intention of the legislature. A court confronted with a conflict between a provision of Community law and a subsequent Act of Parliament, would, it is argued, on both grounds be obliged to give effect to domestic law.[56]

Whether the courts would do so depends ultimately on the judicial response to the fact of membership. It is too early to say with any confidence whether the courts will deny the capacity of Parliament to abrogate or diminish rights conferred by Community law. In the absence of any express reference to the European Communities Act 1972 the Court of Appeal has accorded priority to Article 119 of the EEC Treaty against a conflicting and subsequent

[56] See *e.g.* Hood Phillips, *Constitutional and Administrative Law* (6th ed., 1978), p. 99.

provision of an Act of Parliament.[57] Yet in the same case Lord Denning M.R. added: "If the time should come when our Parliament deliberately passes an Act with the intention of repudiating the Treaty or any provision in it or intentionally of acting inconsistently with it and says so in express terms then I should have thought that it would be the duty of our courts to follow the statute of our Parliament."[58] In one important sense, however, concern with this issue and the related question of the capacity of the United Kingdom to withdraw from the Communities, and as a consequence to reassert the legislative supremacy of the Queen in Parliament, misses the fundamental point, which is that so long as membership continues Community law *does* form part of the law applicable within the United Kingdom; that the government is *obliged* by the Treaties to refrain from seeking the enactment of legislation inconsistent with Community law and has done so; and finally, that if the precedent of the Court of Appeal is to be followed and built upon, that obligation is *enforceable* in proceedings before domestic courts.

It should be emphasised that these limitations are confined to the scope of Community law. Although in terms of the Treaties that scope is envisaged as an increasing one, membership by itself has no implications for the doctrine outside the boundaries of the Communities' competence. What, however, of the possibility of other limitations?

## *A BILL OF RIGHTS?*

During the 1970s the proposal that a Bill of Rights should be enacted for the United Kingdom attracted a considerable degree of support. That support covered a wide range of the political spectrum and reflected an equally wide range of concerns. On the positive side proponents of the proposal argued that greater status should be accorded to certain basic or fundamental rights and liberties than previously has been the case. On the negative side some proponents of the proposal argued that, as a corollary, restrictions should be imposed on the competence of Parliament to legislate in defiance of these rights.

Apart from the major question of the content of the rights and liberties to be protected, this proposal raised two other issues with a

[57] *MacCarthys* v. *Smith* [1980] 3 W.L.R. 929.
[58] [1979] 3 All E.R. 325, 329.

direct bearing on the doctrine of the sovereignty of Parliament.[59] The first of these issues was whether these rights and liberties should be given some special status or entrenched against subsequent legislative attempts at their variation or abrogation. Secondly and relatedly, would such limitations be enforceable? In particular, would they be legally enforceable with the consequence that the judiciary would be vested with the power to review the validity of legislation which it was claimed was incompatible with the rights and liberties laid down? Some proponents of a Bill of Rights have seen no need for its entrenchment or judicial enforcement. The legislative recognition accorded to these rights would by itself be sufficient to prevent or deter their subsequent variation or abrogation.[60] Others have argued the case for their limited entrenchment against implied variation or repeal along the lines of section 2(4) of the European Communities Act 1972. Still others have argued in favour of "a constitutional law which it is the duty of the courts to protect even against the power of Parliament."[61] The support which emerged for a Bill of Rights during the 1970s was insufficient to overcome the widespread lack of agreement which the debate revealed both on the question of the content of the rights and liberties to be protected and the questions of their entrenchment and enforcement. For the moment, at least, the issue is in abeyance.

[59] For an excellent review of the general issues, see Wallington and McBride, *Civil Liberties and a Bill of Rights* (1976).
[60] See *e.g.* Zander, *A Bill of Rights?* (1975).
[61] Scarman, *English Law—The New Dimension* (1974), p. 20.

CHAPTER TWO

# INSTITUTIONAL ARRANGEMENTS FOR THE PREPARATION OF LEGISLATION

While the formal elements in the legislative process—Queen, Lords and Commons—have remained unchanged, one of its notable features over the last century has been the marked expansion in the number of bodies engaged in the various aspects of the preparation of legislation. These range from the Office of Parliamentary Counsel through Cabinet committees to more recently established bodies such as the Law Commissions. A common feature of all of these institutional arrangements is that they have been established by government as a consequence of its assumption of responsibility for the initiation of legislation.

Individually they reflect a variety of concerns, including, initially, the preparation of the government's legislative programme, the drafting of individual Bills and the form of the statute book. Since their establishment these arrangements have been progressively refined, and to them has been added a further concern: law reform. The creation and refinement of these arrangements comprise the subject-matter of this chapter.

## THE PREPARATION AND IMPLEMENTATION OF THE LEGISLATIVE PROGRAMME

### *THE CONTENT OF THE PROGRAMME*

From the period immediately preceding the Second Reform Act until the 1920s, the task of determining the content of each Session's legislative programme was undertaken by the whole Cabinet,[1] but following the radical changes introduced in the Cabinet's structure during the First World War, new arrangements were made. In 1918 the Home Secretary, Lord Cave, set up a Home Affairs Committee (H.A.C.) to deal with all matters of domestic policy. Initially it dealt with items of general administration, but from 1922 to 1939 it gradually became responsible for recommending to the Cabinet the content of the legislative programme, on the basis of proposals

[1] Mackintosh, *The British Cabinet* (3rd ed., 1977), pp. 259, 262–263.

which had received prior Cabinet approval. The Cabinet would consider these recommendations and make adjustments to them as its policy and the state of the parliamentary timetable required. However, the Cabinet drew no institutional distinction between the content of the programme and the form of individual Bills, and so the Home Affairs Committee additionally became the forum for the examination of draft Bills before their introduction in Parliament. During the Second World War, these two tasks were performed by the Home Policy Committee (H.P.C.), later renamed the Legislation Committee.[2] These arrangements reflected the gradual transformation in the Cabinet's role from a body which took decisions to one which primarily co-ordinated the taking of decisions by committees of itself.[3]

When the Labour Government took office in 1945 committed to a massive programme of social reconstruction, these arrangements were revised. Herbert Morrison, then Leader of the House of Commons, argued that the composition of the Legislation Committee made it difficult for it to decide which Bills should go into the programme, as all the Ministers present were themselves competing for places on it. In addition, it was expected to vet draft Bills. What was sought were modifications giving the key members of the government responsible for the programme—the Leaders of the two Houses and the Chief Whips—much closer control over its formulation. Accordingly, Morrison argued, it was essential to separate those with a vested interest in getting proposals onto the programme from the decision as to what its contents would be. In addition, "it was desirable to separate the task of shaping the legislative programme from the work of examining actual Bills."[4] To this end, a Future Legislation Committee (F.L.C.) was established. Its principal members were the Leader of the House of Commons, as Chairman, the Leader of the House of Lords, and the Chief Whips of both Houses. The Committee was designed to be a "small and impartial planning tribunal"[5] which would decide between the competing departmental claims. The task of examining draft Bills was left with the larger Legislation Committee, which became generally responsible for implementing the details of the programme.

Despite this differentiation of the Cabinet structure for the

[2] Wilson, *The Cabinet Office to 1945* (1975), paras. 414, 521 and 946.

[3] Described by Mackintosh, *op.cit.*, Chap. 10.

[4] Morrison, *Government and Parliament* (3rd ed., 1964), p. 234. See also Donoghue and Jones, *Herbert Morrison: Portrait of a Politician* (1973), p. 355 and Walkland, *The Legislative Process in Great Britain* (1969), pp. 57–58.

[5] Morrison, *ibid.*

purpose of preparing the legislative programme, its content remains to a remarkable extent unplanned. Crossman criticised the arrangements as "hopelessly unsatisfactory. It just gets itself filled up by Departments listing the things they want to do and fighting to get the maximum time for each. There is no Government plan for a balanced policy."[6] Earlier, he described a meeting of the Future Legislation Committee:

> "A vast concourse—some thirty people—had been gathered together, and some eighty to ninety Bills were listed in various classes of priority . . . The meeting was a bit ludicrous: we were supposed to consider priorities but couldn't, since it was obvious that everyone was deeply committed to his own particular measure whether it was a minor piece of legal reform . . . or a really major piece of our programme. If you go there briefed by your Ministry you can only say, 'My Bill is equally important'."[7]

Subsequent arrangements reflect a continuing desire to keep control over the content of the programme within a small group, the key figures being the Leader of the House of Commons and the Chief Whips,[8] even if larger ministerial committees have some say in the matter. Between 1974 and 1976, the task of preparing the programme was "masterminded by the Lord President of the Council"[9] (who was also the Leader of the House of Commons) before being approved in substance by the Queen's Speech Committee (Q.F.) and formally by the whole Cabinet. Subsequently the Future Legislation and Legislation Committees were merged to form a new Legislation Committee (L.G.), chaired by the Leader of the House of Commons and including the Law Officers and Chief Whips as its permanent members. Its responsibilities were to determine the programme in conjunction with the Queen's Speech Committee, and to examine draft Bills.[10] The present Conservative Government appears to have reverted to the earlier practice of creating separate committees for the discharge of these functions. One committee (Q.L.), chaired by the Leader of the House of Commons is responsible for future legislation and the preparation of the Queen's Speech,[11] while a second, standing

[6] Crossman, *The Diaries of a Cabinet Minister* (1976), Vol. 2, p. 168.
[7] *Ibid.*, Vol. 1, p. 59.
[8] The Leader of the House of Commons may for example delete items from the Queen's Speech, as happened with the Local Government (Miscellaneous Provisions) Bill 1980.
[9] Wilson, *The Governance of Britain* (1976), p. 129.
[10] *The New Statesman*, July 17, 1978.
[11] *The Times*, February 10, 1981.

committee, the Legislation Committee, chaired by the Lord Chancellor is responsible for the implementation of the programme[12]

The objective of these arrangements, to institute efficient control over the content of the programme, is also reflected in the various efforts of these committees to develop criteria for determining what Bills should be included. The task of shaping the programme usually begins during the previous session. This is so firstly because all legislative proposals must be considered and approved by the appropriate policy committee of Cabinet before a Minister can seek a place in the programme, and secondly because it takes time to agree the content of the programme, to prepare and issue instructions to the draftsman, and to draft and approve Bills. These tasks have to be performed in the context of the allocation of all the other government and non-government business which occupies the parliamentary timetable. In a normal parliamentary session there are about 160 working days for this business. Just under half of that is taken up with government legislation; the other half is taken up with such items as the debate on the Address in reply to the Queen's Speech, debates on government expenditure and executive actions, private Members' time, question time, debates on the adjournment and so on.

All attempts to devise criteria for determining what Bills shall be included in the programme begin by making an allocation for annual financial legislation; principally the Finance Bill which incorporates the Budget proposals and requires about 20 days to complete its stages—the single largest allocation—and the Consolidated Fund and Consolidated Fund (Appropriation) Bills. There remain fifty-sixty working days to be allocated between major government commitments (representing its manifesto and campaign promises) and departmental interests. As room will usually be found for the former (though this may lead to congestion and unusually long sessions such as in 1967 and 1979—1980), the allocation of the rest of the programme is devoted to departmental proposals promoted by Ministers in competition with one another. In an attempt to reduce this element of competition, the Home Affairs Committee devised a classification for the purposes of its recommendations to Cabinet. After annual Bills, this basically distinguished between urgent or essential Bills representing major government policies and useful Bills representing departmental proposals of no great political importance.[13] This classification was adopted by

[12] H.C. Deb., Vol. 967, ser.5, col. 179 (May 24, 1979).
[13] Wilson, *The Cabinet Office to 1945, op.cit.*, para. 521.

the Future Legislation Committee,[14] but Crossman's observations and the failure of his own efforts at reform[15] suggest that the programme is as likely to be determined by arguments based on political expediency as anything else.

By whatever means the appropriate committee employs, a list of Bills is prepared in order of priority having regard to dates when instructions to the draftsman can be ready, the time the drafting will take, and to the Chief Whip's estimate of the approximate dates on which the Bills must be introduced to pass through their parliamentary stages. This list is then presented to the Cabinet for formal approval; this occurs in a normal session during the Easter recess. Once approved, the main features of the programme are incorporated into the Queen's Speech for the opening of the new session. Where the Queen's Speech is the first of an incoming government, its preparation will take place contemporaneously with the shaping of the programme.

## *THE IMPLEMENTATION OF THE PROGRAMME*

The government's assumption of responsibility for the initiation of legislation raises the immediate problem of the translation of its proposals into legislative form. Centralised arrangements for the drafting of Bills were established only gradually in response to the unsystematic and expensive practices of the early nineteenth century. These arrangements culminated in the establishment of the Office of Parliamentary Counsel in 1869, which now has a monopoly over the drafting of government Bills. Of necessity, these arrangements continue to be of primary importance in the implementation of the government's programme. In addition, its implementation has given rise to the creation of further arrangements designed to co-ordinate the preparation and progress of Bills.

[14] Morrison, *op.cit.*, pp. 235–236, 245–246. See also Walkland, *op.cit.*, p. 60.

[15] Crossman's proposal was: "Instead of each Minister trying to get as many of his Bills into the session ahead, we should work backwards from the election. The first question to be asked in planning the programme is what we want to see in the election manifesto. The second question is what measures would be suitable for White Papers or even for draft Bills to be published in the year before the election but which wouldn't become law. Having got this part of the election programme prepared we should then ask, what measures do we have to put on the statute book because they must come into operation at once." *Op.cit.*, Vol. 2, pp. 169–170; and Vol. 3, p. 70.

THE DRAFTING AND SCRUTINY OF BILLS

## The Office of Parliamentary Counsel

Most eighteenth century legislation was privately sponsored, affecting local or private interests only; government legislation was largely confined to financial and public order matters. Government Bills were generally drafted either by Chancery barristers or, following the Treasury's example in 1790, by counsel employed on a more permanent basis by individual departments. However, as the burden of preparing legislation increased following the Reform Act 1832, government departments made more regular arrangements.[16] In 1837 the Home Secretary, who was ordinarily responsible for the most important legislative measures, appointed a barrister full-time to draft his department's Bills. But as departments appointed different draftsmen, some of whom had very little legal training, the results of their efforts varied considerably: "The trouble was that there were too many cooks, and they spoilt the broth."[17]

Despite the presence of some very able draftsmen such as Symonds, Coode and Thring, the variations in drafting styles and techniques meant that conflicts and inconsistencies between particular legislative provisions were legion. No one had any responsibility for ensuring that the legislation which was presented to Parliament would be correctly assimilated to the existing corpus of statute law. Bentham had identified a wide range of imperfections in the drafting of eighteenth century statutes, and the remedies he proposed[18] (which included the establishment of a centralised drafting agency) were pursued by two of the specialist draftsmen who were employed by government departments; Arthur Symonds who worked for the Board of Trade and Henry Thring who in 1860 was appointed official draftsman to the Home Office. However although Symonds in particular drew the attention of successive Statute Law Commissions between 1836 and 1856 to the necessity for centralised drafting arrangements, his proposals were not acted upon.[19]

The financial implications of the absence of any centralised control over the content of Bills provided the necessary impetus for change. In the absence of control, there simply was no check on the financial consequences of proposed measures. A Minister could introduce a Bill the financial implications of which would disrupt

[16] Griffith, "The Place of Parliament in the Legislative Process" (1951) 14 M.L.R. 279, 285–286.

[17] Parris, *Constitutional Bureaucracy* (1969), p. 174. See also Ilbert, *Legislative Methods and Forms* (1901), pp. 80–85.

[18] *Of Laws in General* (1970), pp. 1, 232–246.

[19] Carr, 'The Mechanics of Law Making' (1951) 4 C.L.P. 122.

the budgetary allocations made for that year. Less significantly, the Chancellor of the Exchequer, Robert Lowe, was concerned about the costs incurred by departments employing both full time, and occasional, drafting assistance:

> "The increase of late years in the number of Bills which have in every session to be introduced by H.M. government is so great, and the attention which some of the more important require during their progress, so onerous, that . . . it has become necessary to call in other professional gentlemen of the highest eminence. To such gentlemen . . . large fees are of course paid and in consequence the cost . . . has become a considerable item."[20]

In order to control both these financial implications, the Office of Parliamentary Counsel to the Treasury was established in 1869, with Lord Thring as its first appointment.

### *The Establishment of a Drafting Monopoly*

From the late Victorian period until the First World War, Ministers and groups of Ministers played a substantial part in the preparation of Bills, with one of the two draftsmen in the Office being brought in to assist them to draft clauses[21] but by the end of the war the principle had become established that government Bills, except those relating to Scotland,[22] were to be drafted by the Office. This monopoly, together with the increase in government legislation required the addition of a third draftsman in 1917, a fourth in 1930 and further regular additions throughout the thirties.

During this period difficulties began to arise concerning the timing of instructions from departments to the Office of Parliamentary Counsel in such a way as to ensure a regular and orderly flow of Bills at times when the government wanted to introduce them in Parliament. Despite the fact that the programme was subject to the scrutiny of the Home Affairs Committee and of the whole Cabinet, "there was liable on occasions to be some confusion between departments and Parliamentary Counsel, with the former complaining that the latter were in arrears, and the latter being overpressed, with some feeling that they had had no proper instructions from departments, and were without sufficient knowledge of the priority they should attach to the various measures."[23] As the Office had

[20] From the Treasury Circular which established the Office of Parliamentary Counsel, P.R.O. T29/614 Minute 2245 (February 8, 1869).

[21] Walkland, *op.cit.*, p. 56. For instance, Lord Halsbury L.C. drafted the Companies Act 1900; see *Hilder* v. *Dexter* [1902] A.C. 474, 477.

[22] See below, pp. 32–33.

[23] Wilson, *The Cabinet Office to 1945, op.cit.*, para. 521. See also Ram, "The Improvement of the Statute Book" (1951) 1 J.S.P.T.L. 442, 447.

been established within the Treasury, its authority was required before a department could issue instructions to the draftsmen, and so

> "to remedy the situation, a Treasury circular was issued in 1935 that authority for Paliamentary Counsel to be employed would be given for those Bills which constituted the main items in the government's legislative programme, and only for such other Bills as had received Cabinet approval in principle and for which the Chief Whip was satisfied that there was a reasonable chance that parliamentary time would be found."[24]

The full significance of these developments only became apparent with the massive increase in government legislation after the Second World War.

*The Present Establishment and Duties of the Office*

Since its creation, the Office of Parliamentary Counsel has acquired a prestige and status which places it among the highest levels of government.[25] In 1980 there were 20 full-time and three part-time draftsmen, arranged as follows: one First Parliamentary Counsel (Sir George Engel); one Second Parliamentary Counsel; six Parliamentary Counsel; three Deputy Parliamentary Counsel; six Senior Assistants and six Assistants.[26] The number of full-time draftsmen is expected to rise to 24.[27] Of the current establishment, four full-time and three part-time draftsmen are on temporary secondment to the Law Commission, which also has its own full-time draftsmen.

Bills which relate exclusively to Scotland, and those parts of Bills applying to England, Wales and Scotland which relate especially to Scotland, are drafted by members of the Lord Advocate's Department. Responsibility for Scottish Bills was expressly excluded from the Office of Parliamentary Counsel when it was established, but two years later the Treasury authorised the appointment of a Parliamentary Draftsman for Scotland. This post was transferred to the Lord Advocate's department in 1925. By 1978 there were 12 full-time and two part-time staff. In addition to their other drafting duties, the Scottish draftsmen perform a variety of other tasks in their capacity as legal secretaries to the Lord Advocate, such as assisting the Scottish Law Officers, advising government depart-

[24] Wilson, *ibid.*

[25] See the account of a former Parliamentary Counsel, Sir Harold Kent, *In on the Act* (1979), pp. 163, 164.

[26] Bennion, *Statute Law* (1980), p. 18. Until 1967 only barristers were eligible to be members of the Office, but in that year solicitors were included; see (June 1967) 64 Law Soc. Gaz. xxxv, 293.

[27] H.L. Deb., Vol. 409, ser.5, col. 1585 (June 5, 1980).

ments on Scots law and working on the implications of international conventions and Community law for Scottish legal practice. Like their counterparts in London, the draftsmen may also be called upon to advise Ministers on the necessity or constitutionality of proposed legislation.[28]

The Office of Parliamentary Counsel is unique in the civil service in that although it is directly and essentially concerned with matters of the first political importance, its distinctive functions are not under the control of any one Minister. While it works to a Minister's instructions on any particular Bill, these instructions cannot be issued without the authority of the Cabinet committee responsible for the implementation of the programme, and its administration is subject to the Prime Minister as head of the Civil Service.

The primary function of Parliamentary Counsel is to prepare Bills for the government's legislative programme, although they also have some responsibility for private Members' legislation.[29] This function has a number of aspects, of which the most significant is the translation of a department's instructions into legal provisions which will give legal effect to the government's policies and comply with the parliamentary rules of public Bill procedure. We examine the performance of these tasks in Chapter 4. The draftsman of a Bill is also responsible for ensuring that during its parliamentary stages the Minister is properly advised on the legal effects of the Bill and of proposed amendments to it, and for redrafting, where necessary, those amendments which the Minister is prepared or compelled to accept.

From the government's point of view the advantages of these centralised institutional arrangements for the preparation of its Bills are beyond question. The arrangements conduce to uniformity and consistency in drafting technique, a reasonably efficient use of limited resources, direct control over the progress of preparation of Bills, familiarity between Counsel and senior departmental civil servants with each other's particular concerns, an invaluable collective experience, and perhaps most important, a virtual guarantee that the government's policies will be given legal effect.

[28] Report of the Renton Committee, *The Preparation of Legislation,* Cmnd. 6053 (1975), paras. 3.3–3.4 (hereafter, Renton). On the difficulties associated with drafting Anglo-Scottish legislation, see Renton, Chap.12; and for the Government's response to its recommendations (32–38), H.L. Deb., Vol. 412, ser.5., col. 192 (July 22, 1980). Separate arrangements were established in Northern Ireland; see Renton, para. 3.5.

[29] See below, p. 134. Two minor exceptions to this monopoly are the Consolidated Fund and Consolidated Fund (Appropriation) Bills which are common form and are prepared by the Treasury.

## The Scrutiny of Draft Bills

While Ministers were involved in the preparation of Bills, the government was in a position to ensure that they were drafted so as to give legal effect to its policy.

> "Before 1914 the Prime Minister and the Cabinet still took far greater interest in, and were far more influential in preparing, the main heads of most Bills of medium importance than is the case today, a situation which reflects the rather amateur and informal organisation of pre-1914 Cabinets and the comparatively lighter load of administrative and legislative supervision which they were responsible for than that which is borne by modern Cabinets."[30]

However, the separation of the function of formulating legislative proposals from that of drafting Bills, which was implicit in the creation of the Office of Parliamentary Counsel and its gradual establishment of a drafting monopoly, created the need for arrangements to ensure congruence between Bills as drafted and prior Cabinet decisions.

As we have seen, the function of examining draft Bills fell initially to the Home Affairs Committee.

> "It generally met under the chairmanship of the Lord Chancellor, and was attended by most of the ministers dealing with civil affairs at home, by the Law Officers, the Chief Whip, Parliamentary Counsel and a number of officials from departments. The Committee met as drafts of Bills were taking their final form, made detailed adjustments to them within policies already settled and made recommendations to the Cabinet for authority for their introduction in Parliament."[31]

Under the first post-war Labour Government these tasks were undertaken by the Legislation Committee. Although it "would examine a Bill not normally from the point of view of policy but from the standpoint of general structure, proper legal wording, fairness, good sense in carrying out the intentions of the Government, and general acceptability as a workable measure,"[32] the distinction between policy and form is one which is not always easily made. At one time this Committee did in fact try to re-open policy matters, in the guise of making drafting easier, but this practice has not on the

[30] Walkland, *op.cit.*, p. 57.
[31] Wilson, *The Cabinet Office to 1945, op.cit.*, para. 521.
[32] Morrison, *op.cit.*, p. 250.

whole persisted following instructions that the Committee should confine itself to drafting matters.[33]

Vetting the form and substance of a Bill is a task which when it is performed is undertaken by the Lord Chancellor and the Law Officers, but because of the traditional confidentiality which surrounds the composition, terms of reference and operation of Cabinet committees during the life of a government, it is difficult to obtain an accurate account of the current extent of the scrutiny of draft Bills; but we may suppose that it varies according to their complexity and political importance.

## MANAGEMENT OF THE PROGRAMME

In addition to the drafting and scrutiny of Bills there are other tasks involved in the implementation of the programme, such as deciding when to introduce a Bill in the session and in which House, for which arrangements need to be made. "As the emergence of stronger Cabinets with reliable voting support in the Commons and the ever-increasing pressure from different groups for executive activity resulted in more proposed legislation"[34] so difficulties emerged in the management of the programme. To a limited extent these difficulties could be overcome by making maximum use of parliamentary time. As we shall see in Chapter 5, this continues to be an aim of all governments.[35] In addition, successive governments have sought to make the most effective use of internal resources, and as we have seen, to create new, or to modify the existing, institutional arrangements for their use.

In relation to the management of the programme, attempts were made by the Home Affairs Committee and the Treasury during the thirties to systematise its planning and implementation. The classification devised by the Committee for the purposes of determining which Bills should be included in the programme which we described above, was also intended to serve the additional purpose of indicating the order of priority in which Bills should be prepared and introduced. Under the first post-war Labour Government, the Legislation Committee became responsible, in addition to the vetting of Bills, for deciding the time and place of their presentation to Parliament.

[33] Mackintosh, *op.cit.*, p. 527. The difficulties inherent in attempting to separate questions of policy from questions of drafting are illustrated by Crossman, *op.cit.*, Vol. 1, pp. 387, 520 and Vol. 2, p. 248 and Castle, *The Castle Diaries 1974–1977* (1980), pp. 53–54, 298–299, 718.

[34] Cromwell, *Revolution or Evolution : British Government in the Nineteenth Century* (1977), p. 161.

[35] See below, pp. 107–110.

Management of the programme now involves a number of functions: regulating the flow of instructions to the Office of Parliamentary Counsel during the session; reviewing the progress being made in the preparation of Bills and sanctioning Ministers and departments who fail to adhere to the timetable;[36] approving the introduction of Bills the need for which was not anticipated before the Queen's Speech; determining the government's attitude to private Members' Bills; ensuring that Bills comply with the parliamentary rules governing public Bill procedure; authorising their introduction and fixing the date and place of their first reading; and monitoring their progress through their subsequent parliamentary stages. All of these functions, and their centralised control have arisen from the government's need to ensure that its programme is completed within the constraints imposed by the parliamentary timetable.

## THE CONDITION OF THE STATUTE BOOK

Complaints about the condition of the statute book were by no means uncommon before the nineteenth century, but it was not until then that any significant attempts were made to remedy them. These complaints embraced a wide range of grievances, and particular emphasis was placed upon the absence of any adequate publishing and indexing system. Most new legislation amends existing provisions, and if these are difficult to locate, the task of preparing Bills is at best delayed or worse prone to error. From the point of view of the government, and of the citizen, the law needs to be accessible and known.

Considerations such as these prompted a House of Commons' Select Committee to recommend in 1800 that work begin on publishing an accurate and comprehensive set of the statutes in force.[37] This task was undertaken between 1810 and 1828, but it soon became apparent that an initial and considerable obstacle was the presence of many "obsolete" and "unconsolidated" enactments. The remedies which were devised were to initiate programmes of

[36] *e.g.* Crossman, *op.cit.*, Vol. 2, pp. 557–558; Castle, *op.cit.*, pp. 296, 331, 420 and Kaufman, *How to be a Minister* (1980), pp. 60–66.

[37] There were a number of privately published collections of the statutes, but these were of varying accuracy. The recommendations of the 1800 House of Commons' Select Committee resulted in the establishment of the Record Commission, which produced an authoritative collection of statutes from 1235 to 1713 called *Statutes of the Realm*. Eighteenth and nineteenth century statutes were published in sessional volumes from 1801 under the title *Statutes at Large*, and *Public General Statutes* were issued from 1831.

statute law revision and of consolidation.[38] Both were initially conceived narrowly: statute law revision involved the repeal of statutes no longer in force, while consolidation was confined to the *verbatim* or verbal re-enactment of statutory provisions relating to a subject, contained in a number of different existing statutes, those provisions in turn being repealed. Nevertheless both proved to have controversial aspects. It was for example often difficult to determine the precise effect of subsequent statutes on existing statutory provisions. It was therefore a matter of debate whether a provision had or not been repealed. The conception of consolidation could be extended to include not only the verbal re-enactment of provisions, but also re-drafting them so that they were consistent in their arrangement and use of language. Moreover, both statute law revision and consolidation were seen as inviting the codification of the law, an undertaking which was regarded by some—in particular the judiciary—as quite undesirable given the profound consequences it would have for the development of the common law and the role of the courts.[39]

Statute law revision and consolidation were considered by a number of Commissions, the first of which was established in 1834, appointed on an ad hoc basis over the next 40 years. By the last quarter of the nineteenth century however, the bureaucratic requirement of systematic procedures for the revision, consolidation and publication of statutes was acknowledged, and the government instituted arrangements which remained largely unchanged until the creation of the Law Commissions in 1965. A primary feature of these arrangements is the way in which the initially narrow conceptions of statute law revision and consolidation have been expanded to include, in the case of statute law revision, the repeal of statutes "no longer of practical utility," and in the case of consolidation, consolidation to include minor improvements and later, substantive amendments. This expansion has taken place with the approval, or at the instigation, of the government, with the result that significant changes in the law can now be brought about under the technical umbrella of "law reform"; and, because statute law revision and consolidation Bills are subject to special parliamentary procedures, without impinging on increasingly crowded parliamentary timetables.

In the following sections we describe the development of statute

[38] These arrangements are comprehensively described in Ilbert, *op.cit.*, Chap. 4. See also Lord Simon of Glaisdale and J. Webb, "Consolidation and Statute Law Revision [1975] P.L. 285, and Hughes, *The British Statute Book* (1957), Chap. 8.

[39] On codification see Hahlo, "Here lies the Common Law" (1967) 30 M.L.R. 241 and Diamond, "Codification of the Law of Contract" (1968) 31 M.L.R. 361.

law revision and consolidation and the responsibilities of the Law Commissions and of the Joint Committee on Consolidation etc. Bills for these matters, before returning to the arrangements for the publication of statutes.

### *STATUTE LAW REVISION AND CONSOLIDATION*

The first Statute Law Commission was instructed to prepare two statutes digesting the whole of the criminal law, the first incorporating all statutory provisions and the second incorporating common law principles; to consider the possibility of amalgamating these two; and generally to inquire how far it might be expedient to consolidate other branches of the law. Despite the publication of a number of reports including a draft criminal law Bill, no legislation emerged from this Commission or its successor appointed in 1845. In 1853 Lord Cranworth L.C. appointed a Statute Law Board with the aim firstly of revising the statute book by the expurgation of defunct Acts and secondly of consolidating statutes in actual operation. The appointment of this Board was part of Lord Cranworth's ambitious programme to produce a "Code Victoria," but like the Statute Law Commissions, no legislation was forthcoming. The reasons for this were that in the case of the digest of criminal law, the judiciary were strongly opposed to codification, while in the case of the Statute Law Board, the Commissioners themselves were in profound disagreement as to whether to begin with statute law revision or with consolidation. A further Statute Law Commission was appointed in 1854 superseding the Statute Law Board, but as parliamentary opposition to this succession of Commissions grew, because of the lack of results and what was claimed to be a waste of money, Lord Campbell L.C. refused to reappoint it in 1859.[40]

Three Statute Law Revision Bills based on previous Commissioners' reports were enacted in 1856, 1861 and 1863, and between 1863 and 1894 22 further Statute Law Revision Acts were passed, but they were not always mere technical exercises involving the deletion of obsolete enactments. For example, introducing the Statute Law Revision Bill 1861, Lord Campbell L.C. said that its preparation was a "difficult and delicate duty, for no lawyer, however, laborious had been his studies, could take upon himself to state what statutes were now in force, and what had been repealed."[41] Particular concern

[40] See Simon and Webb, *op.cit.*, p. 290. Seven major Acts consolidating almost the whole of the criminal law were passed in 1861 based on the work of the first Statute Law Commission.

[41] Parl. Deb., Vol. 161, ser. 3, col. 1058 (February 28, 1861).

was expressed about the accuracy of these judgments and about the absence of any further provision for the detailed examination of such Bills, but the Lord Chancellor did little more than assure his critics that those who had prepared the Bill had been very careful in their research.[42] Similar concerns were expressed about the Statute Law Revision Bill 1889 which proposed the repeal of statutes enacted in Queen Victoria's reign.[43] MPs argued that the Bill should be examined by a Select Committee as had originally been mooted in 1864; and the implementation of this suggestion in 1890 was the origin of the arrangements established two years later for the parliamentary consideration of Statute Law Revision—and thereafter—of Consolidation Bills.

Set against the background of its attempts during this period to alter the rules of parliamentary procedure so as to afford more time to, and allow quicker dispatch of, the legislative programme, the practical problem with Statute Law Revision Bills for the government was clear; how to find a method of considering them which, "whilst maintaining Parliamentary control, would avoid opening them to detailed revision of their substance on the floor of either House."[44] This was achieved by the establishment in 1892 of a procedure whereby these Bills would be referred to a Joint Committee of both Houses after their Second Reading. If approved by the Committee, the completion of the rest of their parliamentary stages was entirely formal; this procedure thus represented an advance for the government in its efforts to promote statute law revision at a minimum cost to itself in terms of parliamentary time.

On the other hand, this procedure reduced the opportunity for the parliamentary consideration of Statute Law Revision Bills, and when the practice of referring Consolidation Bills to the Committee began in 1894, parliamentary opposition increased. In the case of Consolidation Bills, the problem was one of definition: could amendments, however minor, be included? The distinction between Bills which merely re-enact existing provisions and those which consolidate and amend had been recognised by the Statute Law Commission of 1854,[45] but it did not acquire parliamentary significance until 1897, when an MP successfully opposed the committal of the Post Office (Consolidation) Bill to the Joint Committee on the grounds that it was not possible to consolidate

[42] *Ibid.*, col. 1059.
[43] Simon and Webb, *op.cit.*, p. 291.
[44] *Ibid.*, p. 290.
[45] First Report of the Statute Law Commission, C. 1963 (1855), 3; see also Simon and Webb, *op.cit.*, p. 289–290.

anything which was put into different words; "different words, however similar to the existing words, necessarily involved some change in the law."[46] The result was a substantial decline in the number of Consolidation Bills presented to Parliament; no further Bill was introduced until 1911.

## THE EXPANSION OF STATUTE LAW REVISION AND CONSOLIDATION

The task of the Joint Committee was, and still is to examine Statute Law Revision and Consolidation Bills committed to it; the key issue is the definition of these two enterprises.

Statute law revision had been conceived by the Statute Law Commissioners of the mid-nineteenth century as being limited to "weeding away all those enactments that are no longer in force,"[47] but the working criteria of the Joint Committee became broader than this. Apart from proposals to remove from the statute book enactments which had been expressly repealed, a Bill would be approved by the Committee if it proposed the repeal of statutes which were obsolete, spent, unnecessary or superseded. There was no statutory basis for these categories. Instead they evolved through practice. In many cases the judgment that an enactment was "obsolete," etc., was based on departmental advice, and thus such Bills represented opportunities for a government to enact legislation having substantive effect without committing parliamentary time on the floor of the two Houses. During the first half of this century the responsibility for initiating and introducing Statute Law Revision Bills lay with the Lord Chancellor, who was also the Chairman of the Joint Committee. A number of such Bills were enacted, but there were no systematic attempts, as have been subsequently instituted by the Law Commissions, to treat statute law revision and consolidation as devices to be used together to improve the condition of the statute book.

Whereas the scope of statute law revision was gradually extended, the opportunities to consolidate legislation without a considerable expenditure of parliamentary time continued to be limited by the restrictive definition of consolidation adopted in 1897. Only in 1949 was the restriction relaxed when the Consolidation of Enactments (Procedure) Act provided for the inclusion of "corrections and

[46] *Ibid.*, p. 292.
[47] Parl. Deb., Vol. 171, ser. 3, cols. 775, 786 (June 12, 1863; Lord Westbury L.C.).

minor improvements."[48] This Act was the product of the greater emphasis placed on consolidation both during the Second World War, when responsibility for this matter was transferred to the Statute Law Committee, and immediately thereafter, when a Consolidation Branch was established within the Office of Parliamentary Counsel,[49] and of the difficulties which the Office had experienced in attempting to draft Consolidation Bills within the 1897 limitation. This limitation meant, in the words of Lord Jowitt L.C., that such Bills should "reproduce exactly the existing law with all its blemishes and imperfections."[50] To cope with this, the draftsman adopted, in Kent's words "a ghastly process known as 'consolidating the doubt,' *i.e.* he does his best to reproduce the exact state of ambiguity of the existing law, which is by no means always simply a question of reproducing the words of the previous Act."[51] These difficulties were to some extent alleviated by the 1949 Act, which in section 2 defined "corrections and minor improvements" as follows:

> " 'Corrections and minor improvements' means amendments of which the effect is confined to resolving ambiguities, removing doubts, bringing obsolete provisions into conformity with modern practice, or removing unnecessary provisions or anomalies which are not of substantial importance, and amendments designed to facilitate improvement in the form or manner in which the law is stated, and includes any transitional provisions which may be necessary in consequence of such amendments."

Criticisms were also made by Parliamentary Counsel and the Statute Law Committee, which was responsible for the publication of statutes and to which responsibility for statute law revision had along with consolidation, been transferred in 1942, of what they

[48] According to Lord Gardiner, the Act was prompted by an after dinner speech he gave in 1947 to the Society of Labour Lawyers, in the presence of the then Lord Chancellor, Lord Jowitt; see H.L. Deb., Vol. 366, ser. 5, col. 987 (December 10, 1975). However, its enactment may be seen as part of the much broader process of rationalisation of legislative methods carried out by the Labour Governments of 1945–51. Other aspects include the rationalisation of private legislation procedure and the restructuring of the Cabinet committees dealing with the legislative programme described above, pp. 10–11 and 26; the enactment of the Statutory Instruments Act 1946, below p. 142 and the introduction in the Parliament Act 1949 of further limitations on the power of the House of Lords to delay Bills, below pp. 127–128.

[49] The background is described in Kent, *op.cit.*, pp. 163–164. For the Statute Law Committee, see below pp. 47–48.

[50] H.L. Deb., Vol. 155, ser. 5, col. 1172 (May 27, 1948).

[51] Kent, *op.cit.*, p. 30.

regarded as the restrictive categories of permissible statute law revision. What they wanted was the opportunity to repeal other measures so as to facilitate consolidation and the publication of the third edition of *Statutes Revised.* Although the expansion the definition of statute law revision did ease pressure on the parliamentary timetable, the enterprise itself was not treated as being of the same importance as consolidation, and no further changes were made in its definition until the establishment of the Law Commissions in 1965.

## THE LAW COMMISSIONS' RESPONSIBILITIES

In their First Programme on Consolidation and Statute Law Revision,[52] the Law Commissions took the view that although consolidation, which they described as "the process of combining the legislative provisions on a single topic into one coherent enactment"[53] would in itself simplify the law and make it more easily accessible, it was more appropriate to think of consolidation and statute law revision as complementary techniques. The Commissions were critical of the restrictive definitions of both statute law revision and consolidation, and proposed substantial extensions to them. Statute law revision should, they argued, include the repeal of statutes on the ground that they are *no longer of practical utility.*

> "As originally understood, statute law revision was designed to facilitate the production of a revised edition of the statutes by striking out unrepealed provisions which had become inoperative. There was a great deal of this to be done, since early statutes often contained no express provisions for repeal at all or merely repealed "all previous Acts so far as inconsistent with this Act." This type of statute law revision is now done concurrently with the amendments by the Repeal Schedule in the amending Act. There is still room for it, for instance where temporary provisions have expired or where there has been

[52] The statutory duties of the Law Commissions include "the elimination of anomalies, the repeal of obsolete and unnecessary enactments, the reduction of the number of separate enactments and generally the simplification and modernisation of the law," Law Commissions Act 1965, s.3(1). Responsibility for statute law revision was transferred to them from the Statute Law Committee.

[53] The Law Commission, First Programme on Consolidation and Statute Law Revision (1966) Law Com. No. 2, para. 2. See also the Law Commission's Second Programme (1971) Law Com. No. 44, paras. 15–16, and the Scottish Law Commission's First (1966) Scot. Law Com. No. 2, Second (1973) Scot Law. Com. No. 27 and Third (1978) Scot Law Com. No. 46, Programmes.

some change of circumstance such that the facts on which an Act operates can no longer occur, and it is still the practice to have Statute Law Revision Bills at intervals to deal with matters of this sort, as well as with oversights in Repeal Schedules or in previous Statute Law Revision Acts. The scope of statute law revision has of recent years been somewhat extended, but we think there is room for a still more forceful approach; we propose to work systematically through the existing statutes with a view to recommending the repeal not only of matter which can be treated as inoperative but also *of matter that no longer serves a substantial purpose.*"[54]

Bills of this new type are called Statute Law (Repeal) Bills, and since 1969, the Law Commission has published ten reports on Statute Law Revision (seven in conjunction with the Scottish Law Commission) which have resulted in the enactment of nine Statute Law (Repeal) Acts. Altogether these have repealed over 2,300 separate enactments, including 947 whole Acts.[55] To reiterate the point made earlier, the decision that an enactment no longer serves a substantial purpose is clearly by no means a merely technical one; for example, in the light of the inner-city rioting of the summer of 1981, some people would dispute the judgment that the Riot Act 1714 which was repealed in 1967 was no longer of practical utility.[56] Nevertheless, this illustrates how substantive decisions about the desirability of retaining certain enactments are now taken in a context which treats such decisions as essentially concerned with the *formal* presentation and compilation of the statute book.

Similarly, the Law Commissions thought that the existing definitions of consolidation were too narrowly framed to permit the preparation of satisfactory programmes of consolidation. Accordingly they recommended a third procedure whereby the Law Commissions prepare a Command Paper "which contains Recommendations for changes in the law which are deemed desirable in order to secure a satisfactory consolidation of the relevant subject matter."[57] These Recommendations may involve amendments to the existing law which go well beyond the "corrections and minor improvements" authorised by the 1949 Act. Unlike the parliamentary

[54] The Law Commission, First Programme on Consolidation and Statute Law Revision, *ibid.*, para. 14, emphasis added.

[55] The Law Commission, Fifteenth Annual Report 1979–80 (1981) Law Com. No. 107, Appendix 5. See also Sir Michael Kerr, "Law Reform in Changing Times" (1980) 96 L.Q.R. 515, 525.

[56] The Criminal Law Act 1967, s.10 and Sched. 3 Part III, and the Statute Law Repeals Act 1973, s.1(1) and Sched. 1 Part V.

[57] Simon and Webb, *op.cit.*, p. 254.

procedures for other Consolidation Bills, those parts of a Bill which contain such Recommendations may be amended by either House after they have been considered by the Joint Committee.[58] In practice it is rare for such a Bill, once it has been approved by the Joint Committee, to be amended during its subsequent stages.

Consolidation may thus now take three forms: (1)pure consolidation, that is verbal or *verbatim* re-enactment without altering the substance of the law;[59] (2) consolidation with corrections and minor improvements under the Consolidation of Enactments (Procedure) Act 1949; and (3) consolidation with amendments to give effect to Recommendations of the Law Commissions. Depending on their form, consolidating statutes may serve either or both of two purposes. Pure consolidation is only intended to have an organisational effect upon the statute book, in the sense of making it tidier and easier to use; whereas consolidation of the latter two types are in addition intended to effect substantive changes in the law. Major programmes for consolidation were prepared by the Law Commission in 1966 and 1971 and by the Scottish Law Commission in 1966, 1973 and 1978.[60] Since its creation, the Law Commission has been responsible for the enactment of well over 100 Consolidation Acts, of which 19 have been based on Recommendations prepared under its new procedure. The Scottish Law Commission, which acts in conjunction with the Law Commission on Bills not relating exclusively to Scotland, has also been responsible for over a dozen Consolidation Acts applying only to Scotland over the same period.

Very few Consolidation Bills are based on proposals which come from the Commissions themselves. They are under a statutory duty to prepare programmes at the request of a Minister, and this typically involves consultation both with the proposing department and others likely to be affected by the consolidation. In addition, proposals may be made by other bodies such as the editorial staff of *Statutes in Force*, the Office of Parliamentary Counsel, or in Scotland, the Lord Advocate's Department, and some consolidation takes place in the normal process of preparing government Bills. In the case of proposals involving legislation of major size or complexity, the Commissions may set up a working party with representatives

[58] Erskine May, *Parliamentary Practice* (19th ed., 1976), pp. 524–525.

[59] Contemporary practice may involve not just literal transcription, but some modernisation of language, and the use of different drafting techniques; see Lord Simon, *Farrell* v. *Alexander* [1977] A.C. 59, 83.

[60] See above, n.53.

from the relevant departments, as was done for example with the proposal to consolidate public health legislation.[61]

The drafting of Consolidation Bills is undertaken by parliamentary draftsmen. In England, responsibility is divided according to the complexity of the programme between members of the Office of Parliamentary Counsel who are seconded to the Law Commission, and the Consolidation Branch of the Office. Where the legislation can be dealt with speedily, it is drafted in the Office; but if by virtue of the volume of the legislation or the difficulty of the subject matter it is likely to take some time to prepare, the Bill is prepared by the Commission's draftsmen. An example is the Highways Act 1980 which occupied two draftsmen for two years.[62] In Scotland, drafting of Consolidation Bills is the responsiblity of the Lord Advocate's Department.

Initially four draftsmen were seconded to the Law Commission. One additional appointment was made in the following year, but it is rare that all five have been available for any prolonged length of time. The draftsmen are often recalled to the Office to complete the preparation of programme Bills; this is particularly the case when a new government has been elected. This is one of the factors which prevents much acceleration in the current progress of consolidation. Where there is a conflict of priority in the preparation of Bills the government attaches greater importance to the enactment of the main items in its programme. In 1980 there were four full-time and three part-time draftsmen available to the Law Commission, and the government's view then was that no additional resources could be made available for the purpose of consolidation.[63]

The pace at which consolidation can occur is influenced by other factors.[64] Firstly, the draftsmen at both Commissions have other reponsibilities to perform, notably the preparation of draft law reform Bills. Secondly, as we have seen consolidation is not always a simple matter of taking sections from existing statutes and re-

[61] The Law Commission, Ninth Annual Report 1973–74 (1974) Law Com. No. 64, para. 55. The importance of consultation with affected groups was illustrated in 1980 when the Royal Association for Disablement and Rehabilitation objected to the Social Welfare (Local Services) Bill when it reached the Joint Committee on the grounds that it had not been consulted about the proposed transfer of sections from the Chronically Sick and Disabled Persons Act 1970. The Committee decided to defer consideration of the Bill *sine die*; The Law Commission, Fifteenth Annual Report, *op.cit.*, para. 2.47 and *The Guardian*, July 10, 1980.

[62] The Law Commission, Fourteenth Annual Report 1979–80 (1980) Law Com. No. 97, para 2.50.

[63] H.L. Deb., Vol. 410, ser. 5, col. 1591 (June 25, 1980).

[64] See generally Renton, *op.cit.*, Chap. 14; and The Law Commission, Thirteenth Annual Report 1977–78, (1977) Law Com. No. 92.

enacting them *verbatim* in a new Bill. It is sometimes necessary to enact amending legislation before the provisions can be consolidated. In such cases the Commissions have to obtain the Legislation Committee's approval for the inclusion of such amendments in one of the programme Bills. Although usually non-contentious, such clauses may be opposed, in which cases Ministers may be unwilling to agree to their inclusion. Thirdly, departments themselves may have other priorities, and where some new legislation is possible in a given area, a Minister may be unwilling to see a consolidation programme go ahead. Finally, it is unlikely that the Joint Committee could cope with a greater output of Consolidation Bills without some enlargement of its membership or change in its procedures.

## THE JOINT COMMITTEE ON CONSOLIDATION BILLS

The Joint Committee on Consolidation etc. Bills is set up each Session. It comprises 12 members each from the Lords and the Commons, the Chairman usually being a Lord of Appeal in Ordinary. Its function is to provide that measure of parliamentary control over Bills which is consistent both with the doctrine that nothing must be enacted which changes the law without parliamentary approval and with the purpose for which it was originally set up, namely to examine and approve Statute Law Revision and Consolidation Bills separately from the normal legislative process, thus saving time for the government. There are now five types of public Bills which are automatically referred to the Committee after their Second Reading in the first House;

(*a*) pure consolidation; or
(*b*) consolidation with permissible corrections and minor improvements made pursuant to the 1949 Act; or
(*c*) consolidation with amendments which accurately reflect of the Law Commissions Recommendations; or
(*d*) permissible Statute Law Revision, *i.e.* enactments proposed for repeal only on the grounds that they are obsolete, spent, unnecessary or superseded; or
(*e*) permissible Statute Law (Repeal), *i.e.* enactments proposed for repeal only on the grounds that they are no longer of practical utility.[65]

[65] Simon and Webb, *op.cit.*, p. 297, and Erskine May, *op.cit.*, pp. 683–684. The terms of the Committee were amended in 1980 to allow it to consider (draft) Orders in Council which require an affirmative resolution before they are made or can continue in operation and which, but for the provisions of the Northern Ireland Act 1974 would in the Committee's opinion have been enacted by a Consolidation or Statute Law Revision Bill; see H.C. Deb., Vol. 991, ser. 5, cols. 716–834 (October 30, 1980).

Unless the Committee can certify to both Houses that the Bill falls within one of these categories, or can amend it so that it does, the Bill cannot proceed under the special procedure. If the Committee approves the Bill, the rest of its parliamentary stages are, with limited exceptions, entirely formal.

## *THE PUBLICATION OF STATUTES*

The Statute Law Committee was set up in 1868 "to make the necessary arrangements and to superintend the work of preparing an edition of the Statutes Revised"[66] which would contain only those Acts which were in force at the time of publication. The first volume was completed and published in 1870, coincidentally with the first edition of the *Chronological Table* and *Index of Statutes* prepared by Lord Thring. Thereafter the first edition of *Statutes Revised* comprising the public general Acts in force at the end of 1878, as amended, was completed in 1885. It reduced the number of published volumes of statutes from 118 to 18. Further Statute Law Revision Acts were passed during this period, and work began on the second edition of *Statutes Revised*, the first 16 volumes of which were published between 1888 and 1901. The edition was completed in 1929.

The Statute Law Committee originally comprised a small group of parliamentary and other officials including the Lord Chancellor and First Parliamentary Counsel, but it gradually increased in size as its responsibilities grew. In 1891 what is now the Statutory Publications Office was set up by the Committee to be responsible to it for the preparation of editions of the *Chronological Table of the Statutes*, *Index to the Statutes* and *Statutes Revised*. During the Second World War, responsibility for statute law revision and consolidation, which had lain with the Home Affairs Committee, was transferred from it to the Statute Law Committee. Under its new terms of reference it was directed "to consider the steps necessary to bring the Statute Book up to date by consolidation, revision and otherwise, and to superintend the publication and indexing of Statutes, Statues Revised and Statutory Instruments."[67] To deal with these additional responsibilities, its membership was increased

[66] See Renton, *op. cit.*, para. 5.1.
[67] *Ibid.*, para. 5.2.

in 1946 to include the Attorney-General, the Lord Advocate, three or four of the Permanent Secretaries of departments most concerned with legislation, a number of Law Lords and other legally qualified members of both Houses of Parliament, Speaker's Counsel and the Counsel to the Chairman of Committees, and a little later, the Treasury Solicitor, into whose department the Statutory Publications Office was incorporated in 1956. The Lord Chancellor is the Committee's chairman.

The third edition of *Statutes Revised* was published in 1950, containing in chronological order all the Public General Acts from 1235 which were in force at the end of 1948. In 1965 the Committee's responsibilities for statute law revision and consolidation were transferred to the Law Commissions, and since then, its primary responsibilities have, as were originally conceived, been concerned with the publication of statutes and indexes thereto. Its role is essentially twofold. First it supervises various aspects of the form and publication of statutes, in particular the work of the Statutory Publications Office which comprises the editorial staff who compile and edit the statutes. Secondly it authorises new editions and classifications of statutes. The first volumes of *Statutes in Force*, which supersedes *Statutes Revised*, and is based on a classification by subject matter, were published in 1972 and was completed in 1981. The Renton Committee made no proposals for the reform of the existing arrangements governing the publication of statutes, but it did express the view that the Statute Law Committee's functions might be extended to include the continuous review of their structure and language.[68]

## LAW REFORM

There is a basic difficulty about a concept of law reform distinguishable from the promotion of general changes in the law. Reform is, at least to the extent that there is pre-existent law, inherent in the law-making process. Nevertheless, the expression is generally understood to be concerned with a more specialised area of activity than this, even if its boundaries are vague and imprecise. It comprehends reform of the substance and the form of the law and of the institutions of the legal system, typically where these matters fall within the traditional preserves of lawyers and have been developed by case law rather than legislation. Sir Michael Kerr, a former

[68]See below, p. 106.

Chairman of the Law Commission, has defined law reform as comprising "recommendations for changes and improvements in any part of the law which can appropriately be put forward by a body of lawyers on the basis of legal principle and pragmatic common sense, after due public consultation."[69]

As with statute law revision and consolidation, it would be wrong to characterise law reform as a technical exercise having no political implications. Although the concept of law reform can be supported on the basis of the technical nature of the areas of law involved, and on the inadequacies, if not the unacceptability, of the judicial process as a means of promoting desired changes in the law, "law reform" or "lawyer's law" can give rise to conflicts which are as sharp as those traditionally associated with general legislation. Nevertheless, as with the arrangements for statute law revision and consolidation, the use of legal expertise in the preparation of "law reform" Bills may allow them to be presented as "technical" or "purely legal." This in turn means that discussion may be more restricted, with only lawyers participating,[70] and that some parliamentary time may be saved.

These points are illustrated by the way in which a number of reform measures affecting the substance of the criminal law have been dealt with over the past few years; in particular the introduction of statutory definitions of conspiracy in 1977,[71] of amendments to the offence of criminal deception in 1978,[72] of changes in the law relating to the arrest and detention of suspects in Scotland in 1980,[73] and in 1981, of changes in the law governing contempt of court[74] and criminal attempts.[75] Many of the proposals contained in these measures were based upon the recommendations of permanent or ad hoc law reform bodies, and the Bills incorporating them were for the most part presented as matters of "law reform" or of "lawyer's law." Yet they were, to put

[69] Kerr, *op.cit.*, p. 516. See also Farrar, *Law Reform and Law Commissions* (1974), p. 1.

[70] A large number of the MPs who are appointed to the Commons' standing committees established for such Bills have legal qualifications.

[71] Criminal Law Act 1977.

[72] Theft Act 1978.

[73] Criminal Justice (Scotland) Act 1980.

[74] Contempt of Court Act 1981.

[75] Criminal Attempts Act 1981. With the exception of this measure, all these Acts were introduced in the House of Lords. As Consolidation and Statute Law Revision Bills invariably have their First Reading in the Upper House, as do many other "law reform" measures, the decision to introduce a Bill in the Lords is a tactic which may help to present a measure as being a matter of "lawyers' law."

it mildly, controversial, and raised difficult issues of criminal policy. Nor are controversy and policy conflicts confined to areas of public law; proposals for changes in such areas of private law as breach of confidence, liability for defective products, implied terms in contracts and in Scotland, diligence,[76] may equally provoke disagreement. Regarding proposed changes in family law, Crossman wrote:

> "This afternoon Gerald Gardiner [the Lord Chancellor] brought forward at Home Affairs a Divorce Bill to implement the reforms recommended by the Law Commission. He said rather airily that he thought that this had been so widely accepted not only by the Law Commission but by the Archbishop's committee that it was bound to get through without any controversy. This was greeted with a hearty roar of laughter by the Secretaries of State for Wales and Scotland who said there'd be plenty of disagreement."[77]

Individual government departments are responsible for the initiation of changes in the law falling within their areas of administration. In addition, the Lord Chancellor's Office in England and Wales and the Lord Advocate's Department in Scotland have a general responsibility for changes in those areas of the civil law and its administration which do not fall within the responsibilities of other departments. Changes introduced by these departments have frequently been based upon reports of ad hoc committees, but it was not until quite recently that these arrangements were placed on a more permanent basis. In 1934 the Lord Chancellor, Lord Sankey set up the Law Revision Committee, revived after the war in 1952, as the Law Reform Committee "to consider, having regard especially to judicial decisions, what changes are desirable in such legal doctrines as may be from time to time referred to it." In Scotland, an informal group appointed by the Lord Advocate did similar work until 1955 when it was formally appointed as the Scottish Law Reform Committee, but this lapsed on the establishment of the Scottish Law Commission. In 1959 the Home Secretary, R.A. Butler, set up the Criminal Law Revision Committee "to examine such aspects of the criminal law of England and Wales" as the Home Secretary might refer to it, and "to consider whether the law requires revision and to make recommendations." The Department of Trade established a Company Law panel in 1980 to review

[76] Diligence is a debt-collecting procedure; see Scottish Law Commission, Fifteenth Annual Report 1979–80 (1980) Scot. Law. Com. No. 61, para 2.2.

[77] Crossman, *op.cit.*, Vol. 2, pp. 495–496. See also Lord Hailsham L.C. "Obstacles to Law Reform" (1981) 34 C.L.P. 279, 281–282.

and report on desirable developments of company law and proposals for changes designed to improve the operation of the Companies and related Acts "in the light of modern conditions and practices," and on anything else referred to it by the Department.

The Law Commissions' establishment under the Law Commissions Act 1965 represents the most far reaching commitment to a separate notion of law reform. They are specifically charged with the duty of keeping under review all the law with which they are respectively concerned "with a view to its systematic development and reform, including in particular the codification of such law, the elimination of such anomalies . . . and generally the simplification and modernisation of the law."[78] In contrast to the bodies examined above they may examine branches of the law and formulate proposals for their reform on their own initiative pursuant to programmes approved by the Minister, as well as at the request of the Minister. In England and Wales, the Law Commission has been chaired successively by four High Court judges, and the other Commissioners, who are also full time appointments, have generally constituted a common law Q.C. with criminal law experience, a practising solicitor with experience in property law and two legal academics specialising in other areas. The Commissioners are supported by a legal staff from the civil service, parliamentary draftsmen seconded from the Office of Parliamentary Counsel and administrative and library staff.[79] Similar arrangements exist in Scotland.[80]

The Law Commissions have generally sought to avoid controversy both in the branches of law which they have selected for examination and through a process of extensive consultation on the basis of working papers prefatory to the issue of a report. How controversial their proposals are depends of course to a considerable extent on how successfully their recommendations are depicted as a matter of "pure" law reform. Their conservatism in the selection of issues for examination is reinforced by the exercise of the ministerial veto; where the Law Commission proposed the institution of a broad enquiry into administrative law by a Royal Commission or a committee of comparable status its proposal was rejected by the Lord Chancellor.[81] Perhaps for these reasons the Commissions have not dealt directly with tax, labour law or company law. They have instead concentrated on subjects typically falling within the

[78] Law Commissions Act 1965, s.3(1).
[79] Kerr, *op.cit.*, pp. 522–523.
[80] Scottish Law Commission, Fifteenth Annual Report, *op.cit.*, paras. 1.1 – 1.6.
[81] The Law Commission, *Administrative Law* (1969) Law Com. No. 20.

traditional scope of law reform: family law, contract, property and criminal law. Within these areas, the Law Commission had by 1980 published 102 Reports and 76 Working Papers; of the 56 Reports containing law reform recommendations, 39 have been enacted in whole or in part.[82]

The effect of these arrangements has been to mobilise lawyers' expertise within institutional frameworks specifically designed to promote different aspects of law reform. They do not however infringe the government's monopoly over the formulation of policy; rather they increase the range and variety of advice available to it. Even in this latter respect these bodies do not enjoy a monopoly over particular aspects of law reform. The Criminal Law Revision Committee, for example, has no monopoly of reform of the criminal law; proposals for change continue to be made ad hoc by departmental and inter-departmental committees, and since 1965, by the Law Commissions.

At the end of the day the implementation of their recommendations depends upon the government. This dependancy may limit the nature of their recommendations, and in the case of the Law Commissions, their choice of subjects. Even where their recommendations are endorsed by the government, this does not guarantee their enactment. Ministers have been increasingly reluctant to press for their inclusion on the programme, for this may result in the loss of other departmental Bills which may appear more pressing. The Law Commissions have consequently turned to backbench Members to sponsor legislation. Thus although successive governments have made arrangements for law reform which encourage specialisation and the diffusion of tasks, the legislative initiative remains with the Cabinet; and this is as true of the apparently technical changes in the law associated with consolidation, statute law revision and law reform, as it is of the government's major political commitments.

[82] Kerr, *op.cit.*, p. 527.

CHAPTER THREE

# THE PRE-PARLIAMENTARY STAGES

C.K. Allen observed in *Law in the Making* that: "The elements which contribute to the framing of much modern legislation are numerous and diverse. They are bound to be so in crowded communities where public opinion is not usually one collective and unanimous sentiment, but is fragmented among many different sections and interests."[1]

His observation was echoed by the Lord President of the Council and the Government Chief Whip in evidence to the Select Committee on Procedure in 1971:

> "The origin of Bills and the manner of their preparation are as diverse as the Bills themselves. Some Bills derive directly from a political decision or a commitment in a manifesto . . . Others grow naturally out of the ordinary work of Government Departments; in such cases the start of preparations for a new Bill may be hardly distinguishable from the continuing process of administering the existing law. Departments maintain close contact with local authorities and others concerned in the administration of the various services and many proposals for the amendment of the law come to notice in this way. Memoranda from professional and trade associations, academic studies, articles in the Press, letters from Members and the public all contribute suggestions for legislation. It would often be impossible to disentangle the threads and say with confidence where a particular provision in a Bill originated.[2]

Given the wide range of types of Acts which we identified in Chapter 1 and the inherent diversity in their origins and manner of preparation, it would be virtually impossible within the space of one chapter to deal exhaustively with every aspect of the pre-parliamentary stages of the legislative process. Rather we shall attempt to outline what we regard as their dominant and recurrent features.

[1] (7th ed., 1964), p. 433.

[2] *The Process of Legislation*, Second Report from the Select Committee on Procedure (1971; H.C. 538), Appendix 5, para. 5. For an earlier analysis along similar lines see Jennings, *Parliament* (2nd ed., 1957), pp. 183–234.

There are two dominant features which exercise a continuous and pervasive influence on the processes by which legislative initiatives are decided upon and formulated. The first which we have already emphasised, is the responsibility of government for the initiation of almost all of the legislation that is enacted in the United Kingdom. The second is that government in exercising that responsibility normally seeks to mobilise the co-operation and agreement of groups affected by its proposals. In general terms, therefore, we see the pre-parliamentary or deliberative and preparatory, stages as being characterised by a continuous interplay between government and outside groups. This is the case in both the determination and formulation of legislative initiatives. Accordingly in this chapter we shall examine first the part these participants play and, then, the main features of the process leading up to the formal preparation of a Bill to be introduced in Parliament.

## THE ROLE OF GOVERNMENT

In Chapter 1, we saw that responsibility for the formulation and introduction of the greater part of the legislation enacted in the United Kingdom rests in practice with government. It is now accepted that government has not only the right but is also under a duty to bring forward a prepared programme of legislation for each parliamentary session. In this sense we described legislation as a function of government. Accordingly, although as the quotations at the beginning of this chapter suggest, an individual enactment may be attributable to any one or several of a wide variety of sources, it is the government which in a very real sense constitutes the formal source of, if not the inspiration behind, virtually all legislation.

In examining the origins within government of legislative proposals it is useful to distinguish between two of its constituent elements: the party or elected element represented by the Cabinet, and the permanent or administrative element, the civil service. Although the Cabinet is responsible for determining the content of the legislative programme for each session, it is the source of only a limited number of the proposals put forward. "In an average session legislation for which a mandate has been given occupies only a fraction of the time spent on Bills."[3] Rose estimates that only 8 and 13 per cent. respectively of the Bills introduced by the 1970–74 Conservative Government and by the 1974–79 Labour Governments can be attributed to their respective election manifestos.[4] The great

[3] Eckstein in *Patterns of Government* (Beer and Ulam ed., 1965), p. 133.
[4] *Do Parties Make a Difference?* (1980), pp. 70–72.

proportion of Bills, 81 and 75 per cent. respectively, originated within government departments, the remaining proportion being accounted for by legislation enacted in response to unexpected events such as the Rolls Royce Purchase Act 1971, the Prevention of Terrorism Act 1974 and the Drought Act 1976.[5] These figures do not distinguish the qualitative significance of each element's contribution and, given that a party's electoral programme is not definitive of the range and extent of its policies, they probably underestimate the size of the party element's contribution to the legislative programme. Nevertheless they do indicate the importance of the permanent element in government as source of legislative proposals.[6]

The part played by each element in the preparation of the legislative programme cannot, however, be measured solely in terms of the origins of Bills. As the examples of legislative proposals brought forward in response to unexpected events illustrate, the preparation of individual proposals depends on the successful linking of both elements. Proposals emanating from the Cabinet will be prepared by the responsible department in consultation with other departments whose responsibilities and interests may be affected. The response of the responsible department or of other departments may lead to the modification, deferrment or even abandonment of proposals. Conversely, departmental proposals depend for their progress initially on convincing the Minister of the desirability, if not the necessity, of their introduction and thereafter on the Minister's success in securing the agreement of his Cabinet colleagues.[7] The picture which emerges of the preparation of the legislative programme is thus a complex one which has as its focal point the institutional arrangements at Cabinet level outlined in the previous chapter. Essentially its preparation involves a two-way process. On the one hand, proposals emanating from the party element are relayed from the Cabinet to departments for consideration, consultation and preparation and, on the other hand, given the limited parliamentary time available, departmental proposals which have secured ministerial support vie with one another for inclusion in the programme.[8]

[5] Eleven per cent. in each case, *ibid.* See also Jennings, *op.cit.*, Appendix 2.

[6] When a government has been in office for some time it may be impossible to say whether party policies stem from departments or *vice versa*, Jennings, *op.cit.*, p. 204.

[7] The process is well described by Morrison, *Government and Parliament* (3rd ed., 1964), pp. 237–238.

[8] See above, pp. 25–29.

## THE ROLE OF OUTSIDE GROUPS

It is perhaps commonplace to observe that much of the legislation initiated by government has been moulded by the unceasing efforts of interested groups who seek to imbue formal legislative initiatives with their own interests and ideas. While concentration on their role alone would, in view of the control which government exercises over access to the legislative process and the preparation of legislation, present a highly misleading picture of the legislative process, their influence cannot be ignored. As Walkland observes, "the formal policy processes of British government are not carried out in a vacuum. The Departmental structure is increasingly characterised by an agency-clientele relationship with powerful organised interests; Departments are usually wise to take note of the attitudes of those pressure groups, whose adherence to official policy is often vital to its success."[9] If, given its responsibility for the initiation of legislation, competition within government is one of the characteristic features of the establishment of legislative priorities, one of the recurrent features of the preparation of individual enactments is the involvement of outside groups, whether public or private.

A distinction is normally drawn between two types of groups, "sectional" or "interest" groups and "promotional" or "cause" groups. Sectional groups perform a wide variety of functions on behalf of their membership. In relation to the political and legislative processes, their function involves the promotion and protection of the interests and points of view of the particular section of society which they represent. They cover, if not evenly, the whole spectrum of society ranging from local groups such as tenants' or residents' associations to major groups such as the Trade Union Congress and the Confederation of British Industry. Their significance and influence vary markedly. Of particular significance, however, are "producer groups" consisting of financial, industrial, trade union and professional interests such as the TUC, the CBI, the National Farmers' Union, the National Union of Teachers, the British Medical Association and the Law Society.

Promotional or cause groups on the other hand have an almost exclusively political function in that their activities are restricted to the defence and promotion of specific causes arising from a given set of common attitudes among their membership. Among such groups, we would include organisations such as the Howard League for Penal Reform, the National Council for Civil Liberties, the Royal Society for the Prevention of Cruelty to Animals, the National

[9] *The Legislative Process in Great Britain* (1969), p. 22.

Anti-Vivisection Society, Justice, the Abortion Law Reform Association, the Society for the Protection of the Unborn Child and the Lord's Day Observance Society.[10] This distinction between sectional and cause groups, while valuable, is not a rigid one. The protection and furtherance of their members' interests may involve sectional groups in work of a promotional nature. Cause groups may be supported by and provide a vehicle for the representation of sectional interests. Moreover, some cause groups, such as those concerned with welfare and environmental issues—Shelter, Friends of the Earth and the Child Poverty Action Group—may seek to combine representative as well as promotional functions.

Given that the function of these groups is the representation and furtherance of their members' interests and views, it is axiomatic that their influence in relation to legislation may be negative as well as positive, involving them both in initiating proposals for legislation as well as in reacting to legislative initiatives, either through outright opposition or, as is more common, through seeking to amend them. Perhaps the clearest illustration of their negative influence was provided by the opposition of the Trade Union movement to the 1966–70 Labour Government's proposals for industrial relations legislation embodied in the White Paper, *In Place of Strife*, an opposition which led ultimately to the abandonment of the proposed legislation.

Clearly the likely extent of an outside group's involvement in the preparatory stages of a Bill will depend in part upon its subject matter. The Howard League for Penal Reform has no direct interest in legislation dealing with the economy or industrial relations, whereas the CBI and the TUC clearly do. Equally one would not expect the latter to be directly concerned with legislation dealing with penal policy. In general, however, the breadth of sectional and in particular producer groups' involvement in the preparatory stages of the legislative process is much greater than that of cause groups. In the absence of the direct and permanent access to government enjoyed by sectional groups, cause groups' efforts are more visibly directed towards influencing the media and lobbying MPs.[11]

How can we account for the greater likelihood of sectional group involvement in the preparation of legislation? Most commonly it is attributed to a shared pluralist conception of authority on the part of government and outside interests. Thus Beer attributes their greater

[10] On the growth of promotional groups, see Kimber and Richardson, *Pressure Groups in Britain* (1974).

[11] Mackintosh, *The British Cabinet* (3rd ed., 1977), p. 573.

involvement to "the widespread acceptance of functional representation in British political culture."[12] Acceptance of functional representation has in turn meant that: "It has now almost become a convention of the constitution that the interests likely to be affected by developments in public policy have, through their representative associations, a right to be consulted by policy makers," and that governments "are regarded as having a corresponding duty to consult before taking final decisions."[13] This is undoubtedly correct. However, it should not be allowed to obscure the extent to which shared expectations as to the way in which public, including legislative, power will be exercised are themselves the product of government's increased dependence on the acquiescence if not the active co-operation of these groups in the attainment of its policy objectives and of the tacit or explicit recognition of the power which their control of the resources involved affords them to "limit, deflect and even frustrate government initiatives."[14]

Commentators rightly emphasise the benefits derived from the involvement of these groups by both the groups themselves and government. For the groups, their involvement constitutes a procedural guarantee that their interests and views will be given a hearing if not reflected in the content of proposals. For government, on the other hand, the groups' expertise and advice may be crucial to the formulation of workable proposals and their acquiescence, if not active co-operation, may be equally vital to the successful implementation of proposals. These groups are thus important and necessary channels of communication which parallel, but do not supplant, representation through the electoral system. Without their activity, Finer observes, party rule would be "a rigid and ignorant tyranny," and public administration "a rigid and stupid bureaucracy."[15] To the extent that their privileged position in relation to government creates a danger that interests other than those immediately involved might well be ignored, adequate safeguards are seen as existing in the fragmented and often competing nature of groups, together with the independent authority enjoyed by government, which, reinforced by its responsibility to party and Parliament, enable it to resist their demands and give it the capacity to impose its own conceptions of the general interest.[16] However, a number of factors suggest this assessment may be overly

[12] *Modern British Politics* (1965), p. 329.
[13] Smith, *Policy Making in British Government* (1976), p. 56.
[14] Mackintosh, *op.cit.*, p. 578.
[15] *Anonymous Empire* (2nd ed., 1966), p. 113.
[16] See *e.g.* Walkland, *op.cit.*, p. 36; Hanson and Walles, *Governing Britain* (3rd ed., 1980), pp. 162–164.

sanguine. These include the declining electoral appeal of the two major political parties, the failure of successive post-war governments' economic policies upon which so much else depends, and the limits to group tolerance and public authority respectively revealed by, for example, attempts to reform industrial relations or control prices and incomes by legislation.[17]

This analysis of the role of sectional groups in relation to policy making as well as legislation illustrates that where defined interests are involved which government is either unwilling or unable to coerce, it is, despite the authority which it possesses independently of these groups and its control of the legislative process, somewhat constrained by what is acceptable to the interests involved. "This need to consult and persuade, to secure the support of groups who have the power to block its actions, limits policy options open to government."[18] These considerations apply equally to the manner in which legislative proposals are formulated. Despite the monopoly which government possesses in their formulation, the emphasis is more on discussion, consultation and the accommodation of affected interests than on their coercion. It is "a central feature of British administration that no attempt should be made to formulate a new policy in any matter without the fullest consultation with those who have practical experience in that field, and with those who will be called upon to carry it out."[19]

## THE PREPARATION OF PROPOSALS

The part played by these, the main participants in the pre-parliamentary stages of the legislative process, forms the background to our examination of the preparatory process itself. The enactment of legislation has been described as

> "a continuous process, which begins when the idea for a bill originates whether in an election manifesto, or in the report of a commission or in the administrative shortcomings of existing provisions or in the pressure exerted by certain groups to which the Government is beholden. As the ideas begin to take shape and a place is found for the proposal in the legislative programme, consultations begin with the interests and instruc-

[17] See further: Mackintosh, *op.cit.*, pp. 568–581; Finer, *The Changing British Party System, 1945–1979* (1980); Middlemass, *Politics in Industrial Society* (1979), pp. 430–463.

[18] Lord Croham, quoted in Richardson and Jordan, *Governing Under Pressure* (1979), p. 3.

[19] Sir Edward Bridges, quoted in Mackintosh, *op.cit.*, p. 568.

> tions begin to flow from the Department to Parliamentary Counsel. The Treasury and other related departments having been satisfied, then, several conferences later, the bill will emerge in a more or less complete form and be printed and read a second time."[20]

Although the preparation and enactment of legislation is a continuous process, three distinct elements are involved in the formulation of a detailed proposal: the identification of the issue, investigation and evaluation, and consultation. In practice the manner of preparation of individual Bills is as diverse as their subject matter and these elements frequently overlap or are combined, for example in response to an unforeseen contingency. Nevertheless they are functionally distinguishable. Below we concentrate initially on the identification of the issue and the investigative process, before examining the consultative aspects of the preparation of legislative proposals more fully. The drafting stage which takes place once a detailed proposal has been formulated is examined in Chapter 4.

## *IDENTIFICATION OF THE ISSUE*

All legislation stems from the reactions, whether of political parties, government departments or individual MPs, to circumstances which they perceive as raising issues or constituting problems which require action. Whether circumstances, be they political, administrative, social or economic, are perceived in this way depends on the perspectives of the groups or individuals in question. The perception by groups or individuals of circumstances as requiring action thus constitutes a normative exercise conducted in terms of their values. As such, these reactions may vary both laterally, that is across groups, and sequentially, that is through time. Laterally, not all groups may accept that the circumstances involved raise an issue or constitute a problem, or, where they do, they may not agree on their nature or on what responses are appropriate. Sequentially, the same circumstances may be perceived differently at different times and thus as meriting different responses; sometimes they even may be perceived as raising no issue or problem at all.[21] Reactions, accordingly, are important for two reasons: first they serve to establish whether action is required and secondly, assuming that it

[20] Griffith, *Parliamentary Scrutiny of Government Bills* (1974), p. 90.
[21] For an example see Page, "State Intervention in the Inter-War Period: The Special Areas Acts 1934–37" (1976) 2 B.J.L.S. 175.

is, the form that it should take. As we have seen legislation will be required as a matter of law where the response envisaged involves a change in the law, the raising of revenue or the authorisation of expenditure on a permanent basis. By the identification of the subject matter, therefore, we mean simply the perception of circumstances as undesirable and as thus necessitating a response the form of which requires the enactment of legislation.

The subject matter of some legislation may not itself be at issue. A primary example of this is financial legislation. To survive in office a government must secure legislative sanction for the raising and spending of money through the enactment of annual Finance, Consolidated Fund and Consolidated Fund (Appropriation) Bills. These Bills thus constitute a permanent and vital feature of the work of each legislative session. Even here, however, it is worth noting that while financial legislation derives its general character from the necessity of securing legislative authorisation for the raising and spending of money, its detailed content (although subject to important constraints as a result of the need to ensure the continued financing of government activity) does involve choices and, therefore, may be at issue. Thus, for example, a decision to alter rates of taxation or expenditure in a particular area, although effected through financial legislation may follow a process of investigation, evaluation and consultation which is not substantially different from that followed in the generality of legislation.

Apart from legislation which must be enacted annually the government is free to introduce legislation on such subjects as it thinks fit. Within government such legislation has, as we have seen, two sources: the party or elected element and the permanent element, the civil service. Topics for possible future legislation are typically identified by political parties when in opposition either in response to the policies of the government in office, or as a result of the work of the party's own research and policy-making groups. The party's election manifesto constitutes the most important initial source of inspiration for legislation when elected. Although policies continue to be worked out while in office the proportion of legislation attributable to the party element in government tends to decline over the life of a Parliament.

As we have noted the permanent element is in fact responsible for the majority of the proposals introduced in each Session. Departmental Bills emanate from what Parris describes as "the momentum of government itself,"[22] the discharge by departments of their

[22] *Constitutional Bureaucracy* (1969), p. 95.

responsibilities. "More often than not the need for a Bill emerges in the ordinary course of administrative work."[23] These Bills may take several forms. They may, for example, promote some desirable reform which may be enacted if parliamentary time allows. Such Bills may be used to fill gaps in the legislative timetable or else given to MPs who have secured a place in the ballot for private Members' Bills. More importantly, they may be consequential upon previous legislation, for example, amending it in response to administrative difficulties which have arisen or providing continued authorisation for the exercise of powers or the expenditure of money. Apart from these largely minor Bills, there are also major Bills which concern departmental policies whose form, while influenced by the political process, is not solely attributable to it, for example, in relation to housing, social security, financial assistance to industry, or incomes policy. Bills enacted to give effect to these policies illustrate the fallacy of assuming that because they originate within departments they are necessarily apolitical.

The prohibition of individual resale price maintenance by the Resale Prices Act 1964 is a good example of a measure which was departmental in origin yet of considerable political significance. It also illustrates some of the more general themes which we have discussed.

Resale price maintenance originated during the late nineteenth century and rapidly became a widespread trade practice. Under it suppliers set the price at which their goods were to be sold by retailers. This system of stipulated prices was backed up by judicially sanctioned machinery for their private enforcement. Retailers who failed to observe stipulated prices could be fined by trade association courts and, where the failure was persistent, stop-listed. Suppliers undertook not to supply stop-listed retailers with goods. Between the wars the uniform response of industry to the slump in demand was to reduce capacity and output in an effort to maintain prices. Against a background of overwhelming business and political support for the restriction of competition, the Greene Committee in 1931 endorsed resale price maintenance and recommended against its limitation. It concluded that "the ordinary right of freedom to contract ought not to be withdrawn without some compelling reason."[24]

After the war attitudes towards the restraint of trade underwent a gradual change and the Board of Trade appears to have become convinced of the economic case for the dismantlement of resale price

[23] Ram, "The Improvement of the Statute Book" (1951) 1 J.S.P.T.L. 442, 446.
[24] *The Restraint of Trade* (1931).

maintenance and other restrictive trade practices. "If any one major source of the 1964 Bill can be discerned it lies in the matured policy of this Department."[25] The Board was supported in this policy by the 1949 Lloyd Jacob Committee which concluded that the collective enforcement of resale price maintenance was contrary to the public interest and should be made illegal, but that individual manufacturers should remain free to maintain the end price of their goods.[26] The Labour Government subsequently entered into discussions with manufacturers and traders, but the failure of its attempts to negotiate the voluntary abandonment of collective enforcement and the moderation of individual enforcement revealed that the practice was entrenched and that its restriction could only be secured by legislation. In June 1951 the Government announced in a White Paper its intention of legislating against both forms of resale price maintenance.[27] However, for a government nearing the end of its life the implementation of this intention was a political impossibility.

The attitude of the subsequent Conservative Government towards resale price maintenance was less clearly defined. Part II of the Restrictive Trade Practices Act 1956 prohibited certain forms of the collective enforcement of resale price maintenance, but in an important *quid pro quo* the Act strengthened its individual enforcement against third parties who were not in a direct contractual relationship with the supplier. For the first time suppliers were provided with a legal remedy against retailers who failed to observe stipulated prices of which they had been notified.

The prohibition of collective resale price maintenance was followed by an "insistent" attack on its individual counterpart.[28] This attack was reinforced by the condemnation of the practice in a succession of reports. However, although the increasing emphasis placed on economic growth and consumer protection favoured the Board of Trade's policy, its implementation was made unlikely by the widespread support which existed for the practice among suppliers and retailers and within the Conservative Party. In 1959 the President of the Board of Trade, Reginald Maudling, refused to put a departmental proposal for the prohibition of individual resale price maintenance before the Cabinet because of the likelihood of its rejection.[29] In response to criticism the Government announced the setting up of a departmental committee to investigate the practice.

[25] Walkland, *op.cit.*, p. 30.
[26] Report of the Committee on Resale Price Maintenance, Cmd. 7696 (1949).
[27] *A Statement on Resale Price Maintenance*, Cmd. 8274 (1951).
[28] Pickering, *Resale Price Maintenance in Practice* (1966), p. 216.
[29] Bruce-Gardyne and Lawson, *The Power Game* (1976), p. 86.

The report of this committee was not published but it was widely believed to have recommended the prohibition of individual resale price maintenance, with only limited provision for exemption. No further action was taken until January 1962 when this report was presented "a little airily" to the Cabinet by Reginald Maudling's successor as President of the Board of Trade, Frederick Errol. The report was decisively rejected on the grounds of the political opposition which its implementation would engender.[30]

With the resignation of Harold Macmillan in October 1963, Edward Heath assumed the increased responsibilities of President of the Board of Trade and Secretary of State for Industry, Trade and Regional Development. Apart from the increased political weight which he brought to the office and the Prime Ministerial support upon which he could rely, two factors were crucial to the subsequent prohibition of individual resale price maintenance. The first was Edward Heath's conviction that the retrieval of the political initiative from the Opposition depended upon convincing the electorate that the Government's capacity for innovations in policy was not exhausted. The Board of Trade put forward two possibilities: a new policy on regional economic development and the prohibition of individual resale price maintenance. The principal attraction of the latter was that its results would be more politically immediate than those of the former. The second factor was the result of the ballot for private Members' Bills in which John Stonehouse secured first place. He announced his intention of introducing a Bill to secure the abolition of individual resale price maintenance. This effectively compelled the Government to adopt a position on the issue and provided Edward Heath with an opportunity to seize the initiative. On January 15, 1964 he announced the Government's intention of seeking the prohibition of individual resale price maintenance and on February 25, the Resale Prices Bill received its first reading.

Although the genesis of the Resale Prices Bill illustrates the importance of departmental policies and short-term political considerations in the emergence of legislation, it was equally atypical of the process in that it was marked by the complete absence of consultation prior to its introduction. The controversy which this lack of consultation aroused reveals the strength of the expectation that governments will legislate on the basis of consultation and agreement. In relation to the Resale Prices Bill the lack of consultation meant that the conflict between the Government and organised interests, including their representatives within the

[30] *Financial Times*, January 16, 1964; Bruce Gardyne and Lawson, *op.cit.*, p. 89.

Conservative Party, was fought out during the parliamentary stages of the legislative process. The seriousness of that conflict was emphasised by the abstention of the Opposition from the vote on the Bill's second reading. Twenty Conservative backbenchers voted against the Government and a greater number abstained, the largest revolt within the Party since the fall of the Chamberlain Government in 1940.

Both government departments and political parties are heavily reliant upon sectional and cause groups for the identification of issues upon which legislation may be necessary. Issues are not identified and policies are not formulated in isolation. As Finer observes of political parties, they

> " . . . do not, on the whole, make their policies in a vacuum. Policies are usually framed in opposition not when a party is in power; and in opposition, parties have no civil servants to advise them. Therefore, they have to rely on working parties of their supporters and on their research organisations; but these, in turn, tend to seek advice from those who are competent to give it; *i.e.* the various lobbies. For their part, these lobbies are only too glad to have a party espouse their particular causes. Of course, a party will reject many such supplications; it will alter others to make them harmonise with the claims of the other groups sponsored in its programme; it will moderate all such special pleas to fit the contours of the party's temper, principles and philosophy; and above all it will remember that the party exists to win elections. In short, though party ideology may owe nothing to any sectional groups, the detailed programme usually owes a great deal."[31]

Similarly, government departments rely on groups affected by their policies for the identification of needed reforms and proposals brought forward by departments may reflect the expressed needs of client groups.

Where a group enjoys a close relationship with government in either the party or permanent sense, its task involves impressing upon government the desirability of the proposed legislation. Where it fails to elicit a favourable response, whether out of conviction or expediency, or where it does not enjoy such a relationship it may resort to more visible means of achieving the same end, for example by lobbying the media or MPs in an attempt to create a climate of opinion favourable to the proposed change.[32] Not infrequently, the

[31] *Anonymous Empire, op.cit.*, p. 20.

[32] For an instructive example see Kimber, Richardson and Brookes, "The Deposit of Poisonous Wastes Act 1972: A Case of Government by Reaction" [1974] P.L. 198.

group may succeed in convincing an MP of the desirability of promoting legislation on the issue. Although few of these proposed Bills are enacted, a glance at any list of private Members' Bills is illustrative of the range of issues upon which legislation is sought. Recent examples include: Abortion (Amendment); Constitutional Referendum; Dogs Control; Hare Coursing (Abolition); Mental Health Patients (Rights to Vote); Sex Shops (Control) and Skyline Protection. Some of these issues may be of no more than temporary concern, while others tend to recur on the political agenda. Where issues do recur this is attributable frequently to the efforts of cause groups, their efforts in turn normally being matched and opposed by competing groups, for example the Abortion Law Reform Association and the Society for the Protection of the Unborn Child.

## *INVESTIGATION AND EVALUATION*

The investigation of issues has two aspects. It involves first the determination of whether the circumstances involved raise an issue or constitute a problem which requires the enactment of legislation; in this sense the investigative process constitutes an inherent part of the identification of the issue examined above. Secondly, given acceptance of the desirability or necessity of legislation, it involves the examination and evaluation of alternative strategies for achieving the desired objective; in this sense it constitutes an inherent part of the translation of the reaction into an effective and workable legislative proposal. The investigation of alternatives is most commonly undertaken by government departments in consultation with each other and with outside interests where appropriate. Even where proposals are embodied in the party's election manifesto, they must be reassessed and revised in the light of the administrative practicalities and the economic and political circumstances confronted when in office. Additionally, the government may establish an ad hoc body to investigate whether action, including legislation, is desirable and if so, the form which it should take. These ad hoc bodies may serve as an alternative or a complement to the continuous processes of administration, inquiry and reflection within government departments.

Excluding *standing* investigatory bodies such as the Law Commissions discussed in Chapter 2 these ad hoc bodies may take three main forms: parliamentary select committees, Royal Commissions and departmental and inter-departmental committees. With the government's assumption of responsibility for the formulation of policy and the initiation of legislation during the mid-nineteenth century, parliamentary select committees were gradually replaced by Royal Commissions as the preferred form of investigatory body. During the present century Royal Commissions have been effectively replaced by departmental and inter-departmental committees. Our concern in this section is with the part which Royal Commissions and departmental and inter-departmental committees may play overall in the legislative process.

The first point to note about these bodies is that the initiative in their establishment, the appointment of their membership and the determination of their terms of reference rest with government. Apart from the greater formal authority and status which Royal Commissions are regarded as enjoying by virtue of the manner of their appointment,[33] there are no significant differences between these forms of investigating bodies.[34] The "golden age" of Royal Commissions was undoubtedly during the middle of the last century when, in the period after the industrial revolution, they emerged as the "chief instruments of government investigation and preparation for numerous innovations in social and industrial policy."[35] Much of the framework and responsibilities of modern government can be traced to the investigations of Royal Commissions such as those which preceded the development of the poor law, public health, education, housing, local government and factory legislation. Their rise was meteoric: by the middle of the nineteenth century they were being appointed at the rate of seven a year. In 1859 alone no fewer than 13 were appointed.[36] By the end of the century their use had begun to decline and by the nineteen thirties they were being appointed at the rate of only two a year.[37] This decline has been more than offset by the increasing use made of departmental and inter-departmental committees, over 1,400 of which have been appointed since the beginning of this century.[38]

Broadly speaking these bodies may be charged with either or both of two functions: the investigation of an issue and the making of recommendations either independently of or pursuant to an investigation.[39] Concentration on their overt function alone is, however, potentially misleading. Examination of the reasons under-

[33] They are appointed by Royal Warrant issued to the Commissioners by the Queen on the advice of a Secretary of State, whereas departmental and inter-departmental committees are appointed by a Minister or Ministers.

[34] Wheare, *Government by Committee* (1955), p. 69.

[35] Clokie and Robinson, *Royal Commissions of Inquiry* (1937), p. 1.

[36] Cartwright, *Royal Commissions and Departmental Committees in Britain* (1975), p. 37.

[37] *Ibid.*, p. 39.

[38] *Ibid.*, p. 40.

[39] For a fuller analysis, see *ibid.*, pp. 101–104.

lying their use reveals a negative as well as a positive side to their establishment. As Jennings observed they are established by government "to examine any question for which it cannot find, *or does not want to find*, an immediate solution."[4] This delaying or "symbolic" aspect cannot be ignored in examining the relationship between their establishment and the subject matter of their investigation. Accordingly, apart from examining a problem or issues which the government wants to tackle, but on which it is not committed to any particular policy, Royal Commissions, departmental and inter-departmental committees may also be established, for example, to prepare the way for a policy to which the government *is* already committed,[41] to forestall anticipated criticism or pressure,[42] to pacify critics,[43] to postpone the necessity for action[44] or to kill a proposal.[45]

Recommendations made by these bodies for the introduction of legislation may or may not be acted upon by the government. Being advisory only, they do not restrict the government's freedom in the formulation of policy, and the government retains the same discretion in relation to the implementation of their recommendations as it does in relation to their establishment.[46] Accordingly

[40] Jennings, *op.cit.*, p.211, emphasis added.

[41] *e.g.* the perfunctory examination undertaken by the Balance of Trade Committee which preceded the enactment of the Import Duties Act 1932; Amery, *My Political Life* (1955), Vol. 3, p. 76.

[42] *e.g.* Report of the Royal Commission on Standards of Conduct in Government, Cmnd. 6526 (1976).

[43] *e.g.* Report of the Royal Commission on the Distribution of the Industrial Population, Cmd. 6153 (1939); Report of the Royal Commission on the Press, Cmd. 7700 (1949).

[44] *e.g.* Report of the Royal Commission in Marriage and Divorce, Cmd. 9678 (1955); Report of the Royal Commission on Capital Punishment, Cmd. 8932 (1953); Report of the Royal Commission on the Reform of the Trade Unions and Employers' Associations, Cmnd. 3623 (1968). Summing up the establishment of the last of these Kilroy-Silk observes that the Commission, "provided the excuse for procrastination. The Government could claim to be doing something when, in fact, it was doing nothing. Or rather it had managed to pass what, to it, was a politically dangerous issue on to other shoulders"; in *The Role of Commissions in Policy Making* (Chapman ed., 1973), p. 44.

[45] *e.g.* Report of the Royal Commission on Systems of Election, Cd. 5163 (1910).

[46] See Cmnd. 8214 (1981), Government's reply to the First Report of the Home Affairs Committee (1980; H.C. 23). The Committee, however, was not questioning the government's discretion, but the "dilatory and complacent manner" in which it had responded to a number of reports issued between 1972 and 1978. These reports included the Reports of: the Younger Committee on Privacy, Cmnd. 5012 (1972); the Finer Committee on One-Parent Families, Cmnd. 5629 (1974); the Butler Committee on Mentally Abnormal Offenders, Cmnd. 6255 (1975); and the Lindop Committee on Data Protection, Cmnd.7341 (1978).

where legislation is introduced it may depart significantly from Commission or committee recommendations. On the other hand, the failure to introduce legislation is not necessarily attributable to the government's intention in establishing them. Other factors such as cost, lack of parliamentary time, opposition or the unacceptability of the proposals to the government of the day may have influenced the decision not to act. Nevertheless, their reports may be of longer-term value in contributing to public awareness and in stimulating discussion of the issue.[47]

Because of the essentially advisory nature of all of these bodies, Clokie and Robinson's assessment of Royal Commissions as "a notable example of the wise combination of fact-finding and policy-forming in the modern state,"[48] probably overestimates their significance in relation to the decision-making and legislative processes. Even where legislation is introduced which does not depart significantly from Commission and committee recommendations difficulties arise in attributing that legislation to their deliberations.[49] At best they constitute one among a number of factors contributing to its enactment. What should not be ignored, however, is their significance as a means of involving groups outside government in the decision-making process, either through the inclusion of representatives of affected interests among their menbership, or their dependence upon those interests for the evidence upon which their conclusions are based. As such they "provide a unique channel through which private individuals and interest groups can participate directly in the making of public policy."[50]

## *CONSULTATION*

Once it has been decided that legislation is desirable a detailed legislative proposal must be formulated. This will be undertaken within the responsible department, and the proposal will normally go through a number of drafts. Where Cabinet sanction has been obtained for the introduction of legislation, consultations on the basis of a draft memorandum will take place between the responsible department and other affected departments, including the Treasury. In addition, the formulation of major proposals will be supervised by the appropriate Cabinet policy committee. Where the

[47] Wheare, *op.cit.*, pp. 68–69.
[48] *Op.cit.*, p. 5.
[49] Cartwright, *op.cit.*, pp. 204–206.
[50] *Ibid.*, p. 1; see also Chapman, *op.cit.*, p. 185.

approval of the Cabinet has not been obtained previously it will be sought on the basis of the memorandum as revised in the light of such preliminary consultations as have taken place.[51]

Achieving a degree of coherence in government policy requires that the views of other affected departments be taken into account in the preparation of legislative proposals. Consultation within government at ministerial and senior departmental level is accordingly mandatory. Consultation with outside groups and interests, on the other hand, takes place at the discretion of the government. It may take place on the basis of a Green Paper published with Cabinet approval on which the views of interested parties are sought.[52] Publication of the government's proposals in the form of a White Paper implies, instead, that the government is committed to at least the main principles of the policy outlined and the scope for consultation is correspondingly reduced. More commonly, however, consultation takes place on the basis of informal and private communications between departments, Ministers and affected interests.

In examining this feature of the formulation of legislative proposals we have already noted the extent to which outside groups expect to be and are consulted. "It is a legitimate ground for complaint by any considerable body that they have not been consulted."[53] In evidence to the Select Committee on Procedure in 1971 the Lord President of the Council and the Government Chief Whip stated that:

> "The extent of the consultation with outside interests during the preparatory stages of Bills and the forms which it takes also vary greatly; in some few cases there is no consultation at all. Where local authorities are concerned in the administration of a service, it is normal practice to consult their associations, more particularly on the practical provisions needed to give effect to the broad policy decisions. Similar consultations take place with representative bodies in other fields, sometimes on the initiative of those bodies. In some cases there is an extended process of public consultation, as when legislation is based on the published report of a Royal Commission or Departmental Committee which has taken evidence from the public. Many Bills are founded on White Papers which, even when not debated, provide interested persons with the opportunity to

[51] Ram, *op.cit.*, pp. 446–447, and see further Chap. 4 below.

[52] For example, *Trade Union Immunities*, Cmnd. 8128 (1981); see further Sandford, "Open Government: The Use of Green Papers" [1980] B.T.R. 351.

[53] Mackintosh, *op.cit.*, p. 568.

comment during the formative stage. Reports of the Law Commission, including the text of a draft Bill, are published in advance of legislation and are themselves produced after consultation with interested bodies."[54]

Two features of the consultative process deserve emphasis. First, it need not be confined to any single stage in the preparation of a proposal. A group's influence on a proposal therefore cannot be determined solely by reference to the extent to which it is formally consulted during its preparation. Thus it may, for example, have been the prime mover in the identification of an issue or its views may have been canvassed and reflected in the report of a Royal Commission or departmental committee upon which a Bill is ultimately based. Where the group has not had the opportunity of expressing its views previously, its influence will depend, in part, on the stage of the preparatory process at which it is consulted and, in particular, whether it is consulted before the principles of the legislation have been settled.

> "The most effective time for groups to operate is after a decision to legislate has been taken, but before a Bill has actually been drafted and published. Once the government has publicly committed itself to the main lines of a Bill, disagreement and opposition by interested parties can only usually be manifested by public or Parliamentary campaigns, which groups are not well-fitted to undertake. Given the structure of public decision-making in Britain, in which Parliament plays a distinctly subordinate role, this line of action is usually far less likely to be successful than attempting to persuade the Minister."[55]

Secondly, the extent of the group's influence will depend on the basis upon which it is consulted. There is a fundamental distinction between consultation as involving simply an expression of views, for example on a Green Paper or in response to specific requests, and consultation as involving negotiation or actual bargaining between the parties. Whereas the views expressed in consultation of the former type may or may not be taken into account by the government, the latter implies a much greater involvement of groups in the formulation of the proposal and the effective renunciation by government of unilateral decision-making. As Hartley and Griffith point out:

[54] *The Process of Legislation, op.cit.*, Appendix 5, para. 6.
[55] Walkland, *op.cit.*, p. 38.

> "The Department will tell those whom it chooses to consult . . . what are the broad intentions of the Government, what is sought to be achieved by the bill then being put together, and what means are proposed. On particular matters, or when asked by affected interests, the department may go into more detail, sometimes putting forward alternatives and seeking the opinion of those interested on the various merits of the alternatives. Where, as is often the case, the co-operation of the affected interests is highly desirable in order to make the bill most effective in practice, something very like a bargain may be struck and undertakings may be given on both sides."[56]

Walkland, on the other hand, suggests that: "Negotiation is not an apt description of what happens when major legislation is contemplated . . . "[57] It is, of course true that the government may dispense with the agreement of affected interests, notably those traditionally opposed to it, on major issues of party policy. Nevertheless even in these areas governments do consult in an effort to reach agreement or minimise disagreement. Moreover, major legislation may very well be the result of negotiation between government and outside groups.[58]

## THE ROLE OF PARLIAMENT

Individual MPs and groups of MPs may participate in the initiation of legislation and the formulation of legislative proposals through membership of all-party groups, by bringing pressure to bear on governments drawn from their own party and through the limited opportunities afforded for private Members' legislation. The part which MPs may play must be set against the effective monopoly which the government possesses over the formulation of policy, including legislative proposals. The government's monopoly, reflected in its responsibility for the initiation of legislation, and the domination of the House of Commons by party loyalties, severely limit the part played by the House of Commons as a collective body in the initiation and formulation of legislation. This was not always the case. Prior to their supersession by the increased use of Royal Commissions and later of departmental and inter-departmental committees, the investigations and recommendations of House of Commons' select committees frequently resulted in legislation,

[56] Hartley and Griffith, *Government and Law* (2nd ed., 1981), p. 211.
[57] *Op.cit.*, p. 38.
[58] The Finance Act 1976 is perhaps the best of the many examples provided by the Social Contract between the T.U.C. and the 1974–1979 Labour Governments.

either through their adoption by government or on the motion of committee members themselves. To a limited extent this function has survived. During the present century occasional recourse has been had, invariably at the government's initiative, to what are now termed "pre-legislation" committees. These committees are appointed "to enquire into a public matter with a view to making recommendations on the scope of future legislation on that matter."[59] Notable examples of pre-legislation committees whose recommendations have led to legislation are the 1957–58 House of Commons' Select Committee on obscene publications and the 1966–67 Joint Committee of both Houses on the censorship of stage plays.[60]

In 1967 the Select Committee on Procedure recommended that greater use should be made of these pre-legislation committees. It expressed the general view that: "the House should be brought in at an earlier point in the legislative process so as to allow discussion by Parliament of subjects and details of potential legislation before the Government finally prepare a Bill." To this end it recommended that regular use should be made of ad hoc select committees "to study and report on the specific topics of possible legislation referred to them."[61] Despite being endorsed by the 1971 Select Committee on Procedure[62] this recommendation had little impact. Only three pre-legislation committees were established subsequently—on proposals for corporation tax in 1970–71, tax credits in 1972–73 and a wealth tax in 1974–75[63]—and their experience was not considered to have been uniformly successful.[64]

Although the recommendations made by the 1967 and 1971 Select Committees on Procedure were of little immediate consequence they did reflect the dissatisfaction of some MPs with the exclusion of the House of Commons from the processes of deciding upon and formulating legislative proposals. Accordingly, the failure of the

[59] *The Process of Legislation, op.cit.*, Appendix 1, para. 87. For a complete list of pre-legislation committees established between 1900 and 1970, see *ibid.*, Appendix 1, Part IV, Annex G.

[60] Obscene Publications Act 1959; Theatres Act 1968. Both Bills were introduced by private Members.

[61] *Public Bill Procedure Etc.*, Sixth Report from the Select Committee on Procedure (1967; H.C. 539), paras. 11–14.

[62] *The Process of Legislation, op.cit.*, para. 8.

[63] Independently of the recommendations the House of Lords established a select committee to examine proposals for a Bill of Rights (1978; H.L. 176).

[64] First Report from the Select Committee on Procedure (1978; H.C. 588), para. 2.4. The majority of the recommendations made by the Select Committee on Corporation Tax were incorporated in the Finance Bill 1972. The Select Committee on Tax Credits had less immediate impact.

reforms canvassed left unresolved the questions of whether it is possible for the House of Commons to play any collective part in those processes and, if so, what that part should be. It is possible to detect in the deliberations of the Select Committees on Procedure two reasons for seeking a greater involvement of the House of Commons in the preparatory stages through pre-legislation committes.

Firstly, they would provide a mechanism whereby the considerations and reasoning upon which legislative proposals are based and the part played by outside groups in their formulation might be opened up to greater public scrutiny. This in turn raised the possibility that Bills themselves might receive more informed consideration during their subsequent parliamentary stages. On this basis the proposals were to be welcomed. Apart from the likelihood of government opposition one of the obstacles to their implementation was their impracticability. Given the constraints of the legislative timetable it was difficult to see how they could become, as was envisaged, an established feature of the legislative process. Only in those relatively few areas where time was not a factor would it be possible to have recourse to them. This limitation was affirmed by the 1978 Select Committee on Procedure. "The fact that there is a wide variation in the character of bills, in their degree of urgency and in their size and importance, means that there cannot be a standard procedure for the pre-legislative stage."[65] The Committee concluded that the procedure could only be adopted in the case of Bills which were not urgent.

Even if time were not a factor and pre-legislative committees were established as a feature of legislative procedure, some commentators questioned the value of procedural reforms directed solely to the legislative process to the exclusion of the generality of government activity of which legislation forms only a part.

> "There is an inherent contradiction between [the House of Commons] wanting to 'involve itself at an earlier stage in the preparation of certain kinds of legislation' and spending about half the time of the House examining Bills. For if 'earlier stage' means a formal legislative stage, the likelihood is that there will simply be a Chinese game of names but no real progress; but if it means getting in on the basic processes of inquiry, discussion and opinion-formulation that begin to make legislation seem needed, this can only come through general debates and through reports of committees which, in turn, need debating—

[65] *Loc.cit.*

for all of which time must be found. And more fundamentally the need for legislation emerges from administrative processes. The House will only get in at a significantly 'earlier stage' if it tightens its scrutiny generally of all major processes of administration . . . ."[66]

In the light of this criticism the most significant innovation has been the establishment of the system of departmental select committees in 1979 on the basis of the recommendations made by the 1978 Select Committee on Procedure. Although the Committee accepted that the new committees might consider and comment upon the form and content of proposed legislation and that they might occasionally propose new legislation, it did not envisage their being given any specific responsibility for legislation "especially if this were to disrupt their ordinary programme of scrutiny and oversight."[67]

The second reason why, arguably, the 1967 and 1971 Select Committees recommended the regular use of pre-legislation committees was that they saw them as a means whereby MPs themselves might play an active part in the formulation of legislative proposals. One area in which it was accepted that they might perform a useful role in this respect was private Members' legislation. Given, however, that most legislation is initiated by the government, the emphasis on their regular use suggests that the two Procedure Committees envisaged their establishment to examine issues other than those normally associated with private Members' legislation. Of necessity this would involve them in matters of party controversy. Both Committees took pains to avoid the criticism that the use of pre-legislation committees for this purpose would usurp the government's accepted prerogative in the initiation of legislation. They accepted that the primary initiative in the establishment and determination of the terms of reference of pre-legislation committees should rest with the government. In addition, they emphasised the practical desirability of avoiding matters of party controversy on the grounds that their involvement in such matters would diminish the likelihood of their reaching agreement and of their conclusions being acceptable to the House. Nevertheless they took the view that they could usefully examine the more anodyne aspects of controversial proposals.[68]

[66] Crick, *The Reform of Parliament* (2nd ed., 1968), p. 227.

[67] *Op.cit.*, para. 2.5.

[68] *Public Bill Procedure Etc., op.cit.*, paras. 11–14; *The Process of Legislation, op.cit.*, para. 8.

Despite the limitations which the Select Committees on Procedure accepted would govern the operation of pre-legislation committees, the implicit suggestion that MPs should become involved in the policy-making process was criticised on two grounds. First, it was argued that the proposals were based on a misunderstanding of the respective functions of the government and the House of Commons: the function of the former was to govern; the function of the latter was to scrutinise the actions, including legislative actions, of the former. Accordingly any attempt by the House of Commons to replicate through pre-legislation committees the function of government, except in those areas traditionally associated with private Members' legislation, was misconceived in principle. It could only be pursued at the expense of the critical function of the House of Commons. This in turn led to the second criticism which was that the attempted replication by the House of Commons of the government's function would inevitably draw it into conflict with the government and lead to attempts by the government to control the deliberations and conclusions of pre-legislation committees.[69] These criticisms were endorsed indirectly by the 1978 Select Committee on Procedure which concluded that the value of pre-legislation committees is probably greatest "in areas outside acute party controversy and where there will not be a strong government attitude towards the final Bill."[70]

It is too early to attempt any definite assessment of the functions of the new departmental select committees in this respect. As we have seen the 1978 Select Committee on Procedure did not envisage the examination of legislative proposals as being among their primary functions. Two points, however, may be made. First, where they have examined legislation they have done so on their own initiative. They have thus gone beyond the limits envisaged by the 1967 and 1971 Select Committees on Procedure of examining only those proposals referred to them by the government. Secondly, they have on occasion put forward all-party views on legislative proposals

[69] See *e.g.*, Hanson and Walles, *op.cit.*, p. 84 and Griffith, *op.cit.*, pp. 238–239. It is perhaps indicative of the relationship between government and the House of Commons that the Government favoured the implementation of the recommendation as a means of securing legislation which it would otherwise be unable to introduce, notably on relationships between MPs and public relations firms working for foreign governments, Crossman, *The Diaries of a Cabinet Minister* (1976), Vol. 3, pp. 210, 219, 406–407 and 410.

[70] *Op.cit.*, para. 2.4.

different from those espoused by the government.[71] In doing so they have mounted a direct challenge to the monopoly enjoyed by the government in the formulation of legislative proposals.

## CONCLUSION

Two points may be made by way of conclusion. First, the parliamentary stages of the legislative process are normally subordinate to the antecedent formulation of policy; it is during the pre-parliamentary stages that the main lines and content of proposed legislation is effectively settled.[72] It is this realisation which underlies the frequently expressed view that: "all executive policy and most legislation is conceived, drafted and all but enacted in Whitehall."[73] As, however, we suggested in Chapter 1 it does not follow from this that the parliamentary stages are themselves devoid of significance, and we shall return to this issue in Chapter 5. Secondly, the continuous interplay between government and outside groups in the formulation of legislative proposals underlines our earlier emphasis on the contractual aspects of institutional law-making. In the main, legislation is not "a process solely of command and obedience but of the action and reaction between constitutionally organised initiative on the one hand and social forces on the other."[74] The main feature of that process of action and reaction, as reflected in the efforts of government to secure the agreement of affected interests through consultation and negotiation, is that normally it takes place free from the public gaze.

[71] Most notably on s.4 of the Vagrancy Act 1824; see Fourth Report from the Home Affairs Committee (1980; H.C. 744), which concluded that: "if there is no measure for the repeal of 'sus' foreshadowed in the next Queen's Speech, members of the Committee will themselves place such a Bill before the House." The repeal was effected by the Criminal Attempts Act 1981, s.8.

[72] Griffith, *op.cit.*, p. 14.

[73] Report of the Commission of Inquiry into Industrial and Commercial Representation (1972), p. 5.

[74] Allen, *op.cit.*, p. 427.

Chapter Four

# THE PREPARATION OF A BILL

As we have seen, the formulation of a legislative proposal is undertaken by the civil servants of the responsible government department. Once formulated, its translation into a Bill is undertaken by the draftsmen in the Office of Parliamentary Counsel. Descriptions of the draftsmen not infrequently characterise them as a kind of legal super practitioner. These are encouraged by an apparent similarity between drafting a Bill and drafting private legal texts such as wills and leases, by the false assumption that drafting a Bill and preparing a Bill are synonymous, by the description of the government department as the draftsman's client, and by the fact of his institutional separation and legal background. Although there are similarities between these various activities, it is important to stress that the Office's personnel are, like those who instruct them, civil servants. The draftsman's function and *raison d'etre* are to ensure that the government's policies are given legal effect.

In this chapter we discuss three aspects of the draftsman's involvement in the preparation of Bills. First, we describe in general terms the expectations of the draftsman and his responsibilities in relation to the preparation of Bills; secondly, we examine in some detail what is involved in the drafting process; and lastly we consider briefly the arrangements which exist to ensure the fulfilment of these expectations and to control the discharge of his responsibilities.

## EXPECTATIONS AND RESPONSIBILITIES

All governments have a number of expectations of the draftsman. First he is expected to express the government's intentions as accurately as possible in the Bill. These intentions may be capable of being stated with varying degrees of precision. Where they are capable of being stated precisely, and it is the government's wish that they be so stated, he is in addition expected to ensure that there is as little opportunity as possible for interpreting the Act in any way other than the government wishes. Often the government will want the statute to state precisely what the law is to be, but as we shall see later, it is frequently not possible, and sometimes not desirable, to do this. This first expectation has been described by a former Parliamentary Counsel as the requirement of legal effectiveness.[1]

Secondly, he is expected to ensure that the Bill complies with the parliamentary rules governing public Bill procedure; that is, to ensure that the Bill is procedurally legitimate. These rules specify the conditions which must be met before a Bill can be presented and debated.[2] Thirdly, the draftsman must complete the preparation of the Bill so as to comply with the timetable laid down by the appropriate Cabinet committee for the legislative programme.

Finally, the government expects the draftsman to ensure that the Bill as drafted is compatible with the existing law. Almost every new Bill directly or indirectly refers to or assumes the existence of a wider legal context. The draftsman must endeavour therefore to locate all existing statutory and common law provisions which may be affected by the Bill and take steps to make clear the precise nature of that effect, to present amendments to statutory provisions in as clear and orderly a fashion as possible and to adopt consistent terminology and linguistic usage where appropriate. Fulfilment of this expectation may be easier said than done. Bennion for example has argued that the draftsman's task "is greatly hampered by the chaotic state of the statute book, the lack of arrangement under titles, delays in printing updated official texts, and the absence of computerised search and retrieval systems."[3]

Apart from these general responsibilities, Ministers may have other, more immediate, expectations of the draftsman. For example, a Minister will usually want the Bill to be as brief as possible so as to reduce to a minimum the opportunities for delaying their parliamentary progress. This and other tactical considerations were described by Ilbert in 1901:

> "The Minister in charge of a bill will often insist, and wisely insist, on departure from logical arrangement with reference to exigencies of discussion. He will have considered how he intends to present his proposals to Parliament, and to defend them before the public, and will wish to have his bill so arranged and expressed as to make it a suitable text for his speech. If the measure is at all complicated, he will desire to have its leading principles embodied in the opening clause or

[1] Bennion, *Statute Law* (1980), pp. 25–37.

[2] Following their First Reading, all Public Bills must be submitted to the Public Bill Office of the appropriate House for examination by its officers; see Erskine May, *Parliamentary Practice* (19th ed., 1976), Chap. 21, and Kent, *In on the Act* (1979), pp. 37–38, 197.

[3] *Op.cit.*, p. 36.

> clauses, so that when the first fence is cleared, the remainder of the course may be comparatively easy. In settling the order of the following clauses, he will consider what kind of opposition, and from what quarter, they are likely to evoke. He will deprecate unnecessary length, and will often wish to have his measure so drawn that it can be contained in a single clause or appear on a single page. He will prefer a few long clauses to many short ones, bearing in mind that each clause has, as a rule, to be separately put in committee. His theoretical objections to legislation by reference will often yield to considerations of brevity. He will eschew technical terms, except where they are clearly necessary, remembering that his proposals will have to be expounded to, and understood by, an assembly of laymen. He will bear in mind that members of Parliament, like other Englishmen, have a great respect for precedents, and will prefer a form of expresion borrowed from, or having an analogy in, another Act of Parliament. And he will have learnt that there are certain provisions and expressions at which Parliament instinctively shies, others which it readily accepts. The draftsman has, of course, to bear in mind all these considerations."[4]

These considerations may be as much a matter for the government as an individual Minister, and although written over eighty years ago, this passage still conveys an accurate sense of their implications for the preparation of a Bill.

Apart from the government, the parliamentary audience also has more or less clearly defined expectations, which may be shared, and communicated to the draftsman, by Ministers. These include the expectation that the Bill should be so arranged as to allow orderly debate, that it should be self-explanatory and be as brief as possible.[5] Particular emphasis has traditionally been placed on the requirement that Bills should be self-explanatory.

When faced with a new Bill, an MP wants to be able to discover

[4] Ilbert, *Legislative Methods and Forms* (1901), p. 241.

[5] Brevity is not, however, merely a question of physical proportion; that is, a Bill containing 10 clauses is not necessarily shorter than one containing 15. This is so because brevity has a dimension of comprehensibility. A Bill may be brief because it is readily understood as much as because it is physically short. Given subject matter which is of a certain difficulty, it will take more effort to prepare a long Bill than a short one; but a short Bill whose language and structure is highly complex may be less readily understood than a longer one dealing with a different, less difficult subject. Compression of language is one of the principal obstacles to intelligibility.

from the text itself, first what the Bill is intended to do and secondly how it affects the interests of his constituents or of those interests which he represents. Traditionally the draftsman has responded to this requirement by drafting Bills according to what Lord Thring called "the four corners doctrine": "it is not fair to a legislative assembly that they should, as a general rule, have to look beyond the four corners of the Bill in order to comprehend its meaning."[6] Unintelligible Bills occasion criticism of the government, and so compliance with this doctrine has been one of the draftsman's main responsibilities since the Office was established. However, fulfilment of this expectation has been "one of the most formidable"[7] tasks which he has faced. The main reason for this difficulty is that most MPs are neither lawyers nor familiar with law, whereas the officials and other professional groups who will be implementing the Act are usually one or the other. It is extremely difficult to cater for both groups:

> "The same document has to be designed to satisfy two distinct legislative audiences: first (in point of time) the Parliamentary audience, mainly composed of laymen, whose primary need is to ascertain, with the minimum of labour and preferably no reference to any document other than the Bill itself, what is the general purpose and effect of each clause or section which they are asked to pass; and secondly, the expert lawyers and other professionals who will seek to find in the Act passed a specific answer to each specific question upon which they have to advise or decide. One customer wants a picture and the other wants a Bradshaw."[8]

Finally, as the notion of two distinct audiences indicates, the ultimate users of legislation also have expectations of the draftsman. The expression, "ultimate user" was used by the Renton Committee to refer to the many groups and individuals, official and otherwise, who routinely apply and interpret legislative provisions. The group includes the officials of public institutions such as the courts, tribunals, local authorities and public corporations, and private individuals such as accountants, architects, barristers and solicitors. The ultimate user's demands of legislation are principally that it should be intelligible, and legally certain, that is, precise and clear. Intellligibilty here means that it is possible for the user to assimilate and understand the legislation without undue difficulty. He will

[6] Thring, *Practical Legislation* (1902), p. 8.
[7] Bennion, *op.cit.*, p. 30.
[8] Hutton, "The Mechanics of Law Reform" (1961) 24 M.L.R. 18, 21.

expect that a statute will be drafted and arranged in such a way which makes plain the relevance of its provisions, even those which are complex, to his own or his clients' problems.

One of the most important features of these differing expectations is the extent to which they conflict. First, the expectations of a particular group may be mutually inconsistent. For example, the expectations attributed to ultimate users, that legislation be both intelligible and legally certain are not always compatible. To draft a text that is legally certain, namely, that is unambiguous and leaves as little room as possible for competing interpretations as to its application to particular circumstances, often means that intelligibility—ease of understanding—is sacrificed, or assumes a secondary importance. So far as the government's expectations are concerned, the demands of the legislative timetable may only be met at the expense of hastily drafted clauses which are not legally effective.

Moreover, one group's expectations may conflict with another's. For example, the ultimate user's expectation that an Act should be intelligible may conflict with the emphasis placed by MPs on the four corners doctrine. This is particularly evident where a Bill amends previous legislation. Compliance with the four corners doctrine has often meant that amendments are drafted describing in narrative form the effect of the new provisions upon the old. This style increases the intelligibility of the Bill for MPs, but it may not necessarily be what the ultimate user wants from the Act. He may prefer the amending provision simply to state what word(s) or phrase(s) are to be altered so that he can make a direct substitution onto his own copy of the amended legislation. In pursuance of legal effectiveness the draftsman may see the need for the inclusion of provisions guarding against remote contingencies, but which cause the Minister difficulty during the parliamentary stages. Ministers will usually want their Bills to appear as politically attractive as possible, but legal effectiveness may require the inclusion of provisions which are prosaic or uninspiring.

Given the draftsman's position and primary responsibilities, the government has traditionally resolved these conflicts in favour of its own order of priorities. Accordingly, all other expectations are subordinated to the realisation of legal effectiveness, procedural legitimacy and timeliness. As between legal effectiveness and intelligibility,

> "the test is that when it is passed, and a trained lawyer or judge has mastered its intricacies, the meaning is clear (in the sense of unambiguous) and the intention carried out. Subject to this, the

second object is to make the Bill as intelligible as possible to Parliament and the general public."[9]

The conflict between the government's expectations of the draftsman and the expectations of those others who have an interest in legislation, lies at the root of many of the criticisms which have been made of the present arrangements for its preparation. Some, such as MPs and judges have sufficient status for their complaints to be taken seriously, but it is only recently that other users have been recognised as having a claim in determining what ought to be the draftsman's priorities. Thus the Renton Report recommended that "in principle the interests of the ultimate user should always have priority over those of the legislators"and that "a statute should be arranged to suit the convenience of its ultimate users," but there is little evidence of any change of attitude on the part of successive governments.[10] The reason for this stems from the government's overriding wish "to obtain precise legal effect."[11] For the moment it appears unlikely that changes will be made to the traditional order of priorities beyond those which are interstitial and can be accommodated within the existing system.

## THE DRAFTING PROCESS

While drafting is but one aspect of the preparation of a Bill, it is perhaps the most demanding; certainly it is a highly skilled and technical activity which is the subject of a number of specialist manuals.[12] We do not have the space to deal with the vast range of matters which arise in drafting a Bill in the detail which is necessary to explain their significance and, in many cases, their complexity.

[9] Kent, *op.cit.*, p. 97.

[10] Report of the Renton Committee, *The Preparation of Legislation,* Cmnd. 6053 (1975), recommendations 8 and 19 (hereafter, Renton). The notion of the "ultimate user" is problematic; many statutes have a variety of users, for example the Transport Act 1981 concerns nationalised industry, private companies, the police, drivers, magistrates, and various government departments. Each of these has a different interest in and use for the Act's provisions.

[11] H.L. Deb., Vol. 410, ser. 5, col. 1111 (June 18, 1980).

[12] Coode, *On legislative expression* (Appendix to the Report of the Poor Law Commissioners on Local Tax, 1843, House of Commons Papers, Vol. XX) reprinted in Driedger, *infra* this note, Appendix I; Ilbert, *Legislative Methods and Forms* (1901); Thring, *Practical Legislation* (1902); Russell, *Legislative Drafting and Forms* (4th ed., 1938); Dickerson, *Legislative Drafting* (1954) and *The Fundamentals of Legal Drafting* (1965); Driedger, *The Composition of Legislation and Legislative Forms and Precedents* (2nd ed., 1976); Thornton, *Legislative Drafting* (2nd ed., 1979); and see generally, Commonwealth Secretariat, *Legislative Drafting, Manual and Bibliography* (rev. ed., 1977).

Accordingly, we shall concentrate on four aspects of the drafting process: first, the draftsman's response to his instructions; secondly, the main steps involved in drafting a Bill; thirdly, the difficulties which arise in attaining legal effectiveness and fourthly, the principal criticisms which have been made of the results of the drafting process and the suggestions which have been made for its reform.

## *THE DRAFTSMAN'S RESPONSE TO HIS INSTRUCTIONS*

Instructions to draft a Bill are sent to First Parliamentary Counsel by the responsible Minister on the authority of and in accordance with the timetable agreed by the Cabinet committee. Sometimes First Parliamentary Counsel is consulted about proposed legislation at an earlier stage, but in principle participation by the draftsmen does not begin until instructions are received. With the exception of the Inland Revenue, where the administrative civil servants communicate directly with the Office of Parliamentary Counsel, these instructions are drawn up by the department's lawyers.

Although practice varies, these instructions normally should:

- (i) contain sufficient background information to enable the draftsman to see in perspective and in context the facts and problems which the legislative proposal is intended to meet;
- (ii) state clearly and fully the principal objects of the proposal;
- (iii) state the means whereby the objects are to be achieved; and
- (iv) refer to all known implications and difficulties, whether legal, social or administrative.[13]

The object is to let the draftsman see what is wanted; to provide a target at which the clauses may be aimed. Particular difficulties are caused by the inclusion of a draft Bill or an agreed form of words.[14] Sir Granville Ram, a former First Parliamentary Counsel, observed that nothing was more of a hindrance to the draftsman than being obliged to build what is usually a complex structure around forms of words which have become sacrosanct merely by reason of their having been agreed to in Cabinet or one of its committees. A more serious objection is that such agreed forms of words frequently transpire to be agreements as to words only, concealing the fact that

[13] Thornton, *op.cit.*, p. 105.

[14] This was illustrated by the attempt by the Department of Customs and Excise's Working Party on V.A.T. to prepare a draft Bill to be sent to Parliamentary Counsel as part of his instructions; see Johnstone, "Role of the Administrator in the Preparation of U.K. Legislation" [1980] Stat. L.R. 67.

no real compromise or decision was reached between conflicting views on policy.[15]

When First Parliamentary Counsel receives the instructions he assigns himself or one of the other Parliamentary Counsel to be responsible for preparing the Bill, and then assigns a junior draftsman to assist Counsel. These arrangements may of course vary depending on the complexity, urgency, importance and size of the Bill; typically the Finance Bill is drafted by two Counsel. Each Counsel is likely to be responsible for six to eight Bills in a session. These will include at least one major Bill and in the case of one or more Counsel the whole or a share of the Finance Bill, which itself represents two to three months continual work under a strict timetable.[16] When First Parliamentary Counsel has informed the department which Counsel he has assigned to the Bill, all subsequent communications concerning its progress are conducted through that draftsman.

Different draftsmen have different practices at this stage, but for most of them one of the first steps will be to arrange a conference with the department's administrative and legal civil servants who prepared the instructions. The object of such conferences is to identify aspects of the proposal which are likely to cause difficulty when they come to be translated into legal provisions. These may of course be identified in the instructions themselves. However, the draftsman does not treat his instructions as being non-negotiable. Whether they are clear or unclear he will direct the department's attention to the drafting or legal difficulties which they raise. The resolution of legal difficulties frequently involves issues of policy. Where the issue is of some political importance reference to the Cabinet or one of its committees may be necessary, otherwise policy matters are settled by the Minister. In theory the Minister has the last word on matters of policy and the draftsman the last word on matters of form and law, but the dividing line between policy and drafting, substance and form, is not a sharp one and the draftsman is inevitably drawn into policy decisions.

Descriptions of the relationship between the draftsman and the department show that there is some variation both in practice and in the conception of what that relationship should be. Sir Harold Kent characterised the relationship as a creative one. While recognising that it is the department's role to develop workable and acceptable policies, "the draftsman holds the pen and plays a leading part in

[15] Ram, "The Improvement of the Statute Book" (1951) 1 J.S.P.T.L. 442, 446–447.
[16] Ellis, "The Making and Form of Bills" in Hansard Society, *Parliamentary Government in Britain: A Symposium* (1949), p. 27.

shaping the document."[17] Elsewhere in his account Kent remarks on the fairly broad conception Sir Granville Ram entertained of the draftsman's role, but Kent's experience of encroachment by a department onto what is traditionally regarded as the draftsman's preserve—the wording of a Bill—suggests that this relationship may not be totally one-sided.[18]

A more moderate conception of the draftsman's role can be found in the writings of the American draftsman Reed Dickerson, who wrote, "Although the draftsman is not himself a policy-maker, he can help educate the client so that the client can make informed decisions."[19] While Dickerson envisages a restricted role in policy making for the draftsman, he nevertheless advocates early consultation with him by the policy makers. The purpose is to anticipate drafting and legal difficulties, and in both the United States and Canada[20] the draftsman is frequently consulted at the policy making stage for his views on what is legally necessary and possible in the implementation of policy. In the United Kingdom, First Parliamentary Counsel may be consulted occasionally, in particular on the constitutional propriety of a proposal or when the government is faced with an emergency which it thinks necessitates swift legislative intervention, but such occasions appear to be rare.

Within the Law Commissions the distinction between policy-making and drafting has become blurred as a result of the secondment to them of government draftsmen. Similarly, when they are assigned ad hoc to other law reform bodies such as the Criminal Law Revision Committee, their advice is sought during the policy making stage, but it is unlikely that the existing arrangements will be significantly altered to facilitate such early consultation in a general way. Apart from the political considerations which argue in favour of the maintenance of a theoretical and institutional division of functions, it would be quite impracticable for the draftsmen to participate at the policy making stage as a matter of routine in view of the small size of the Office of Parliamentary Counsel.

In almost all cases, correspondence forms the bulk of the communication between the draftsman and his instructing department; but this will often be supplemented by conferences at which draft clauses will be discussed and possibly modified. Within the limits allowed by the timetable, it is not uncommon for a dozen or more drafts of the Bill to be prepared before it is finally agreed, and

[17] Kent, *op.cit.*, p. 98.
[18] *Ibid.*, pp. 29, 45 and 236.
[19] Dickerson, "How to Write a Law" (1955) 31 Notre Dame Lawyer 14. See also his *The Fundamentals of Legal Drafting*, *op.cit.*, Chap. 2.
[20] Driedger, "The Preparation of Legislation" (1953) 31 Can.Bar.Rev. 33.

for some changes to be made to the department's proposals, in some cases as a result of consultations with other departments. There are always additional policy matters which cannot be known or foreseen until the drafting process is under way, and where there is more than one way of implementing particular aspects of the policy, the draftsman inevitably influences the department's choices.

## *THE MAIN STEPS IN DRAFTING A BILL*

A former First Parliamentary Counsel, Sir Noel Hutton, wrote that the draftsman should "(1) master the subject matter; (2) ascertain in detail what primary and secondary effects the client wishes to secure or avoid; and (3) express the result in plain and unambiguous language."[21] More specifically drafting involves five analytically distinct steps: understanding, analysis, design, composition and scrutiny.[22] We should stress that these steps do not so much represent clearly defined divisions but are rather recognisable points along a continuum. The transition between analysis of the substantive aspects of his instructions and the composition of draft clauses is not an abrupt one, but represents for the draftsman a shift in emphasis in the attainment of legal effectiveness.

The first step, understanding, should be self-explanatory. A draftsman must understand what the law is and what changes are to be made to it. He may draft a clause which is precise and clear, but if it is not what was desired by the department, it is not legally effective. Secondly the draftsman must subject the department's instructions to rigorous analysis, particularly in relation to their impact on the existing law. There are certain proposals to which he must be especially sensitive, and to which it is his duty to draw the attention of the Law Officers:

(i) proposals which affect personal rights and liberties; for example, enabling detention without trial, depriving a person of recourse to the courts, prejudicing pension rights, interfering with electoral rights or restricting freedom of speech;
(ii) proposals affecting property rights; for example, giving officials a right to enter, search, seize or detain private property, or giving powers to requisition or compulsorily acquire property;

[21] Hutton, *op.cit.*, p. 21.
[22] Thornton, *op.cit.*, pp. 104–26. See also Dickerson, "Legislative Drafting and the Law Schools" (1955) 7 Jo. Leg. Ed. 472 and *The Fundamentals of Legal Drafting*, *op.cit.*, Chap. 3.

(iii) proposals for retrospective legislation;
(iv) proposals offending against international law;
(v) proposals of doubtful constitutional competence;
(vi) proposals which are unnecessarily bureaucratic;
(vii) proposals affecting the interest of other government departments or of public bodies;
(viii) proposals affecting prerogative powers.[23]

At the same time, the draftsman must consider the practicability of the proposals, namely whether they are capable of being implemented effectively. Draftsmen become familiar with the administrative implications of different kinds of proposals, and rely upon the experience of civil servants to inform them of what is involved in the day to day implementation of particular provisions. This exchange of information is one of the purposes of the various communications between the draftsman and the department.

The third step is the creation of a scheme for the Bill's contents. To some extent the actual arrangement of clauses is controlled by parliamentary rules and by drafting conventions, but the form is elastic. For example, Lord Brougham's Act of 1850 introduced the requirement that every Act containing more than one prescription should be divided into sections,[24] and rules of public Bill procedure require the long title to be inserted immediately following the year and chapter number. Drafting conventions normally require that the clauses which specify miscellaneous definitions, the short title, the date of commencement, transitional provisions, savings and extent be placed towards the end of the Bill, before the schedules, if any, but the precise order of these clauses in any given Bill may vary. In addition, the draftsman has considerable choice over the order in which the clauses which make up the substance of the Bill appear.

Let us take a hypothetical example of the creation of a scheme for a Bill. Suppose that the draftsman's instructions envisage the establishment of a public body to license certain individuals who wish to engage in a particular activity. The draftsman would first have to be satisfied that the department was clear on the following matters at least: the exact scope of the activities which require licensing; who is eligible and who is disqualified from applying for a licence; the composition, appointment, salaries, powers and liabilities of the licensing body; the procedures for making application for

[23] Thornton, *ibid.*, p. 109.
[24] An Act for shortening the language used in Acts of Parliament 1850 (13 Vict. c. 21), s.2.

a licence; the criteria for determining who is to be granted a licence; the conditions to be attached to the licence; the penalties which may be imposed for breach of those conditions; how the system will be enforced; what fees will be payable; whether there shall be any system of appeal and so on. He may adopt this order for the Bill; alternatively he might begin by establishing the licensing body, specifying its composition, method of appointment and its general responsibilities before going on to specify the licensing procedures. Some of the detail may be included in a schedule to the Act, or provision may be made for its introduction in the form of subordinate legislation.

The results may range from the prosaic to the dramatic. Kent recalls the Home Secretary's scornful reaction to the first clause of the Factories Bill 1937 which read

> "All inside walls and partitions, and all ceilings or tops of rooms, and all walls, sides and tops of passages and staircases . . . shall at least once in every period of fourteen months be washed with hot water and soap or other suitable detergent . . . "[25]

Yet Kent argues that there were very good reasons why it was appropriate to begin in this way: administrative convenience for the Factory Inspectorate; a clear obligation on employers; and a maximum time within which to conduct annual cleaning which was flexible enough to fit in with the practice of spring cleaning and the variation in the Easter holiday. On the other hand, section 1(1) of the Trade Union and Labour Relations Act 1974 provided simply that "The Industrial Relations Act 1971 is hereby repealed," although section 1(2) went on to re-enact many of that Act's provisions. The reason was that the Labour Government had assumed office committed to the total repeal of the 1971 Act, yet wished to retain many of its features. The choice of scheme depends on a great many factors; it is for each draftsman to find the best way of giving legal effect to his instructions whilst accommodating any further demands that may be made of him.

The fourth step is that of composition. In 1924 Ilbert could write that "the composition and language of statutes is a subject which has been comparatively neglected by the authors of legal literature, and on which not very much has been written."[26] The position has changed considerably since then. Apart from Ilbert's own contributions there are now a number of books and manuals written by

[25] Kent, *op.cit.*, p. 88.
[26] Ilbert, *The Mechanics of Law-Making* (1924), p. 91.

draftsmen, both in this country and abroad, which describe the technicalities of drafting.[27] Essentially those technicalities are of two kinds. Some relate to the accurate use of language and grammar; for example, the choice of the tense, mood and voice of verbs, the use of modifiers, the use of definitions and sentence structure. Others have a special legal connotation such as the use of the verb "shall," the creation of remedies for breach of a statutory duty, styles of amendment, effect upon the Crown, references to subordinate legislation and the inclusion of schedules. Composition can also be a highly creative activity, even to the extent of coining new words having specific meanings within the context of a particular statute.[28]

The fifth step is careful scrutiny of the final draft. In practice the process of composition will involve much revision, carried out both by the draftsman, his assistant and by those who instruct him. We have already outlined the arrangements which exist at Cabinet level to scrutinise Bills before they are presented to Parliament, but it should be noted that revision frequently continues beyond this point. The pressure to comply with the government's timetable means that the draftsman may have insufficient time to find the exact formulation to give legal effect to his instructions, in which case changes inspired by the draftsman may have to be introduced in the form of amendments during the Bill's parliamentary stages. Although amendments made during the parliamentary stages may be revised, it may not be easy to assimilate them to the scheme of the Bill.

## *ATTAINING LEGAL EFFECTIVENESS*

As we have seen, the government's first expectation of the draftsman is that he should express its intentions as accurately as possible in the Bill. A Bill which does not achieve this is not legally effective. We should stress that legal effectiveness does not necessarily imply legal certainty: a Bill which accurately expresses the government's intentions is not necessarily one whose provisions will be clearly and precisely stated. Occasionally a government will want a Bill to be uncertain.[29] Certainty is a question of degree and can be increased or reduced as a matter of policy. The government may wish to conceal the fact that it was unable to secure the agreement of groups affected by the legislation; to enable compromises to be reached

[27] Above, n.12.
[28] *e.g.* "patrial" in the Immigration Act 1971, s.2(6).
[29] Miller, "Statutory Language and the Purposive Use of Ambiguity" (1956) 42 Virginia Law Rev. 23 and Bennion, *op.cit.*, pp. 132–135.

between those implementing the legislation and those subject to it; to obscure politically sensitive measures; or to reduce the opportunities to challenge the exercise of the powers conferred, for example in their application to changing or unforeseen circumstances. In so far as it is the government's intention to introduce uncertainty, it is the responsibility of the draftsman to give legal effect to it, even if the consequence is a reduction in clarity and precision.

Bearing in mind that legal effectiveness and legal certainty are analytically distinct, there are a number of difficulties which may impede the attainment of legal effectiveness. Some of these are inherent in the enterprise of "subjecting human conduct to the governance of rules"[30]; some arise from the conflicting expectations which are held of the draftsman; some arise from the condition of the statute book and yet others flow from the judicial reactions to legislation.

## INHERENT OBSTACLES

In almost all cases it is simply impossible for policy-makers or draftsmen to foresee every combination of circumstances to which their rules might apply. This "relative ignorance of fact" in turn makes it difficult to define the exact scope of any proposed rules.[31] Frequently these difficulties are catered for by defining the activity or matter in question in broad terms, by reserving a power to make further rules by way of subordinate legislation, and by conferring a discretion on a named authority, for example, the courts, a tribunal, an administrative agency or civil servants to apply the rule in specific cases. That discretion may be qualified to a greater or lesser degree, for example by requiring that it be exercised "reasonably."

Some of the many instances of these common features of United Kingdom legislation are the prohibition of "*anti-competitive practices*", whose meaning is to be determined by the Office of Fair Trading and the Monopolies and Mergers Commission;[32] the power conferred on the licensing authority not to renew a gaming licence on the grounds that the holder is "not a *fit and proper* person"[33]; the

[30] Fuller, *The Morality of Law* (1969), p. 106.

[31] Hart, *The Concept of Law* (1961), p. 124: "It is a feature of the human predicament (and so of the legislative one) that we labour under two connected handicaps whenever we seek to regulate, unambiguously and in advance, some sphere of conduct by means of general standards to be used without further official direction on particular occasions. The first handicap is our relative ignorance of fact: the second is our relative indeterminacy of aim."

[32] Competition Act 1980, s.1.

[33] Gaming Act 1968, s.2(1), Sched. 2, para. 20(1)(*b*).

obligation on a local authority if they "have *reason to believe*" that a person is homeless to make "*appropriate* inquiries" which include "such inquiries as are *necessary to satisfy* the authority" that the person is homeless[34]; the power conferred on a court not to make a possession order in respect of a protected tenancy "unless the court *considers it reasonable* to make such an order and . . . the court *is satisfied that suitable alternative accommodation is available* . . . "[35]; and the obligation on "every employer to ensure, so far as is *reasonably practicable*, the *health, safety and welfare at work* of all his employees."[36] Such instances could be multiplied many times. The uncertainty in the application of these provisions to specific cases may be progressively reduced through the development of precedents, statements of intended administrative practices and the promulgation of subordinate legislation.

Apart from ignorance of fact and indeterminacy of aim, there is a third difficulty which affects the drafting of *all* rules, even where the policy-maker and draftsman are well informed about the circumstances to be provided for and have a clear conception of the scope of the rule. This difficulty is the inherent indeterminacy of language. Rules by definition describe categories of the persons, things and conduct to which they apply. Legislation makes a maximal use of general classifying words such as "buyer," "occupier," "family", "goods," "property," "public place," "uses," "permits," and when used in this way, language is, as Hart points out, "irreducibly open-textured."[37] All classifying words have a core of settled meaning and a penumbra where their meaning is indeterminate; the price to be paid for their use in legislation is uncertainty at the borderline. What, for example is the meaning of the word "family"? Is the unmarried partner of a protected tenant under the Rent Act 1968 a member of the tenant's "family" and so also entitled to protection?[38]

These three difficulties are inherent; nevertheless it has been argued that their effect could be lessened in a number of ways, such as the adoption of drafting techniques which place greater emphasis on making the rules more intelligible, an increase in the establishment of the Office of Parliamentary Counsel, technological improvement of the statute book and the development of a coherent and

[34] Housing (Homeless Persons) Act 1977, s.3(1) & (2).
[35] Rent Act 1977, s.98.
[36] Health and Safety at Work etc. Act 1974, s.2.
[37] Hart, *op.cit.*, p. 124.
[38] *Dyson Holdings* v. *Fox* [1975] 3 W.L.R. 744. See now the Rent Act 1977.

systematic code of interpretation by the judiciary. We consider some of these suggestions in later sections in this and subsequent chapters.

## CONFLICTING EXPECTATIONS OF THE DRAFTSMAN

Earlier in this chapter we described the various expectations held of the draftsman by different groups and pointed out their potential incompatability. It will be apparent that drafting a Bill to meet the government's priorities of legal effectiveness, procedural legitimacy and timeliness is carried on under circumstances which may not conduce either to the careful consideration and resolution of the many technical and policy issues which arise or to the realisation of the expectations of the draftsman held by MPs and the ultimate users. Moreover, the government's own expectations of the draftsman are as we have seen not mutually compatible. In his evidence to the Renton Committee, Sir Anthony Stainton, then First Parliamentary Counsel, remarked that the requirement of timeliness in particular is a serious constraint which

> " . . . makes for an undigested text, and a logical structure which is imperfectly worked out. Moreover, the pressure makes it difficult for the drafting team to prepare material to help in understanding the Bill when it first appears. Even drafting an Explanatory Memorandum may be a considerable task for a big Bill. The preparation of the occasional White Paper by way of giving more detailed explanations of the text can be a burden so great that it interferes with the main object of getting the Bill right."[39]

This and the other pressures on the draftsman which arise from the demands made of him apply differentially with regard to particular Bills. However, in the absence of an increase in the size of the Office or a reduction in the volume of legislation, it is unlikely that these pressures will be significantly relieved.

## THE CONDITION OF THE STATUTE BOOK

It has been argued for many years that the unsatisfactory condition of the statute book is itself a source of difficulty. Two criticisms may be distinguished. First it is argued that successive governments have devoted insufficient resources of time and expertise to statute law revision, consolidation and the production of sets of revised statutes. Secondly, it is argued that insufficient effort has been made to group

[39] Renton, para. 7.12.

provisions relating to one subject in one place, and that the system of chronological arrangement in no way eases the task of text collation. Thus "it becomes increasingly difficult to locate the relevant Acts on any given topic, and, more seriously, once the relevant Acts have been located they may well be found to be distributed among three or four separate volumes, so that reading them together becomes—physically as well as mentally—a formidable task."[40] Clearly, this may prejudice the draftsman's ability to discover what the law is, although most of the criticisms of the statute book have come from its users.

As we saw in Chapter 2, progress has been made in coping with these criticisms, firstly by the establishment of the Law Commissions as a focal point for consolidation and the preparation of Statute Law Revision and Statute Law (Repeal) Bills, and secondly by the publication of *Statutes in Force* in which statutes are classified by subject-matter. Nevertheless, criticism of the difficulty which may be experienced in ascertaining the law governing a particular subject at a particular time has not ceased. Some critics see the problem primarily as one of resources, and argue in favour of their increased expenditure, for example in a "crash" programme of consolidation. Others place greater emphasis on matters of technique, and advocate the adoption of the principle of "one Act, one subject" and of a system of textual amendment. Classification by subject-matter permits, it is argued, maximal use of textual amendment and rapid consolidation. Despite some agreement that the present system is unsatisfactory, the desirability and feasibility of these qualitative changes are matters of some controversy,[41] and they are discussed more fully below.[42]

## THE INFLUENCE OF STATUTORY INTERPRETATION

Although the processes of drafting and enacting legislation are analytically separable from its interpretation, a necessary connection exists between the two which gives rise to a further difficulty in achieving legal effectiveness. One of the most important influences on drafting styles has been the approach adopted by the judiciary to

[40] *Ibid.*, para. 6.13.

[41] As are proposals for the quantitative extension of existing resources. See Statute Law Society, *Statute Law: The Key to Clarity* (the Stow-Hill Report, 1972) and *Statute Law: A Radical Simplification* (the Marshall Report, 1974). For criticism of them see the Stow-Hill Report, Appendix B. The debate is continued in Renton, *passim*; and Statute Law Society, *Renton and the Need for Reform* (1979).

[42] See below, pp. 100–103.

the interpretation of statutes. In Mitchell's words: "Forms of draftsmanship are often the consequences of the methods and rules of judicial interpretation."[43] In 1969 the Law Commissions expressed the relationship in this way

> "It would . . . be an oversimplification to look solely to improvements in this field [the form and arrangement of the statute book and the drafting of legislation] without regard to the rules of interpretation which have been developed by the courts. It would be more accurate to say that there is an interaction between the form of a communication and the rules by which it is to be interpreted. If defects in drafting complicate the rules of interpretation, it is also true that unsatisfactory rules of interpretation may lead the draftsman to an over-refinement in drafting at the cost of the general intelligibility of the law."[44]

Indeed, the continued use of these allegedly unsatisfactory rules of interpretation is still offered as an explanation, if not an excuse for the draftsman's lack of positive response to recommendations for change in drafting technique.[45]

Fiscal legislation offers a prime example of the interaction identified by the Law Commissions. Its detail and complexity are in part attributable to the narrow approach which the judiciary have traditionally adopted to its interpretation. The basis of this approach was clearly expressed by Lord Wilberforce in *Vestey* v. *I.R.C.*

> "Taxes are imposed upon subjects by Parliament. A citizen cannot be taxed unless he is designated in clear terms by a taxing Act as a taxpayer, and the amount of his liability is clearly defined. A proposition, that whether a subject is to be taxed or not, or that, if he is, the amount of his liability is to be decided (even though within a limit) by an administrative body, represents a radical departure from constitutional principle."[46]

Given this view, it is therefore not surprising that

[43] "Reflections on *Law and Orders*." (1958) Juridical Review 19, 24.

[44] The Law Commissions, *The Interpretation of Statutes* (1969) Law Com. No. 21, Scot Law Com. No. 11, para. 5.

[45] See H.L. Deb., Vol. 410, ser.5, cols. 1111–1114 (June 18, 1980) and H.L. Deb., Vol. 416, ser.5, cols. 777–778 (January 28, 1981).

[46] [1980] A.C. 1148, 1172.

"... those responsible for the drafting of taxing statutes have in turn attempted to ensure that 'abuses' of the tax system—*i.e.* cases where it is considered that a person ought to have fallen within the charge to tax but on a literal construction of the original legislation he has failed to do so—should not occur in the future; review of one form of abuse necessarily entails anticipation of the counter-measures which taxpayers might adopt in the future to avoid falling within the revised charge, and the legislation is therefore so framed that if it tries to cover the original abuse, any counter-measures, and any other forms of abuse which the draftsman or those instructing him can foresee or envisage in that context. Such an approach inevitably entails complexity ..."[47]

Although the judiciary have on occasions modified their narrow approach to the interpretation of anti-avoidance provisions[48] it is indisputably the case that much of the detail and complexity of fiscal statutes is due to the historical predominance of this approach.

More generally the alleged failure of the judiciary to give effect to the intention expressed in statutes has resulted in the adoption of the detailed drafting style which is characteristic of United Kingdom legislation. Earlier commentators placed particular emphasis on this alleged failure:

"There is a whole science of interpretation better known to judges and parliamentary draftsmen than to members of the Legislature itself. Some of its rules cannot be well accounted for except on the theory that Parliament generally changes the law for the worse and that the business of the judges is to keep the mischief of its interference within the narrowest possible bounds."[49]

The frustration felt by the draftsman and the legislature where the judiciary did take too restrictive an approach to an Act is recorded by Graham-Harrison:

"We find that when an Act comes before a court it is quite often held to mean something which we never intended, and we are told that this interpretation is inevitable, in view of well-established rules applicable to the construction of Statutes; it seems to us, however, that these results are arrived at by subtleties and an excessive ingeniousness of argument which

[47] Clark, "Statutory Drafting" [1980] B.T.R. 326, 327–328.
[48] *e.g.* the House of Lords in *Ramsay* v. *I.R.C.* [1981] 2 W.L.R. 449.
[49] Pollock, *Essays in Jurisprudence and Ethics* (1882), p. 85.

are out of place in construing legal documents prepared as Acts of Parliamentary necessarily are."[50]

This judicial failure was originally explained in terms of an "excessive predilection for common law doctrines"[51] and a consequent hostility to legislation as a source of law. "If—as must be reluctantly conceded—drafting statutes has become largely an attempt to restrain these 'hydra-headed presumptions of the courts in favour of the common law,' piecemeal, illadjusted and at times unintelligible legislation is bound to result."[52] The Law Commissions have criticised this view as no longer giving "a wholly fair impression of the present theory and practice of the British courts."[53] While this may be so, the likely judicial response continues to be one of the most potent influences on drafting styles and techniques. It is sometimes argued that drafting would become easier if judges were to adopt a purposive approach to the interpretation of statutes. We explore this argument more fully in Chapter 7.[54]

## *CRITICISMS OF THE DRAFTING PROCESS AND SUGGESTIONS FOR REFORM*

Given the potency of these difficulties it is hardly surprising that the government's primary objective of legal effectiveness may not be achieved. Irrespective of this failure, however, the conflicting expectations of the draftsman mean almost inevitably that the product will be criticised. The most vocal critics have been the ultimate users, who argue that in trying to meet the government's requirements of legal effectiveness and timeliness, the draftsman produces legislation which is neither legally certain not intelligible. In too many instances legislation is linguistically obscure or complex, overelaborate in its specification of the matters provided for, structurally unsound and unhelpfully arranged.[55] Particular criticism has been directed at the methods of amendment adopted by the draftsmen.

[50] "An Examination of the Main Criticisms of the Statute Book and of the Possibility of Improvement" (1935) J.S.P.T.L. 9, 13.

[51] The Law Commissions, *op.cit.*, para 10.

[52] Scarman, *Law Reform : The New Pattern* (1968), p. 51.

[53] *Loc.cit.*

[54] See below, pp. 198–200.

[55] These criticisms are described in Renton, Chaps. 6–8.

## METHODS OF AMENDMENT

Amendment can be carried out essentially in one of two ways. The first, textual amendment, achieves the desired result by specifying the words or phrases which are to be deleted from and/or added to the provision being amended. This method allows the user to make the appropriate substitutions directly onto a copy of the affected statute, as the following example shows.[56] Section 149 (1) and (3) of the Town and Country Planning Act 1962 read:

"149.—(1) Subject to the following provisions of this section, in these provisions 'owner-occupier,' in relation to a hereditament, means a person who—

(*a*) occupies the whole or part of the hereditament in right of an owner's interest therein, and has so occupied the hereditament or that part thereof during the whole of the period of six months ending with the date of service, or

(*b*) occupied, in right of an owner's interest, the whole or part thereof of the hereditament during the whole of a period of six months ending not more than six months before the date of service, the hereditament, or that part thereof, as the case may be, having been unoccupied since the end of that period.

(3) In these provisions 'resident owner-occupier,' in relation to a hereditament, means an individual who—

(*a*) occupies the whole or part of the hereditament as a private dwelling in right of an owner's interest therein, and has so occupied the hereditament or that part thereof, as the case may be, during the whole of the period of six months ending with the date of service, or

(*b*) occupied, in right of an owner's interest, the whole or part of the hereditament as a private dwelling during the whole of a period of six months ending not more than six months before the date of service, the hereditament, or that part thereof, as the case may be, having been unoccupied since the end of that period."

In Section 38 of the Town and Country Planning Act 1968 these subsections were textually amended as follows:

Section 149:

"In subsections (1)(*a*), (1)(*b*), (3)(*a*) and (3)(*b*), for the words 'the whole or part' (whenever occurring) there shall be substituted the words 'the whole or substantial part'."

[56] The example is taken from Renton, para 13.3.

Textual amendment has not however, been generally liked by MPs for whom the amending provision (which is usually all that appears in the Bill) is virtually meaningless and thus difficult to discuss. Accordingly, as we noted earlier, the draftsman has, in compliance with the four corners doctrine, frequently adopted the method of non-textual amendment. This "consists of a narrative statement in the amending law stating the effect of the amendment. The amending law does not in so many words purport to amend the principal law, nor does it merge with it and lose its separate existence on enactment as an amending law generally does when the direct method is followed."[57] Section 149 of the 1962 Act was also amended non-textually by section 37(3) of the 1968 Act, as follows:

> "For a person to be treated under Section 149(1) or (3) of the principal Act (definitions of blight notice provisions) as owner-occupier or resident owner-occupier of a hereditament, his occupation thereof at a relevant time or during a relevant period, if not occupation of the whole of the hereditament, must be, or, as the case may be, have been occupation of a substantial part of it."

On occasions users may prefer non-textual amendment,[58] but its adoption has increasingly been criticised on the grounds that it does not provide an obviously authoritative statement of what the law is to be. Instead the user will have to read the amending section carefully and make his own amendments on a copy of the principal Act if he wishes to have an authoritative version in one place. This of course can be time-consuming and can generate error. As the Renton Committee said, "Whether an Act is amended non-textually or textually, the reader must acquaint himself with the provisions both of the original Act and the amending Act until he is provided with a consolidation of the statute law on the subject in question,"[59] but critics argue that this process of conflation—reading related enactments together so as to arrive at an authoritative text—is greatly hampered by the non-textual method.[60] This is so because successive amendments overlay their predecessors but without necessarily repealing them or providing the reader with a clear statement of the law as amended.

From the perspective of achieving legal effectiveness, the drafts-

[57] Thornton, *op.cit.*, p. 295.

[58] The Education Act 1980 is an example of a "four corners" Act.

[59] Para. 13.4.

[60] See in particular Bennion's written evidence to the Renton Committee, reproduced by the Statute Law Society, *Renton and the Need for Reform* (1979), pp. 31–44.

man's choice between the two methods will be based primarily on that which best achieves this goal. Even here, however, and discounting the users' interests, non-textual amendment coupled with the untidy way in which legislation is accumulated in the statute book, is said to make the retrieval of existing provisions affected by a Bill awkward and prone to error.

The Renton Committee recommended that the textual amendment should be used as generously as possible,[61] but there are a number of obstacles to the implementation of this recommendation. First, a great deal of existing legislation is amended non-textually and is thus not suitable for the textual method. Secondly, the non-textual method is sometimes the only practicable way of effecting amendments. In particular, adoption of the textual method would in some cases greatly increase the length of the Bills and the time taken to prepare them. For example, Schedule 1 to the Parliamentary Commissioner Act 1967 which dealt with the Commissioner's pension rights, incorporated by reference only, the provisions of the Superannuation Act 1965. That Act contained 106 sections and eight operative schedules. As Hutton commented, "the alternative of setting out even the relevant provisions would have been quite unacceptable."[62]

In addition, if the textual method were commonly used, many Bills would have to be accompanied by memoranda explaining to MPs the effects of the amendments. MPs are accustomed to non-textual amendment and are likely to be opposed to its replacement. An alternative to such textual memoranda is the incorporation in the Bill of a Keeling Schedule, re-enacting in textual form the affected provisions as amended.[63] This device is rarely used. It is thought to be suitable only "where the changes made by the Bill in the previous enactments are exclusively textual amendments or repeals; and even then it is not used if the previous enactments have been amended non-textually, by any intervening Act."[64] Moreover, like the preparation of textual memoranda, this device increases the work involved in the preparation of a Bill, as well as substantially increasing its length. Finally, although the textual method enables the user to make the appropriate changes to a copy of the amended Act so as to achieve an authoritative

[61] Renton, recommendation 41.

[62] Hutton further comments ironically that "It may surprise some of the more recent critics of legislation that it is not so long ago since [textual amendment] was Public Enemy No. 1"; "Legislative Drafting in the United Kingdom" (1979) *The Parliamentarian* 253, 257.

[63] *e.g.* Guardianship Act 1973, Sched. 2, Pt. II.

[64] Renton, para. 13.22.

statement of the law in one place, such direct substitution can be laborious and where the affected Act is heavily amended, physically impossible to achieve on the printed page. Despite these obstacles, greater emphasis is being placed on the use of the textual method.

## EVALUATION

It is difficult to evaluate the cogency of the various criticisms of the drafting process at a general level. One of the reasons why we have dealt at some length with methods of amendment and with the criticisms made of the non-textual method is to underline the fact that these issues are not susceptible to simple solutions. They typically involve a number of factors, many of which, like the government's requirement of timeliness, originate outside the drafting process, yet have a profound impact upon it. It is undoubtedly the case that particular experiences can substantiate the criticisms that statutory provisions may be obscure, complex, unintelligible, over-elaborate, and unhelpfully structured and amended. It is, however, neither instructive nor appropriate to present such experiences as evidence supporting the argument that they are of general application. The intelligibility of any section depends upon the context in which it appears, the user's familiarity with its subject matter and the circumstances of individual cases to which it may apply. Many provisions are quite unintelligible when presented out of context and without reference to particular facts. Legislation is not intended to be read in a vacuum. Nor is it appropriate to expect legislation to be understood directly by all those whom it affects. Complaints that legislation is complicated are frequently misplaced:

> "There is always the complaint that legislation is complicated. Of course it is, because life is complicated. The bulk of the legislation enacted nowadays is social, economic or financial; the laws they must express and the life situations they must regulate are in themselves complicated, and these laws cannot in any language or in any style be reduced to kindergarten level, any more than can the theory of relativity. One might as well ask why television sets are so complicated. Why do they not make television sets so everyone can understand them? Well, you can't expect to put a colour image on a screen in your living-room with a crystal set. And you can't have crystal set legislation in a television age."[65]

[65] Driedger, "Statutory Drafting and Interpretation" *Proceedings of the Ninth International Symposium on Comparative Law* (1971), pp. 71, 78; quoted in Bennion, *op.cit.*, p. 96.

Nevertheless it is a sufficient indictment of the drafting process if a user who is familiar with the subject matter of a provision cannot, after a reasonable expenditure of intellectual effort and within a reasonable time, make sense of it in relation to a given set of circumstances. Where this is the case it is important to identify the conditions which give rise to such occurrences, with a view to minimising their influence where practicable. As we have tried to explain, these conditions are numerous, complex and interdependent. They derive from the complexity of the subject-matter and from the differing and conflicting expectations and demands placed upon the draftsman. In these terms current criticism generally has been sympathetic in its appreciation of the constraints which the political process and the shortages of time and expertise impose upon him. Where the draftsman has been criticised, there has been disagreement both as to the cogency of the supporting evidence and as to the appropriateness of the proposed reforms.[66]

## REFORM

We do not have the space to deal in detail with the many suggestions that have been made for the reform of the drafting process. Some have been touched upon in this and Chapter 2. We propose merely to mention the main suggestions, and to indicate some of the difficulties which they encounter. The suggestions have been concerned with two matters: the resources available to the draftsman and the product itself. These raise a number of issues that do not fall squarely within the drafting process, yet which, as we have seen, significantly affect it. In many instances, reform of the drafting process could not take place without regard to these wider implications.

Increasing the available resources has been seen as one means of improving the statute book, in particular through more intensive programmes of consolidation and statute law revision, backed by access to computer technology for the storage and retrieval of statutory provisions. As we have seen, neither consolidation nor statute law revision are mere technical exercises which could be expanded by a simple quantitative extension of resources.[67] In addition, both are liable to be subordinated to the government's overriding emphasis on the completion of its legislative programme.

[66] See the evidence of Sir J. Fiennes, a former First Parliamentary Counsel, given to the House of Commons Select Committee on Procedure 1970–71, reproduced by the Statute Law Society, *The Key to Clarity*, *op.cit.*, Appendix F, pp. 47–59.

[67] Above, pp. 36–44.

The kind of technological innovation associated with word processors and micro-chip computers has been adopted by governments in other countries and by private organisations here; but it appears to excite little interest in those responsible for the preparation of legislation in this country.[68]

Most of the suggestions for reform of the product itself have been directed at what have been identified as the five leading characteristics of United Kingdom statutes: prolixity, complexity, poor arrangement, excessive particularity and pragmatism.[69] A number of remedies have been proposed, and their implementation would, in most cases, require substantial changes in current drafting practices and arrangements. They include: the use of "purpose" clauses;[70] the adoption of a style of drafting that emphasises brevity and ease of understanding through the use of clauses which state what principles are to be applied in the specific cases decided by courts, tribunals and other authorities[71]; the use of modes of presentation other than prose;[72] the adoption of the principle of "one subject, one Act," a deliberate preference for textual amendment, the use of more informative supplementary memoranda, and a preference for the interests of the ultimate users over those of the legislators.

It is difficult to generalise about the appropriateness of these remedies. Moreover our willingness to do so is tempered by the recognition that, in the words of Lord Cross

> " . . . in truth the debate as to the respective merits of the two systems [common and civil law styles of drafting] is somewhat academic because . . . there is not the remotest likelihood of Parliamentary Counsel voluntarily abandoning their system of drafting or the government compelling them to do so."[73]

The key factors which must be acknowledged are the pragmatism of the Office of Parliamentary Counsel and the inertia of govern-

[68] On the use of computer technology for legal purposes see Tapper, *Computers and the Law* (1973), and Niblett, *Computer Science and the Law* (1979).

[69] Dale, "Statutory Reform : The Draftsman and the Judge" (1981) 30 I.C.L.Q. 141, 145. See also Samuels, "Improving the Quality of Legislation" (1974) 3 Anglo-American L.R. 523, and Robson, "Legislative Draftsmanship" (1946) 17 *Political Quarterly* 330.

[70] *e.g.* Wildlife and Countryside Act 1981, s.37 and generally, Renton, para 11.8. For the government's reaction see H.L. Deb., Vol. 412. ser.5, cols. 1588–1589 (August 7, 1980).

[71] This style is commonly associated with the civil law tradition; see Dale, *op.cit.*, and *Legislative Drafting : A New Approach* (1977); and Smith, "Legislative Drafting : English and Continental" [1980] Stat. L.R. 14.

[72] *e.g.* Consumer Credit Act 1974, Sched. 2; Finance Act 1965, Sched. 6, para. 24 (4).

[73] Cross, review of Bennion, *Statute Law* [1981] Stat. L.R. 122, 123.

ment. The draftsman's prime concern is to draft a clause which gives legal effect to what the government wants, and no more. The words he uses and the style he adopts will be geared to achieving that objective: a statement of purpose or the use of some method of presentation other than prose will be selected because they are a more effective means of performing a particular job.[74] In this sense the draftsman is not concerned to generalise their use. For the draftsman, the overriding concern is legal effectiveness and the primary obstacle to its attainment continues to be the shortage of time within which the programme must be completed. Although the draftsman may make a conscious effort to use these remedies where appropriate in preference to the inherited system, no general change in drafting practice could come about in the absence either of there being more time at the draftsman's disposal to consider alternative formulations of a clause or of the government sanctioning change.

Accordingly, the government's attitude to the practice of and arrangements for, the drafting of its Bills is critical.[75] It is difficult to believe that it is not in its interests to consider actively the feasibility and desirability of these various remedies. However, the government is not the only body which displays no great enthusiasm for the subject of reform of the drafting process: the Commons' debate on the Renton Report, which was the first investigation of the subject for nearly a century was attended by only a handful of Members.[76] In part this may be attributable to the perception that the subject is a matter of legal expertise only. It is true that the drafting process presents aspects which are technical, but the success of the government's policies depends to a considerable extent on the effectiveness with which drafting is carried out.

## SCRUTINY OF DRAFTING

As we have seen, elaborate arrangements exist at Cabinet level to ensure that draft Bills express the government's intentions as accurately as possible.[77] Beyond these arrangements there is no

[74] This point cannot be emphasised too strongly; draftsmen seek an economy of words in the formulation of a Bill's clauses, what Bennion calls "the cutting edge," *op.cit.*, p. 95.

[75] The Labour Government's reaction to the recommendations of the Renton Committee for example, not surprisingly displayed a primary concern for allowing the draftsman sufficient discretion in the choice of drafting technique so as to achieve legal effectiveness H.L. Deb., Vol. 366, ser.5, cols. 956–963 (December 10, 1975), and H.C. Deb., Vol. 899, ser.5, cols. 114–120 (November 10, 1975).

[76];H.C. Deb., *ibid.*, cols. 127 and 167.

[77] Above, pp. 34–35.

formal provision for the scrutiny of the drafting of Bills other than those provided by the parliamentary stages of the legislative process.[78] Sometimes errors do become apparent during the parliamentary stages, in which case it is possible for the draftsman to prepare an amendment. Inevitably, however, the consideration of form and drafting is subordinated to the consideration of policy during these stages, and drafting errors usually come to light only when someone has to apply a defective provision. Various suggestions have been made for the provision of additional opportunities for the scrutiny of draft Bills. Thus the Renton Committee considered a number of proposals recommending the introduction of such arrangements either before a Bill is presented to Parliament, during its parliamentary stages or thirdly, following its completion of those stages.[79]

So far as pre-presentation scrutiny is concerned, the Committee's view was that departmental choice as to whom it consulted about drafting should be left unconstrained. It is reasonable to suppose that the government would not welcome the possibility of disagreement with an independent scrutinising body and the consequent delay in the progress of Bills. The Renton Committee also rejected the proposal that there should be a separate parliamentary stage specifically allocated for scrutinising the drafting of Bills. One of the primary justifications which was given for this conclusion was the undesirability of increasing the draftsman's burdens.

However, the Committee did recommend the adoption of two procedures designed to facilitate changes in the language or form of a Bill before it came into force. The first was that on application by the sponsor of a Bill, the Speaker and the Lord Chancellor could certify that amendments which came within a narrowly defined category would, if incorporated in the Bill, constitute improvements of a drafting nature. This procedure would be available where a Bill had completed its parliamentary stages but had yet to receive the Royal Assent. The proposed amendments would be printed on the Order Paper, giving Parliament the opportunity to reject or accept them, but without debate.[80]

[78] The Public Bill Offices of the two Houses of Parliament are concerned only with a Bill's procedural legitimacy; above, n.2.

[79] Renton, paras. 18.26–18.42. See also Jennings' suggestion of a drafting committee, *Parliament* (2nd ed., 1957), p. 447.

[80] This proposal was supported in principle by the 1978 Select Committee on Procedure, but it also wished to see the inclusion of safeguards against the introduction of substantive amendments; First Report from the Select Committee on Procedure (1978; H.C. 588), para 2.44. This recommendation has not been implemented.

The second procedure was intended to allow changes to be made in the form and arrangement of a Bill, either before or after it received the Royal Assent, but before its commencement. Under this procedure a Bill or Act which was obscure or otherwise defective in point of form could be rewritten in clearer language. Renton envisaged a body similar to the Joint Committee on Consolidation Bills being responsible for this task. In 1977 the Government introduced an Acts of Parliament (Correction of Mistakes) Bill. This Bill was prompted by the accidental deletion of three lines in the Rent (Agriculture) Bill 1976 when the Commons were considering, on a guillotine motion, one of the 129 Lords' amendments. The Correction of Mistakes Bill was strongly criticised for its failure to define "mistake"; and there was concern lest changes in substance could be authorised under its procedures in the guise of changes in form.[81] The Bill was subsequently withdrawn. In the event that errors do appear after a Bill has received the Royal Assent, they can only be corrected by amending legislation.[82] In the view of the 1978 Select Committee on Procedure, this is the only proper course which can be taken.

Finally, it should be noted that the Renton Committee recommended that the Statute Law Committee should have responsibility for keeping the structure and language of statutes under continuous review, as part of a general and continuing oversight of legislation, with the aim of achieving long-term improvement in the standards of drafting and in the arrangement of the statute book.[83] As with other suggestions, however, the government apparently does not wish to authorise reviewing procedures beyond those which presently exist.

[81] The 1978 Select Committee on Procedure was opposed to the recommendation for this reason; *ibid.*, para. 2.45.

[82] The mistakes in the 1976 Act were corrected in the Rent (Agriculture) (Amendment) Act 1977.

[83] Renton, para. 18.40 and recommendation 108.

Chapter Five

# THE PARLIAMENTARY STAGES

The government's responsibility for the initiation of legislation raises the fundamental problem of how to distribute the limited parliamentary time available in such a way as to allow the government the chance to enact its legislative programme, while at the same time preserving sufficient opportunities for the consideration of individual measures brought forward as part of that programme. Sir Courtenay Ilbert summarised the problem thus:

> " . . . on the one hand, how to find time within limited parliamentary hours for disposing of the growing mass of business which devolves on the Government; and on the other hand, how to reconcile the legitimate demands of the Government with the legitimate rights of the minority, the despatch of business with the duties of Parliament as a grand inquest of the nation at which all public questions of real importance find opportunity for adequate discussion."[1]

## "THE DEMANDS OF THE GOVERNMENT"

The legislative process takes place within an institutional framework of rules and their interpretation which define *inter alia* the relationship of government to the arrangement and conduct of parliamentary business. The increasing control exercised by government over the parliamentary stages of the legislative process may be traced through the successive amendments made to these rules as set out in the standing orders of the House of Commons. In particular their amendment reflects the government's acquisition of the control of parliamentary time at the expense of backbench Members, and, under the pressure of expanding legislative commitments, the rationalisation and intensification of the use of that time in an attempt to have individual proposals enacted as expeditiously as possible, thus securing the completion of the government's legislative programme.

The establishment of government control over the parliamentary timetable was a gradual development, hastened in its later stages by the systematic obstruction practised by the Irish Home Rule Party

[1] Introduction to Redlich, *The Procedure of the House of Commons* (1908), Vol. 1, xxi.

under the leadership of Parnell. During the early years of the nineteenth century Ministers enjoyed no greater rights than private Members, except in relation to finance. Two days of the week were customarily assigned to government business, but this was regarded as a concession and it was not until 1846 that this practice was officially recognised in the standing orders of the House of Commons. Thereafter "by slow degrees the rules of procedure were made more subservient to the needs of the Government."[2] Its share of parliamentary time increased steadily until with the passing of Balfour's "Parliamentary railway timetable" in 1902 the principle had become established that the daily programme should be arranged by the government. Then, as now, subject to minor exceptions in favour of private Members, the parliamentary time available was entirely at the disposal of the government.[3]

The effective consolidation of the government's position required in addition that its use of parliamentary time should be protected from obstruction by private Members. This end was achieved by the adoption of a number of procedural devices which were designed to truncate debate and ensure that the will of the majority would prevail. Foremost among these devices were the closure, the power to select amendments and allocation of time orders. The closure was introduced in 1881 in response to obstruction on the Coercion Bill by the Irish Home Rule Party. It is of general application and in its modern form it allows discussion to be ended on a motion to that effect provided that the Speaker, at his discretion, accepts such a motion and that at least one hundred Members vote in its favour.[4] The power to select amendments and allocation of time orders date from the same period and are specific to legislation. The former enables the avoidance of repetition in the discussion of amendments[5], whereas the latter, the most drastic of these forms, permits the establishment of a fixed timetable during which the consideration of the individual stages of a Bill must be completed.

These developments were the logical outcome of the government's emergence as the chief initiator of legislation and as such they constitute the parliamentary counterpart of the developments discussed in Chapter 2. Summarising the changes that had taken place during the course of the nineteenth century Redlich wrote:

[2] *Ibid.*, Vol. 3, p. 194.
[3] S.O. No. 6.
[4] S.O. No. 30. For the history of the closure see Jennings, *Parliament* (2nd ed., 1957), pp. 127–131.
[5] Introduced in its modern form in 1919, S.O. No. 33. For the background to its introduction, see Jennings, *op. cit.*, pp. 240–241

"Parliamentary procedure is the only department in the constitution of State and Parliament where the old conventions and forms, silently shaped in the seventeenth and eighteenth centuries, and elsewhere studiously protected, have been ruthlessly set aside from motives of political serviceableness, and where the new political division of strength has also received adequate new legal expression. The order of business in the House of Commons, the actual political sovereign of the empire, has of necessity been converted from a weapon to be used against Crown and Government by the representative assembly of the people into a *political weapon of the Ministry* . . ."[6]

Walkland emphasises the point: "The Standing Orders adopted by the House in the last half of the nineteenth century by and large recognised that government in Britain had become party government, and that the dominant party could expect to control not only the working of the executive, but also the deliberations—and, largely, the conclusions of Parliament."[7]

After 1902 the focus of reform shifted to the intensification of the use of the time required. The most significant consequence of this shift in emphasis for legislative procedure was the differentiation of the legislative structure of the House of Commons through the greatly extended use of the "rudimentary" system of standing committees which had been in existence since 1882.[8] The expansion of their role in the legislative process was presaged by the reversal of the existing presumption as to the method of dealing with public Bills at their committee stage. In 1907 the House of Commons approved a government proposal based on recommendations made in the Second Report of the 1906 Select Committee on Procedure, to the effect that all Bills, with the exception of Finance, Consolidated Fund and Appropriation Bills, and Bills for confirming provisional orders, should be sent to a standing committee after their second reading unless the House ordered otherwise. At the same time the number of standing committees was increased to four, including one to consider all Bills relating to Scotland, and the closure was extended to their proceedings.

Although the theory underlying these reforms was that reference to standing committees would become the normal method of dealing with Bills after their second reading, these reforms had little

[6] *Op. cit.*, Vol. 1, p. 210, original emphasis.

[7] *The Legislative Process in Great Britain* (1969), p. 68.

[8] Walkland, "Government Legislation in the House of Commons," in *The House of Commons in the Twentieth Century* (Walkland ed., 1979), p. 247; Redlich, *op.cit.*, Vol. 3, pp. 207–217.

immediate impact. Up to the beginning of the Second World War the majority of Bills, including most notably those which were politically controversial, continued to be considered on the floor of the House. During the inter-war period only minor reforms were made to the committee system. Their cumulative effect was to produce "a committee system with the minimum competence necessary to deal with the legislative burden of the period."[9]

As with the other developments we have discussed, the size of the legislative programme for post-war reconstruction provided the necessary impetus for the removal of this disparity between theory and practice. The wartime Coalition Government's view that the parliamentary time available for reconstruction legislation had to be increased, led to the establishment in December 1943 of a sub-committee on parliamentary procedure of the internal Machinery of Government Committee.[10] The deliberations of this sub-committee were continued in public by the Select Committee on Procedure appointed by the Labour Government in 1945. In its First Report which dealt mainly with standing committees, the Committee accepted a Government proposal whereby the only Bills not *automatically* referred to a standing committee would be: those Bills provision for the reference of which had been made in 1907; Bills requiring to be passed with great expedition; "one clause" Bills not requiring detailed examination in committee; and Bills of "first class constitutional importance." In addition, it recommended that the limit on the number of standing committees be removed, their size be reduced, and that the standing orders relating to allocation of time orders be extended to their proceedings.[11] This final recommendation proved to be the most politically contentious. As Morrison pointed out, however, it was only the logical counterpart of the proposal that politically controversial Bills should be referred to standing committees.[12] The Committee's recommendations were subsequently embodied in sessional orders after its Report had been approved without a division by the House of Commons.

Two recurring features of these developments merit emphasis. First, the main impetus for reform throughout the period has stemmed from governments, mainly under the pressure of their own legislative commitments. This is seen most clearly in the case of the

[9] Walkland, "Government Legislation in the House of Commons," *op. cit.*, p. 260. The most important reform introduced was the extension of the standing orders relating to the selection of amendments to their proceedings in 1934.

[10] The history is recounted in Lee, *Reviewing the Machinery of Government 1942–1952* (1977), pp. 116–128.

[11] First Report from the Select Committee on Procedure (1946; H.C. 9).

[12] *Government and Parliament* (3rd ed., 1964), p. 224.

reforms introduced by the 1945 Labour Government. Secondly, reform has often been supported by the Opposition front bench, partly no doubt because they recognise the practical advantages which will accrue to them in the enactment of their own legislative commitments. Against this background Select Committees on Procedure have played a largely supportive role, mediating between the demands of the government and the traditional rights and opportunities accorded to backbench MPs.[13]

## "THE RIGHTS OF THE MINORITY"

Any increase in the government's control of the parliamentary timetable inevitably restricts the rights and opportunities accorded to backbench Members. The only recognised limits to the reform of legislative procedure are those set by convention, in relation to the protection of minorities. This convention that "the power of the majority should not be used to steamroller into silence the protests of the minority"[14] is explained by Redlich in the following way:

> "The majority holds the great advantage of being able to realise its wishes in the institutions of government; but, on the other hand, for this very reason the minority ought to have all conceivable rights of expressing its views and aims, and ought to be allowed free use of all permissible weapons of speech and political tactics in its fight against the expression of the wish of Parliament which is a consequence of possessing a majority. For it is just as much the interest of the nation to ascertain whether the majority can maintain itself as such against an able and powerful attack and make proper use of the great privilege of conducting the government, as it is to take care that the will of the ultimate majority shall be treated as the will of the nation. *Protection of the minority is, therefore, in the British Parliament no mere privilege of the minority for the time being: it is a vitally important institution developed in the highest interests of a nation ruled by Parliament.* The majority for the time being has no true interest in weakening the principle for it has always to expect the day when it will in turn be the minority and will need this palladium as a means of advocating its own party conception of the interests of the state."[15]

[13] Walkland, "Government Legislation in the House of Commons," *op. cit.*, pp. 252, 264.
[14] Butt, *The Power of Parliament* (1969), p. 318.
[15] *Op. cit.*, Vol. 1, p. 131, original emphasis.

As the chief beneficiary of this convention the official Opposition is allocated a certain proportion of parliamentary time, namely 29 supply days.[16] Moreover, the residual capacity which it retains to this day, to hinder the fulfilment of the government's programme gives it an important role in the establishment and maintenance of the parliamentary timetable. Although as we have seen the whole of parliamentary time is at the disposal of the government, its use is not determined unilaterally. Rather it is settled through a continuous process of consultation and negotiation between the Chief Whips of both major parties. The part which these arrangements may play in the completion of the government's legislative programme was clearly illustrated in August 1975, when the Government secured the Opposition's agreement to an extension of the parliamentary session until late November, by which time the new session should normally have begun. A number of Bills awaited completion of their parliamentary stages and, in addition, the Government had just introduced a new Bill, the Remuneration, Charges and Grants Bill, as part of its counter-inflation policy. In return the Opposition exacted a commitment from the Government that in the following session no "seriously controversial" Bills would be introduced after Easter.[17] Without the Opposition's co-operation the Government would have experienced greater difficulty than in fact it did in enacting its full programme for the session. Exceptionally co-operation between the major parties breaks down. In May 1976 the Opposition suspended co-operation through the usual channels after the Government had successfully carried a motion suspending the application of the standing orders relating to private business to the Aircraft and Shipbuilding Industries Bill which the Speaker had ruled was prima facie hybrid. Normal co-operation was not resumed for several weeks.

Using Bagehot's terminology, Crossman described timetabling as an "efficient secret."

> "The Cabinet is naturally content to accept the co-operation of the Shadow Cabinet in getting its business through. As for the Shadow Cabinet, since its main desire is to become the real Cabinet as soon as possible, it has a strong common interest with the Government in preserving a system under which it shares four-fifths of the parliamentary time with the Government—thereby reducing to a minimum the time available to private members and rebel groups in either of the two big

[16] S.O. No. 18.

[17] Wilson, *The Governance of Britain* (1976), pp. 144–145.

> parties. Thus Cabinet control of Parliament is exerted—at a price. The Government can only obtain the actual connivance of the official Opposition by sharing with it the planning of the timetable, and the responsibility for keeping the debates within the time limits they have agreed upon. This requires the continuous and intimate co-operation of the Government and Opposition Chief Whips through the usual channels."[18]

These arrangements lend a high degree of artificiality to the parliamentary stages of the legislative process. The formal stages cannot be understood apart from the prior informal discussions which take place within and between the parties, during which the issues of the amount of time to be spent in discussion, the clauses to be considered and amendments to be moved may all be decided upon. Describing the office of Private Secretary to the Government Chief Whip through which the "usual channels" operate, Crossman wrote: "It's as though there had been one staff sergeant major running the British and German Staffs in World War I and it's this which really keeps the House of Commons running and enables us to have so few misunderstandings between the two Chief Whips on either side."[19] Thus, the government formally possesses the capacity to dominate the legislative process through its party majority, the realisation of its legislative aims only being constrained by the procedural opportunities afforded to individual MPs to participate in the process whether through signifying their assent or opposition to individual proposals or seeking their amendment. In practice, however, the emphasis is on inter and intra-party co-operation and agreement in determining, if not the substance of these proposals, at least the form in which (and the extent to which) they will be considered. The rules by which effect may be given to the majority party's domination remain in the background as an incentive to agreement and as a partial substitute for it should co-operation break down.

## PUBLIC BILL PROCEDURE

Although Bills can be introduced in either the House of Commons or the House of Lords the effective scope for their introduction in the House of Lords is limited by the House of Commons' exclusive privilege in relation to the granting of supplies and the imposition

[18] *Inside View* (1972), pp. 61–62; Jennings, *op. cit.*, pp. 151–160.
[19] *The Diaries of a Cabinet Minister* (1976) Vol. 2, p. 625.

and appropriation of charges, a privilege which ordinarily necessitates the introduction of Bills with financial implications in the lower House. In addition Bills which are likely to raise political controversy usually originate in the House of Commons. Thus the Local Government, Planning and Land Bill 1979 was withdrawn from the House of Lords and re-introduced in the House of Commons in response to Opposition demands backed by the threat of the withdrawal of co-operation. Consolidation Bills and "law reform" Bills on the other hand are normally introduced in the House of Lords.

The pre-eminence of the House of Commons in this respect lends a degree of imbalance to the parliamentary session. The work of the House of Lords tends to be concentrated towards the end of the Session when a backlog of Bills may have built up waiting to complete their stages. In 1972 a minor relaxation was effected under Standing Order No. 58A to the House of Commons' privilege in relation to finance which facilitated the introduction of such Bills in the House of Lords.[20] Where speed is vital Bills may be introduced concurrently, as happened in the cases of the Commonwealth Immigrants Act 1968 and the Northern Ireland (Temporary Provisions) Act 1972.

## *INTRODUCTION AND FIRST READING*

Bills may be introduced in the House of Commons by one of two methods: by order of the House or by written notice under the provisions of Standing Order No. 37(1). Introduction by order of the House is exceptional, being reserved mainly for two classes of Bills: those founded upon financial resolutions, notably Consolidated Fund Bills and Finance Bills; and Bills introduced under Standing Order No. 13, the "Ten-Minute Rule," which modified the practice of introducing Bills on a motion for leave. Bills introduced under Standing Order No. 13 are invariably introduced by private Members.[21]

The majority of Bills are presented by written notice. Under this procedure an entry appears on the order paper stating the long and short titles of the Bill and the names of its promoters. At the commencement of public business on the day assigned for a Bill's first reading the Speaker calls the Member who either hands a "dummy bill" to the Clerk, or, if he is a Minister, moves its presentation. The Clerk then reads the short title of the Bill without

[20] Erskine May, *Parliamentary Practice* (19th ed., 1976), p. 483.
[21] See below, p. 132.

any question being put. This constitutes its formal first reading. At the same time, a day is fixed for its second reading and it is ordered to be printed.[22] Before being printed and distributed the Bill is examined by the Public Bill Office to check that it complies with the rules of the House.[23]

Apart from its purely formal first reading which is intended to give notice of the proposed measure, there are four further stages through which a Bill must pass in each House before it receives the Royal Assent: the second reading stage, the committee stage, the report stage and, finally, the third reading stage. Although these stages are treated "as inter-connected portions of a single process of consideration, each stage is regarded as having its own peculiar function and to a certain extent its own more or less limited range of debate."[24] As we shall see, however, this rational conception of the functions of the various stages may be upset by more overtly political considerations flowing from the political context within which the Bill is considered. For the government the essential significance of these stages lies in the fact that they represent procedural hurdles to be overcome before effect can be given to its legislative intentions. At the same time they provide it with an opportunity to explain and, if necessary, reconsider its proposals; in this latter sense they represent an extension of the consultative process allowing more time for the attainment of agreement. On the other hand from the point of view of opponents of the proposals, the stages provide opportunities to oppose or modify the government's intentions. Where opposition is based on inter-party divisions, they also provide the Opposition with an opportunity to establish its own credentials as an alternative governing party in the eyes of the electorate. These factors mean, first, that it is difficult to disentangle the purely formal consideration of the Bill from the process of the continuous political conflict between parties, and secondly, that those values commonly associated with the legislative process, such as the provision of opportunities for the rational and systematic consideration of and the reflection upon the principles and details of proposed measures, may be subordinated to essentially political considerations.

[22] S.O. No. 37(2).
[23] See above, p. 79.
[24] Erskine May, *op. cit.*, p. 496.

## *SECOND READING*

The second reading debate provides an opportunity for the consideration of the principles and policy upon which Bills are based. In practice this means that if a Bill is contentious its supporters and opponents alternatively publicly argue the case for and against the whole Bill or parts of it. Where a Bill is opposed the opposition to it may be carried to the extent of a division on a blocking amendment seeking to postpone its second reading thereby effectively killing it, or on a reasoned amendment expressing opposition to it in principle. But it is exceptional for a government to be defeated on either of these motions. The second reading of the Reduction of Redundancy Rebates Bill was defeated by 130 votes to 129 on February 7, 1977. This victory for the Bill's opponents was however short-lived. The Government secured the enactment of a revised version of the Bill, the Redundancy Rebates Act 1977.[25] For the rest, second reading debates vary markedly "from the formal, the cursory and the brief, to extended examination of the principles and sometimes of the details . . . "[26] In an often quoted passage Erskine May describes the second reading as "the most important stage through which the bill is required to pass; for its whole principle is then at issue, and is affirmed or denied by a vote of the House . . . "[27] The government's command of a majority means, however, that the affirmation of the principle is seldom in doubt. This not only lends a predictable quality to the debate, but also deprives the second reading of much of its functional significance.

> "As a means whereby the House makes an impact on Government bills its [the second reading's] only value is to present an occasion when for the first time in the House a Member or a group of Members can urge the Minister to accept certain changes which they hope to move in committee; and when the Minister may indicate any parts of the bill which he admits may need revision."[28]

There are two alternatives to the taking of the second reading on the floor of the House. First, since 1965 it has been possible on the motion of a Minister for a Bill to be referred to a second reading committee unless 20 or more Members object.[29] The Committee then considers the Bill and recommends whether or not it should be

[25] The last previous occasion upon which a government had been defeated on the second reading of a Bill was on the Rent Restrictions Bill in 1924.

[26] Griffith, *Parliamentary Scrutiny of Government Bills* (1974), p. 27.

[27] *Op. cit.*, p. 497.

[28] Griffith, *op. cit.*, p. 30.

[29] S.O. No. 66.

read a second time. If it so recommends (and an adverse recommendation has never been made) the Bill in question is subsequently given a second reading by the whole House without debate. Although this development parallels the earlier differentiation of the legislative structure of the House of Commons for the committee stage of the legislative process, its impact has been limited. The fact that recourse to it can be defeated by any 20 or more Members means that a minimum agreement between the two major parties is a pre-condition of its use, with the result that, in practice, its use has been restricted to non-contentious Bills.[30]

Secondly, under the provisions of Standing Order No. 67, unless 10 or more Members object, a Bill certified by the Speaker as relating exclusively to Scotland may be referred to the Scottish Grand Committee. This is one of the two Scottish standing committees consisting of all Scottish members and between 10 and 15 additional Members. It considers, but does not vote upon, the principle of the Bill and reports to the House. When the order for the Bill's second reading is read, unless six or more Members have given notice of an amendment, a Minister may move the committal of the Bill to a Scottish standing committee in which case the Bill is treated as having been read a second time. The Welsh Grand Committee, consisting of all Welsh members with the addition of up to five other Members is another committee to which Bills may be referred on the motion of a Minister unless 20 or more Members object. In its operation it is similar to a second reading committee; it reports on the Bill and recommends whether or not it should be read a second time, following which the motion is voted upon without debate.[31]

## FINANCIAL RESOLUTIONS

Where a Bill, other than a financial Bill founded upon an order of the House, involves expenditure or taxation, its financial provisions must be authorised by a resolution of the House proposed by a Minister before they can be considered in committee. The financial resolution is approved on the floor of the House, normally immediately after the second reading.

The government's exclusive initiative in relation to finance severely restricts the scope for the amendment of a financial resolution. No amendments can be moved which would increase the expenditure involved or vary the purposes, conditions and methods

[30] *The Process of Legislation*, Second Report from the Select Committee on Procedure (1971; H.C. 538), Appendix 1; Griffith, *op. cit.*, pp. 25–26.
[31] S.O. No. 72.

laid down for its disbursement; the only permissible amendments are those which serve generally to reduce the amount voted either directly or indirectly through the omission of items of expenditure or the limitation of the purposes for which money may be spent. These restrictions apply throughout the whole of the Bill's passage. Consequently the scope for the subsequent amendment of the Bill depends on how widely the financial resolution is drawn. Following the appointment in 1937 of a Select Committee on Procedure to consider the controversy aroused by the abuse of financial resolution procedure, departments and the Office of Parliamentary Counsel were instructed that financial resolutions in respect of Bills should be

> "so framed as not to restrict the scope within which the Committee on the Bills may consider amendments further than is necessary to enable the Government to discharge their responsibilities in regard to public expenditure, and to leave the Committee the utmost freedom for discussion and amendment of details which is compatible with the discharge of these responsibilities."[32]

Nevertheless, where expenditure is involved money resolutions continue to be very tightly drafted. Thus, for example, to avoid embarrassing amendments increasing the size or scope of the Christmas bonus for pensioners the money resolution to the Pensioners' Payment Bill 1978 simply provided monies "under provisions which . . . correspond to those made . . . by the Pensioners' Payment Act 1977."[33]

## *THE COMMITTEE STAGE*

Under the provisions of Standing Order No. 40(1) all public Bills except Consolidated Fund and Appropriation Bills, and Bills for confirming provisional orders are automatically referred to a standing committee unless the House otherwise orders.

Despite their name, standing committees are constituted as and when it is necessary; up to 10 having been sitting at any one time. Their composition varies between 16 and 50 Members, the average number being 18, who are nominated by a Committee of Selection with regard to their qualifications and the party composition of the House. Each committee is designated by a letter, standing committee A, B, and C, etc., and government Bills take precedence in all of them except standing committee C in which private

[32] H.C. Deb., Vol. 328, ser. 5, col. 1595 (November 9, 1937); Report of the Select Committee on Procedure relating to Money Resolutions (1937; H.C. 149). For the background see Jennings, *op.cit.*, pp. 259–267.

[33] Castle, *The Castle Diaries 1974–76* (1980), pp. 97–98, and Griffith, *op. cit.*, pp. 68–69.

Members' Bills have priority. Distinct arrangements exist for the consideration of Bills relating exclusively to Scotland. They may be referred to one of the two Scottish standing committees which include in their composition at least 16 Scottish Members. In the exceptional circumstances that a public Bill relates exclusively to Wales, the standing committee to which it is referred must include all Welsh Members.

There are three alternatives to the consideration of a public Bill by a standing committee. A motion to have recourse to any one of these must be decided upon without amendment or debate immediately after a Bill's second reading. First, a Bill may be considered in committee of the whole House. This alternative is restricted in practice to: Bills requiring rapid passage; certain financial measures including at least part of each year's Finance Bill, the major clauses of which are taken in committee of the whole House, the remainder being referred to a standing committee; and Bills of constitutional importance. This last term is one of "imprecise content," but it has covered, for example, the Parliament No. 2 Bill 1969, the European Communities Act 1972, the Scotland and Wales Bill 1977, the Scotland Act 1978 and the Wales Act 1978. The justification for retaining these Bills together with part of each year's Finance Bill on the floor of House is that all Members should have the opportunity to participate in the discussion of the details of measures of such consequence. In practice, however, this principle may prove difficult to reconcile with the subjection of a measure to an adequate degree of scrutiny.[34]

Secondly, a Bill may be referred to a select committee. The delay among other factors involved in the referral of a Bill to a select committee has meant that there has been comparatively little recourse to this alternative. Bills which have been referred after their second reading include the House of Commons Disqualification Bill 1955–56, the Obscene Publications Bill 1956–57, the Armed Forces Bills 1965–66, 1966–67 and 1980–81, the Anti-Discrimination Bill 1973 and the Abortion Amendment Bill 1975. The principal advantage of the select committee alternative is that it allows evidence to be heard, following which the Bill is recommitted to a committee of the whole House. The same result can be achieved by recourse to the third alternative, namely, referral of a Bill to a joint committee, that is a committee consisting of the Members of a Commons' and a Lords' select committee deputed to

[34] Following the application of the guillotine only 23 of the 83 clauses and 4 of the 17 schedules of the Scotland Bill were considered before it completed its Commons Stages. Similarly, only 16 of the 84 clauses and 2 of the 12 schedules of the Wales Bill were considered, and see below, p. 138.

meet each other. In relation to public Bills the most significant of these is the Joint Committee on Consolidation, etc., Bills.[35]

The theory underlying the committee stage is that it provides an opportunity for the consideration of the details of the Bill and their amendment consistent with its principle as approved on second reading. Nevertheless, there is a clear conflict between this essentially technical conception of its function and the opportunity which it also provides "to extend political advocacy and opposition beyond the Second Reading stage into the details of legislation."[36] The Opposition's desire to make the passage of government legislation more difficult, the government's unwillingness to allow such obstruction to affect its timetable, and the emphasis of both parties on electoral considerations, may all affect the way in which the task of scrutinising the details of the proposed legislation is approached.

Amendments moved at the committee stage may serve one or more of a wide variety of purposes. The Opposition or government backbenchers may move probing amendments as a means of ascertaining the meaning attached to the provisions of the Bill or of obtaining assurances about how its provisions will be implemented once enacted. Once the information has been obtained the amendment may be withdrawn. If, however, it is regarded as unsatisfactory the amendment may be pressed to a division or form the basis for the moving of a subsequent amendment. Amendments may also be moved with the direct and primary intention of effecting changes in the Bill. Some of these amendments such as those intended to repair unintentional omissions or minor drafting errors may accord with the government's own interests and are thus likely to prove acceptable. Others may be moved with the objective of publicising major points of opposition and may thus serve to bring into sharper focus the conflict over the Bill. These amendments are likely to be resisted unless they attract the support of the government's own backbenchers and thus raise the possibility of its defeat. Less visibly the necessity of securing the co-operation of outside groups may induce the government to make concessions as part of the continuing process of seeking agreement. Outside groups may promote amendments through MPs which are designed to compel the government to defend publicly its refusal to accept amendments sought privately. Under pressure the Minister-in-charge may agree to "look again" with a view to putting forward a compromise on report. Again, amendments may be moved which

[35] See above, pp. 46–47.

[36] Walkland, *The Legislative Process in Great Britain*, *op. cit.*, p. 73.

bear little connection to the substance of the Bill but which rather are intended to slow down its discussion, to embarrass the government or simply to point out the difference between the parties. "The purpose of many Opposition amendments is not to make the bill more generally acceptable but to make the Government less generally acceptable."[37]

Measured in terms of successful amendments, the impact of committee proceedings is comparatively slight: "It has been as rare for ministerial amendments to be rejected as for other Members' amendments to be successfully moved against Government opposition."[38] Griffith's exhaustive analysis of the three sessions 1967–68, 1968–69 and 1970–71 reveals that the overwhelming majority of amendments agreed to, some 93·7 per cent., were moved by Ministers. During the same period only one ministerial amendment failed. Moreover the origins of these successful amendments bears testimony to the marginal impact of committee proceedings on the thinking of government. Usually they reflect a refinement of the original conception of the Bill within the department, particularly where it has been prepared and drafted under pressure of time; and the representations made by outside groups in response to the published Bill. Not suprisingly, Opposition amendments fared much less well, with Government backbenchers amendments doing only slightly better: only 4·3 per cent. and 9·2 per cent. of the amendments moved by the Opposition and Government backbenchers respectively were successful.[39] Griffith concludes that on only 16 occasions during the three sessions was the Government forced to modify a principle of a Bill as a result of proceedings in committee.[40]

During the periods of minority government in 1974 and 1976–1979, the impact of committee proceedings was noticeably greater and was accompanied by some evidence of a weakening in the rigidity of the party system. The Labour Government suffered a series of defeats, notably on: the Social Security Benefits Bill 1975, the Housing Finance (Special Provisions) Bill 1975, the Dockwork Regulation Bill 1976, the Finance Bill 1977, the Scotland Bill 1978, the Wales Bill 1978 and the Finance Bill 1978. For the present these periods remain exceptional, and leaving them aside, it should be emphasised that the lack of impact of committee proceedings flows

[37] Griffith, *op. cit.*, p. 38.

[38] Griffith, "Standing Committees in the House of Commons" in *The Commons Today* (Walkland and Ryle ed., (1981), p. 130.

[39] *Parliamentary Scrutiny of Government Bills*, *op. cit.*, pp. 197–198. Taking into account amendments grouped and discussed but not selected to be moved, Griffith estimates that the more accurate success rate for Opposition amendments was nearer 2 per cent.

[40] *Ibid.*, p. 203.

from the government's possession of a majority and the domination of voting behaviour by party loyalties. As Wheare puts it: "If the government cannot command a majority in the House or in the Committee, something is wrong . . . On British parliamentary principles, it is not merely the usual thing but also the normal thing for the government to win."[41] Nevertheless, the sense of frustration induced by the predictability of much of committee proceedings, coupled with the belief that they are irrelevant to the evaluation of government activity, raise the question whether the time currently spent in committee, assuming it should continue to be spent, could not be used more effectively. The criticisms made of the existing proceedings are conveniently summarised by Crossman. Expanding on what he described as their "inanity" he wrote:

> "It is utterly futile to have this method of taking a Bill to pieces in order to improve it and moreover it's utterly debilitating. The Government backbenchers waste their time in Standing Committee, where they are hardly allowed to speak because that would prolong the business and anything they say may provoke another Tory speech. The Opposition arguments are amateur and bogus, because half the time they don't really understand the details of the clauses they are discussing . . . From time to time dramatic Second Reading debates are staged and the Bill rolls along, getting through without any critical dissection. It is this kind of thing that brings Parliament into disrepute and our modern backbenchers find it quite intolerable. Today they were quite glad and amused to see me there [in Committee] but they realised that as soon as I became interesting and lively progress was slowed down, so the sooner I was got out of the way and the backbenchers could go on writing their letters the better for all concerned."[42]

Proposals for reform have centred on the possibility of departing from the present adversarial character of committee proceedings to a more inquisitorial procedure, based on select committee procedure. The object of these proposals is to increase the information available to committee Members and thus to subject Bills to more informed consideration. As we have seen the 1978 Select Committee on Procedure took the view that while it might be desirable to refer some Bills, particularly those of a technical, non-partisan, or non-urgent character, to permanent or ad hoc select committees, such a course would be inappropriate for the generality of Bills.[43]

[41] *Government by Committee* (1955), p. 154.
[42] *Op. cit.*, Vol. 3, p. 903,
[43] First Report from the Select Committee on Procedure (1978; H.C. 588), para. 2.17.

Instead, it considered that standing committees should be empowered to examine the factual and technical background to the proposed legislation, before proceeding to examine the clauses of the Bill and to debate amendments.

> "In order to achieve this the committee should be free directly to question those who have drafted the proposed legislation and those who will implement it as to the purpose of the legislation, the evidence on which clauses are based, the degree and content of any prior consultation with outside interests, the effects which the legislation is expected to produce, and the problems which will be involved in its implementation. They should also be free to consult those who will be principally affected by the legislation. In our view, this process would not only lead to more informed and better aimed criticism of the text, but also might do away with the need for many probing amendments, might encourage more consideration of the problems of implementation and better drafting in the first place. It also should satisfy the interests principally concerned that proper attention has been paid by Parliament to their opinions about the proposed legislation."[44]

The Committee recommended that Bills might, on the motion of a Minister, be referred to a special standing committee which would be permitted to hold up to three sittings in select committee form before proceeding to clause by clause consideration of the Bill in the normal way. Tentative steps towards the implementation of this modest proposal were taken by the House of Commons on October 30, 1980 when the referral of up to three bills "which raised substantial issues . . . not of acute controversy" to special standing committees was approved as an experiment. Three Bills were considered by special standing committees during the 1980–81 session: the Criminal Attempts Bill, the Education Bill and the Deep Sea Mining (Temporary Provisions) Bill. Whether as a result of this experiment the hope expressed by the Select Committee on Procedure, that this form of committee should become accepted as the normal method of dealing with the committee stage of the great majority of Bills will be realised, remains to be seen.[45]

[44] *Ibid.*, para. 2.18.

[45] *Ibid.*, para. 2.19. Significant changes were made in the Criminal Attempts Bill as a result of the proceedings in committee. During the 1981–82 session the Government indicated its unwillingness to continue the experiment, but the Mental Health (Amendment) Bill was subsequently referred to a special standing committee. See also Griffith, *Parliamentary Scrutiny of Government Bills*, *op.cit.*, pp. 246–252.

## *REPORT STAGE AND THIRD READING*

Once the committee stage has been completed, the chairman of the committee reports the Bill to the House, stating whether or not it has been amended. Where a Bill has been amended the subsequent report stage provides an opportunity for it to be considered in its revised form. Amendments made at the committee stage may be altered, further amendments made, and new clauses added. The majority of government amendments are made at this stage; usually in response to points raised and undertakings given during earlier stages of the Bill's passage, or to reverse defeats suffered at the committee stage whose effects are unacceptable to the government. Thus in the three sessions examined by Griffith, of the 26 defeats suffered by the Government in committee, 14 were reversed on report, three were modified and only nine accepted.[46] The Opposition and government backbenchers may also use the opportunity to renew attempts to effect changes in the Bill.

Where a Bill has been reported from committee of the whole House, without amendment, the report stage is dispensed with and the Bill proceeds directly to its third reading.[47] The reduction in the government's exposure to the risk of potentially damaging defeats which this implies was one of the main reasons for the Government's rejection of all amendments to the European Communities Bill 1972. Bills which have not been considered in committee of the whole House must be considered on report even where they have not been amended.[48] No debate takes place, however, unless further amendments have been proposed.

The innate conservatism of the House of Commons in matters of legislative procedure is clearly illustrated by its unwillingness to contemplate the taking of the report stage other than on the floor of the House, on the grounds that this would involve a departure from the principle that the whole House assumes responsibility for the details of legislation.[49] The suggestion that time would be saved by taking the report stage of less controversial or less important Bills in committee was rejected by the 1946 and 1959 Select Committees on Procedure,[50] before being taken up by the 1967 Select Committee on Procedure.[51] Now under the provisions of Standing Order No. 73,

[46] *Parliamentary Scrutiny of Government Bills, op. cit.*, p. 206.

[47] S.O. No. 50.

[48] S.O. No. 52.

[49] Report from the Select Committee on Procedure (1959; H.C. 92), para. 10.

[50] Third Report from the Select Committee on Procedure (1946; H.C. 189), para. 11; Report from the Select Committee on Procedure (1959; H.C. 92), para. 10.

[51] *Public Bill Procedure Etc.*, Sixth Report from the Select Committee on Procedure (1967; H.C. 539), para. 26.

where a Bill has been considered by a second reading committee or by the Scottish Grand Committee, on the motion of a Minister it may be referred for consideration on report to a specially constituted report standing committee consisting of between 20 and 80 Members or to the Scottish Grand Committee. However, this reform has been "an almost total failure."[52] The Water Resources Bill 1967–68 is the only Bill which has been referred to a report standing committee and there has been no support for the suggestion that their scope should be extended.[53]

The third reading of a Bill is usually moved immediately after the conclusion of its consideration on report. At this stage the Sovereign's assent is signified to Bills affecting the Crown's interest or prerogative if it has not already been given. The third reading is similar in its conception to the second reading, providing an opportunity for the approval or rejection of the final version of the Bill. In addition, amendments of a purely verbal nature not affecting its substance may be made. In theory, however, proceedings are more narrowly confined to matters contained in the Bill; and in 1967 the Select Committee on Procedure recommended that the third reading should normally be taken without debate. Now a third reading debate will only take place if it is requested by six or more Members.[54] The third reading of Consolidated Fund and Appropriation Bills is voted upon without amendment or debate.[55] Where a Bill is controversial a division may take place on a blocking or reasoned amendment. In July 1977 the motion for the third reading of the Local Authority Works (Scotland) Bill was defeated by 105 to 99 votes, but as with defeats on second reading this is an exceptional occurrence. If the motion is carried, the Bill has completed its Commons' stages and it is forwarded to the House of Lords with a message requesting their concurrence.

## *THE LORDS' STAGES*

Despite its subordinate political status the House of Lords constitutes an integral part of the legislature. Within the limits indicated

[52] Griffith, *Parliamentary Scrutiny of Government Bills*, *op.cit.*, p. 252. See also Wheare, *op.cit.*, pp. 158–159; Crick, *The Reform of Parliament* (2nd ed., 1968), pp. 166–167.

[53] Third Report from the Select Committee on Procedure (1975; H.C. 491); First Report from the Select Committee on Procedure (1978; H.C. 588), paras. 2.23–2.24.

[54] In 1971 the Select Committee on Procedure recommended the abolition of the third reading debate but his recommendation has not been acted upon; *The Process of Legislation*, *op.cit.*, para. 37.

[55] S.O. No. 93.

above it provides governments with an alternative forum for the introduction of Bills, and an additional opportunity for their revision and amendment. However, the necessity for securing the approval of the upper House raises the possibility that a government's immediate legislative intentions will be frustrated. In practice this possibility arises only in respect of governments not supported by the Conservative Party, which possesses an inbuilt majority in the House of Lords. Although such defeats have been rare they invariably occasion considerable political tension and call into question the future legislative role of the upper House.

Bills which have completed their passage through the House of Commons, or which are introduced in the House of Lords, go through the same stages as in the House of Commons. Proceedings in the House of Lords are more informal than in the House of Commons and seldom occasion the scenes of party controversy which sometimes mark proceedings in the lower House. In relation to legislative procedure, the main differences between the two Houses are that in the House of Lords there are no standing committees, although exceptionally a Bill may be committed to a public bill committee consisting of 12 or 14 Members,[56] nor is there provision for the curtailment of debate through the selection of amendments or the use of allocation of time orders. In contrast to procedure in the House of Commons substantive amendments may also be made to Bills at their third reading stage.

As in the House of Commons the majority of amendments made are moved by Ministers. Once again these amendments may be made as part of the continuing process of revision within the responsible department; in response to representations made by outside groups; or consequent upon amendments previously made or undertakings given, whether in the House of Commons or Lords, to reconsider issues or questions raised. Less frequently amendments may be carried against the government.

Whatever their origins, amendments made by one House to a Bill introduced in the other House must be reconsidered by the original House. The majority in the original House, that is the government in the case of the House of Commons or the Conservative majority in the case of the House of Lords, may either accept the amendments made as did the Conservative Government in response to amendments made by the House of Lords to the Education (No. 2) Bill 1980 in respect of transport charges,[57] or insist upon the original or a

[56] Griffith, *Parliamentary Scrutiny of Government Bills*, *op. cit.*, pp. 226–228. The Committee stage may be dispensed with for Finance, Consolidated Fund and Appropriation Bills.

[57] H.L. Deb., Vol. 406, ser. 5, col. 1272 (March 13, 1980).

further revised form of the Bill. Where the original House disagrees with or amends the amendments made, they, together with a message indicating the reasons why they are unacceptable, are returned to the other House for reconsideration. This process may be repeated several times until agreement is reached. If agreement cannot be reached the Bill is lost for the session. Thereafter it may be dropped or the provisions of the Parliament Acts 1911 and 1949 may be invoked.

Under the provisions of the Parliament Acts 1911 and 1949 the necessity of securing the approval of the House of Lords may be dispensed with in certain defined circumstances. Two types of Bill are distinguished by the Parliament Act 1911: money Bills and other Bills. In the case of money Bills the Act consolidated the House of Commons' exclusive privilege in relation to proposals for taxation and expenditure by abrogating the right previously claimed by the House of Lords to reject financial legislation. In relation to other Bills the Act replaced the power of the House of Lords to veto legislation by a power to delay the passage of such legislation for a period of two years, subsequently reduced to one year by the Parliament Act 1949.

A money Bill is a public Bill certified by the Speaker of the House of Commons as containing *only* provisions dealing with:

> "the imposition, repeal, remission, alteration or regulation of taxation; the imposition for the payment of debt or other financial provisions of charges on the Consolidated Fund or the National Loans Fund, or on money provided by Parliament or the variation or repeal of any such charges; supply; the appropriation, receipt, custody, issue or audit of account of public money; the raising or guarantee of any loan or the repayment thereof; or subordinate matters incidental to those subjects or any of them."[58]

In the case of such Bills section 1(1) provides that if the House of Lords fails within one month to pass a Bill previously passed by the House of Commons and sent to the Lords at least one month before the end of the Session, the Bill may be presented for the Royal Assent without the consent of the House of Lords havin been secured unless the House ofCommons direct otherwise. The House did so direct in the case of the Land Settlement (Scotland) Bill 1934.[59]

In the case of other Bills section 2 of the Act as amended provides that a Bill may similarly be presented for the Royal Assent if it has

[58] s.1(1) as amended by the National Loans Act 1968, s.1.
[59] Jennings, *op. cit.*, p. 415 n.

been passed in two successive sessions by the House of Commons, and rejected by the House of Lords in each of those sessions, providing that one year has elapsed between the date of its second reading in the House of Commons in the first of these sessions and the date upon which it completed its Commons' stages in the second. A Bill is regarded as having been rejected by the House of Lords if it is not passed without amendment or with such amendments only as may be agreed to by both Houses. The provisions of section 2 cannot be invoked in the case of Bills containing any provisions to extend the maximum duration of Parliament beyond five years, private Bills, Bills for confirming provisional orders or subordinate legisation.

Three Acts have been passed under this provision: the Welsh Church Act 1914, the Government of Ireland Act 1914 and the Parliament Act 1949 itself.[60] In addition its provisions have been invoked, or recourse to them threatened, in respect of the Temperance (Scotland) Bill in 1912 and 1913, the Plural Voting Bill in 1913 and 1914 and, more recently, the Trade Union and Labour Relations (Amendment) Bill in 1975 and 1976 and the Aircraft and Shipbuilding Industries Bill in 1976 and 1977. Further progress on the Plural Voting Bill was prevented by the outbreak of war. In the case of the other Bills a compromise was reached.

The Parliament Act 1911 was a response to the immediate problems posed by the House of Lords' rejection of the Liberal Finance Bill 1909. The Parliament Act 1949 on the other hand was a response to the anticipated rejection by the House of Lords of the Bill for the nationalisation of the iron and steel industry. Both Acts left unresolved the question, among others, of the part, if any, to be played by the House of Lords in the legislative process. Although the preamble to the Parliament Act 1911 asserted that: " . . . it is intended to substitute for the House of Lords as it at present exists a Second Chamber constituted on a popular instead of hereditary basis," disagreements over its powers and composition have meant that this substitution has never been effected.[61] Discussions on the role of the Second Chamber rapidly tend to become polarised between those who regard a reformed upper House as an essential safeguard against a fallible and unchecked Commons, and

[60] In the case of the first two it was not in fact clear that they had been "rejected" by the House of Lords, a motion for the adjournment of their second reading having been carried against the Government; Jennings, *op.cit.*, p. 427.

[61] With what appears in retrospect more than a touch of irony the preamble continued: "Such substitution cannot immediately be brought into operation." The most recent proposals for reform were contained in the Parliament (No. 2) Bill 1969 which was dropped in the face of all party backbench opposition.

those who see it as a threat to the primacy of the House of Commons as the elected chamber and who thus favour its abolition. The all-party conference on the reform of the Second Chamber appointed in 1917 under the chairmanship of Lord Bryce attributed three legislative functions to a reformed upper House:

"1. The examination and revision of Bills brought from the House of Commons, a function which has become more needed since, on many occasions, during the last thirty years, the House of Commons has been obliged to act under special rules limiting debate.
2. The initiation of Bills dealing with subjects of a practically non-controversial character which may have an easier passage through the House of Commons if they have been fully discussed and put into a well-considered shape before being submitted to it.
3. The interposition of so much delay (and no more) in the passing of a Bill into law as may be needed to enable the opinion of the nation to be adequately expressed upon it. This would be specially needed as regards Bills which affect the fundamentals of the Constitution or introduced new principles of legislation; or which raise issues whereon the opinion of the country may appear to be almost equally divided."[62]

The first two of these functions are complementary to the role of the House of Commons in relation to legislation. As regards the first, the pressures imposed by the parliamentary timetable have increased greatly and there is widespread acceptance of the importance of the Lords' stages as providing an opportunity for the tidying up of inadequately scrutinised legislation.[63] As regards the second function, we have already noted the practical advantages which the existence of the House of Lords as an alternative forum for the introduction of Bills affords the government in the timetabling of its legislative programme and the enactment of uncontroversial legislation.[64] By themselves neither of these functions makes the case for a Second Chamber. The House of Lords' revising function only indicates the need for some machinery for the revision and tidying

[62] Cd. 9038 (1918), p. 4.
[63] See *e.g.* Jennings, *op. cit.*, p. 430 and pp. 446–448; Morrison, *op. cit.*, pp. 206–208; Chorley, "The House of Lords Controversy" [1958] P.L. 216 and "Bringing the Legislative Process into Contempt" [1968] P.L. 52.
[64] Maintaining the House of Lords' role in this respect was an important element in the scheme of reform contained in the Parliament Bill 1969 see Crossman, *op. cit.*, Vol. 2, pp. 94, 328.

up of Bills once they have completed their Commons' stages.[65] Its contemporary importance as a forum for the initation of legislation only indicates the need for alternative procedures for the enactment of uncontroversial legislation, provisional order confirmation Bills and private Bills. The third function ascribed to the House of Lords raises the question of what powers, if any, it should have to alter or delay legislation initiated by the government in the House of Commons. This issue lies at the heart of recent controversy about the future of the Second Chamber. Faced with a minority Labour Government during the late 1970s the House of Lords displayed greater confidence about exercising its powers to delay legislation, or using the threat of their exercise to compel the Government to compromise in order to secure the immediate enactment of its proposals. This by itself should be sufficient to ensure that this question does not leave the political stage.

## *THE ROYAL ASSENT*

As we have seen the three-fold assent of the Sovereign, Lords and Commons must be secured before legislative proposals acquire the force of law. Once the text of the Bill has been agreed by both Houses or the provisions of the Parliament Acts have been complied with, the Bill is submitted for the Royal Assent. Although the refusal of the Royal Assent was canvassed between 1912 and 1914 over the Home Rule Bill for Ireland, in practice it has not been withheld since 1707 and its granting is now a matter of form.[66] The Royal Assent may be given by the Sovereign in person but this procedure is now virtually obsolete, not having been used since 1854. Alternatively it may be signified on the Sovereign's behalf by Commissioners appointed for this purpose or, as is now normally the case under the Royal Assent Act 1967, by notification to each House by the Speaker and the Lord Chancellor respectively. The Bill becomes law once the second House has been notified. Different formulae are used for different classes of Bills. Public Bills, which include private Bills other than personal Bills, are assented to with the words "*la reyne le veult*;" financial Bills with the words "*la reyne remercie ses bons sujets, accepte leur benevolence et ainsi le veult.*" Once the Royal Assent has been signified the Bill becomes an Act and is printed individually and in the annual series of *Public General Acts*.

[65] See above, pp. 105–106 and 129.
[66] See especially the discussion in Redlich, *op. cit.*, Vol. 3, pp. 107.

## *PRIVATE MEMBERS' BILLS*

Bills introduced by backbench Members of the House of Commons or of the House of Lords are always public Bills and go through the same parliamentary stages as public Bills introduced by the government. However, the government's control of the parliamentary timetable and its exclusive initiative in relation to finance severely restrict the opportunities for private Members to legislate. While not quantitatively significant, legislation sponsored by private Members nevertheless represents an important substantive contribution to the annual legislative output. The following discussion is principally concerned with private Members' Bills in the House of Commons.

Three broad classes of private Members' Bills may be distinguished.[67] The first class covers minor measures of social regulation, which frequently originate within government departments. The second covers those measures which are designed to amend the existing law where its operation has been unexpected or inconvenient. Again these may originate within a department; but some are based upon recommendations or draft Bills prepared by the Law Commissions or similar bodies. In so far as these two classes of Bills represent departmental policy, they could be introduced by the government, but they are usually not sufficiently important to gain a place on the legislative programme. It is thus not uncommon for such Bills to be introduced as a result of approaches made by Ministers to backbenchers or vice versa.[68] Similarly, the Law Commissions have become increasingly dependent upon private Members to sponsor their Bills. The third class usually attracts most public interest. It covers those controversial measures, usually of a social or moral nature, on which the government prefers not to express a view openly. During the 1966–70 Labour Government a number of such measures were enacted,[69] but both their significance and their success in that Parliament were exceptional.[70] In the 1979–80 and 1980–81 Sessions few such Bills

[67] This classification is based on Richards, "Private Members' Legislation" in *The Commons Today, op.cit.*, p. 137. See also his essay in *The House of Commons in the Twentieth Century, op cit.*, p. 292; and more generally, Bromhead, *Private Members' Bills in the British Parliament* (1956); Herbert, *The Ayes Have It* (1937) and Richards, *Parliament and Conscience* (1970).

[68] See *e.g.* Crossman, *op. cit.*, Vol. 1, pp. 372, 520–521.

[69] The Abortion Act 1967, the Sexual Offences Act 1967, the Theatres Act 1968 and the Divorce Reform Act 1969.

[70] Principally because they received strong covert support from the Government, despite internal disagreement; see Crossman, *op.cit.*, Vol. 1, pp. 561; Vol. 2, pp. 359, 366, 310, 663 and Vol. 3, p. 806.

were introduced; the Abortion (Amendment) Bill 1979 and the Road Traffic (Seat Belts) Bill 1979 attracted a great deal of attention but were unsuccessful. The only "conscience measure" enacted in either session was the Indecent Displays (Control) Act 1981. Most of the successful private Members' Bills—nine in 1979–80 and 15 in 1980–81—fell into the first class, with a few enacting amendments to the existing law.[71]

The government's monopoly of the parliamentary timetable means that a limited amount of time is available for the consideration of private Members' Bills. There have been sessions in which no time has been allowed for them, but at present 10 Fridays, from 9.30 a.m. until 2.30 p.m. are available. Priority in the use of this time is established by a ballot held near the beginning of each session. Twenty private Members' Bills are drawn from the ballot which then have precedence in second reading debates on the first six of these 10 Fridays. On the last four Fridays, precedence is given to the later stages of Bills.

Apart from the ballot, there are two other methods by which a private Member can introduce a Bill in the Commons. The first is under Standing Order 13, commonly known as the "Ten Minute Rule." Under this procedure a Member may introduce and speak to a Bill for 10 minutes after Question Time on Tuesdays and Wednesdays, provided he has been given prior leave. As a large audience, both of Members and of the Press, is guaranteed, such Bills tend to be introduced to make a political point. Almost invariably they do not represent serious efforts to enact legislation, although there are some exceptions.[72] The Transport Act 1962 (Amendment) Act 1981 was introduced under this procedure, but only two of the other 96 Standing Order 13 Bills introduced in the 1979–80 and 1980–81 sessions progressed beyond a first reading.

The second method is that they may be presented in the same way as the majority of government Bills under the provisions of Standing Order 37. It is difficult to generalise about Bills introduced under this procedure. Some represent serious efforts to enact legislation, but they are unlikely to make much progress unless they receive an unopposed second reading, the government provides time for debate, or all the balloted Bills allocated for a particular Friday are

[71] The Deer Act 1980, the Zoo Licensing Act 1981, the Disabled Persons Act 1981 are examples of the first class; the Licensing (Amendment) Act 1980, the Forgery and Counterfeiting Act 1981 and the Matrimonial Homes and Property Act 1981 (these last two were based on Law Commission proposals) are examples of the second. examples of the second.

[72] The Murder (Abolition of the Death Penalty) Act 1965 is a notable example of a successful S.O. 13 Bill.

disposed of before 2.30 p.m. The second and third possibilities are remote. So far as the first possibility is concerned, the sponsoring Member may hope that the Bill will receive an unopposed second reading by putting the question at the close of the main debate, but if any one Member objects, it will be lost.

Securing a place on the ballot by no means guarantees that a Bill will be enacted.[73] The Members who occupy the first six places on the ballot are at least guaranteed that their Bills will be discussed at second reading, for they can each nominate a Friday on which their Bill will take priority. However, although it is usual for three or four Bills to be set down for debate, it is not uncommon for the whole of the sitting to be taken up with the second reading of the first one or two Bills, in which case the Member sponsoring the third or fourth must, as with Standing Order 37 Bills, hope for an unopposed second reading. Under a new procedure introduced in 1979, it is possible, after the sixth Friday, for a sponsoring Member (whether of a balloted Bill, or one introduced under Standing Order 13 or Standing Order 37) to move that his Bill be referred to a second reading committee, but this too can be defeated by the objection of a single Member.[74] It is therefore a matter of some judgment for a Member occupying a lower place in the ballot to determine which Friday to nominate for his Bill's second reading. Moreover, if a Bill is opposed, it is likely that its opponents will endeavour to prolong the debate on a preceding Bill, although it may of itself be quite innocuous, so as to prevent consideration of the contentious Bill. Even where his Bill is debated, the Member faces further obstacles; for example he must ensure that there are enough Members present to secure a vote on the closure. If the Bill's opponents are still speaking just before 2.30 p.m., he must move "that the Question be now put," but, assuming that the Speaker decides that its substance has been adequately discussed, the Bill will be "talked out" unless one hundred Members are present to vote in favour of the motion. Sponsoring a private Member's Bill thus requires a considerable degree of organisation and management if it is not to fail at one of the procedural hurdles.

Although the procedural rules concerning the introduction and consideration of private Members' Bills present considerable obstacles, undoubtedly the single most important factor is the

[73] In the 1979–80 session, six of the successful private Members' Bills had been balloted and the other three were introduced under S.O. 37. In 1980–81 there were seven successful Bills under each procedure, plus one introduced under S.O. 13.

[74] See above, p. 116; but note that where a Minister moves referral to a second reading committee, 20 Members must object for the motion to fail.

attitude of the government. This may be unfavourable, favourable or neutral. The government's attitude is generally communicated to the sponsoring MP by the Chief Whip or the Minister of State in the department most affected by the Bill. A private Member's Bill will be opposed by the government if it conflicts with its policy or if it involves the imposition of substantial administrative burdens on departments.[75] If the government is opposed to a private Members' Bill, its failure is virtually guaranteed. Although it is a tradition of private Members' time that there is no party constraint on attendance or voting, it will frequently be a government Whip who objects to a Bill being given a second reading without debate, or less usually, a Minister may speak against the Bill in debate.[76]

Conversely, government support will generally ensure the Bill's success; a "nod is as good as a whip."[77] The drafting of the Bill will almost always be reviewed by Parliamentary Counsel, government time may be provided, if the programme allows, for the remainder of its stages, and Ministers may speak in favour of it. Where the Bill has financial implications the government may pass the necessary financial resolution for it to be considered in committee. Alternatively, the government may be neutral towards the Bill. In this case it will be reviewed by Parliamentary Counsel only if the Chief Whip takes the view that it is likely to become law; otherwise it is for its sponsor to make such drafting arrangements as he can.[78] Without active government support, its chances of success are slim.

The number of private Members' Bills which are successful each session has remained strikingly constant—around 12 a year—for

[75] As was, *e.g.* the case with the unsuccessful Youth and Community Bill 1980 and the first Disabled Persons Bill 1981. The latter was successful when it was reintroduced with most of the original obligations it imposed on local authorities removed; above, n. 71.

[76] Another common delaying tactic is to table a large number of amendments. Each has to be put as no guillotine or timetable motions are available for private Members' Bills. When opposing the Youth and Community Bill 1980 the Government first sought to amend it in committee by removing all but one of its 14 clauses, and when that failed, tabled 77 amendments at its report stage. Crossman notes how he came under some criticism from other Ministers who objected to his wanting to use private Members' Bills to enact "conscience measures" and supporting them from the Front Bench but at the same time trying to persuade those Ministers who opposed such measures from speaking against them; *op.cit.*, Vol. 2, p. 701; Vol. 3, pp. 306–307.

[77] Jennings, *op. cit.*, p. 198.

[78] The 10 Members who are placed highest in the ballot may claim up to £200 expenses in drafting their Bills. Where they are not redrafted by Parliamentary Counsel, the MP must rely on others such as Parliamentary Agents, Clerks in the Public Bill Office; departmental lawyers or lawyers employed privately by himself or a pressure group on whose behalf he is sponsoring the Bill.

the past 30 years.[79] Although there have been some variations, this number represents what can normally be achieved within the time available. However, the significance of balloted and many Standing Order 37 Bills cannot be measured only in terms of the number which are enacted. Unsuccessful Bills can also be of value. For example, "they may push Ministers into taking more positive action than would otherwise have been forthcoming. These considerations apply especially where protracted negotiations have taken place between pressure groups and government departments."[80] A Bill may thus be withdrawn or allowed to lapse where a Minister gives an assurance that he will initiate an enquiry into the matter, or introduce legislation in a subsequent session. In other cases the sponsor may feel quite satisfied to have attracted publicity to a particular cause. In addition, some private Members' Bills provide an opportunity to debate moral issues which by reason of the government's reticence, would otherwise be unavailable.[81]

So far as successful Bills are concerned, "every Session sees a number of minor but useful Acts passed through private Members' procedure which could not find a place in the Government programme. Apart from the question of the content and influence of private Members' Bills, they also have an effect on the morale and image of Parliament."[82] The opportunities for private Members' legislation allows MPs to participate in the consideration of legislation in a manner quite uncharacteristic of that associated with government Bills. Although the government's attitude can make or break a private Members' Bill, its preparation, the organisation and management of sufficient supporters, the conciliation of opponents and negotiation of the procedural rules are matters which lie almost wholly in the hands of the Bill's sponsors. It is these characteristics which prompt the view that private Members' legislation is "an expression of the pure function of a 'legislature.' "[83]

[79] See H.L. Deb. Vol. 418, ser. 5, col. 509–510 (March 12, 1981).

[80] Richards, "Private Members' Legislation" *op. cit.*, p. 151.

[81] Following the success of "conscience" Bills in 1966–70, the Conservative Party was critical of a system which allowed legislation to be enacted on matters which had not been canvassed at the preceding General Election; but as Richards notes, this objection is essentially anti-parliamentary, and the criticisms, which were limited and tactical, died away shortly thereafter; *ibid.* pp. 149–150.

[82] *Ibid.*, p. 151.

[83] Bromhead, *Britain's Developing Constitution* (1974), p. 137.

## CONCLUSION

Any assessment of the parliamentary stages of the legislative process must start from the twin recognitions that first, Parliament is not an independent decision-making body and that, secondly, what is presented to Parliament in the form of a Bill is in substantial measure a finished product to which the government is committed. Both of these factors restrict opponents' capacity to secure the rejection of proposals or their substantive amendment. The government's possession of a majority, in particular, means that it is seldom compelled to withdraw or to substantially modify measures, and that it is even less frequently defeated.[84]

In terms of their primary purpose, the reforms effected in parliamentary procedure during the course of the last century have been successful in enabling governments to implement their increasing legislative commitments. Whilst the proportion of parliamentary time spent on legislation has remained constant at approximately 50 per cent., the volume of legislation has increased from approximately 200 pages a year at the beginning of the century to over 2,000 pages a year.[85]

What, however, of the conflicting need "to secure full discussion and ventilation of all matters, legislative or administrative, as the condition of giving its assent to Bills . . . "?[86] Although the formal stages of the legislative process have remained substantially unaltered since the last century, the sheer increase in the volume of legislation has undoubtedly meant that the consideration devoted to individual Bills has decreased, despite the concomitant increase in the time spent in standing committee. To a certain extent parliamentary consideration has been replaced by alternative modes of consideration. As we have seen, despite the criticisms made of the drafting of legislation, elaborate arrangements exist within government for the scrutiny of the drafting of legislative proposals to ensure that their intention is expressed as accurately as possible. Equally, consideration of the merits of legislation by Parliament is sup-

[84] The Parliament (No. 2) Bill 1969 remains the outstanding example of a Bill withdrawn in the face of opposition. More recent examples include the Official Information Bill 1980 and the Local Government Finance Bill 1981, which were dropped in anticipation of opposition. Difficulties with the legislative timetable are a more common cause of the failure of legislation, *e.g.* the Petroleum and Continental Shelf Bill 1981.

[85] First Report from the Select Committee on Procedure (1978; H.C. 588), para. 2.31. These figures take no account of the increase in the time spent on legislation off the floor of the House in standing committees, or of the increase in delegated legislation.

[86] Amery, *Thoughts on the Constitution* (2nd ed., 1954), p. 12.

plemented massively by consultation and negotiation with outside groups both before and during the parliamentary stages of the legislative process either with or without the assistance of MPs as intermediaries.

This latter development is one of the most important contributory factors to the contemporary sense of a decline in the importance of Parliament in the legislative process. While the historical accuracy of the view that during the nineteenth century MPs did participate effectively in the legislative process has been questioned on the grounds that the government's domination of the process was as great then as it is now,[87] there is no doubt as to the prevalence of this sense of decline at a time when the legislative process itself and its product have been the subject of increasingly widespread criticism.

Some of these criticisms, such as those of the volume of legislation enacted, are perennial[88]; others cannot be separated from the political content of individual proposals or are an inevitable consequence of the political context within which their consideration takes place. While some MPs may want to play a greater part in the moulding of legislative proposals, others, it must be recognised, may treat their task as being no more than to support their own leadership when in office and to attack the other side when in opposition. Despite the criticisms that are made of the legislative process there is little sign of any significant break in the pattern of reform identified at the beginning of this chapter. The reforms in legislative procedure instituted by Richard Crossman as Leader of the House of Commons during the late 1960s were expressly designed to enable the government to secure the enactment of its legislative programme more quickly. As Crossman asked rhetorically: " . . . is the legislative process designed to enable policies to be translated into law at the speed required by the tempo of modern industrial change?"[89]

For the future, it is difficult to equate these more radical alternatives to the existing system which have been canvassed, such as framework of Bills or compulsory timetabling, with the subjection of government to any greater restraints. Rather their introduction would tend to increase the government's autonomy and the predictability of the legislative process still further. Without any reform in the procedures for considering delegated legislation,[90]

[87] Walkland, "Government Legislation in the House of Commons", *op. cit.*, pp. 249–251.

[88] *Ibid.*, pp. 253–254.

[89] H.C. Deb. Vol. 738, ser. 5, col. 480 (December 14, 1966).

[90] See below, pp. 000–000.

framework Bills would remove a greater proportion of the legislative product from the scrutiny of Parliament. Although compulsory timetabling would deal with one of the more glaring inadequacies of committee proceedings, whereby the initial clauses of Bills are discussed at length and the remaining clauses receive a more perfunctory examination or none at all,[91] it would deprive the Opposition of the power to delay the government's programme. This is the most potent weapon which the Opposition retains as a means of forcing concessions; as Coombes comments:

> "Parliamentary opposition needs effective means of procedural obstruction both as a direct means of influence and as an ultimate sanction. Efficiency is after all relative to the political ends parliament is supposed to articulate. 'Rationalisation' can too often mean simply removing parliament's role as a source of opposition."[92]

Admittedly it can be argued that the over-identification of Parliament with the power of law-making detracts from its function of scrutinising government action generally, and that the time currently devoted to legislation could be spent more effectively in other ways.

> "However much the House improves its procedures for dealing with Public Bills, it must at some stage ask the question whether it is realistic to spend so much of its time on matters that are going to pass anyway—by virtue of the whole party-electoral system of modern British politics—and on matters which represent the last and most unmalleable form of long processes of inquiry, opinion formation and decision-making."[93]

The fate of the system of specialist select committees set up by Crossman as compensation for the reduction in the time spent on legislation suggests, however, that such a reduction need not lead to a concomitant increase in the scrutiny to which government is subject. Consequently it may be that such proposals over-emphasise

[91] *e.g.* the Industrial Relations Bill 1971 completed its Commons' stages with only 39 of approximately 160 clauses and none of its schedules considered; and see the Scotland and Wales Acts, above, p. 119.

[92] Coombes, *The Future of the European Parliament* (1979), p. 79.

[93] Crick, *op. cit.*, p. 227.

the purely enabling as opposed to the restrictive aspects of the legislative process.

> "... [w]e must ask whether the idea of parliamentary democracy is compatible with any system of government other than that in which the actions of public authorities are contained both formally and materially within the rules upheld by elected representatives of the people. The power to review, alter and reject proposed laws, therefore, and even to initiate them, is neither superfluous nor impractical, though it cannot be relied on as the exclusive, or in all circumstances the most effective, method of keeping government under parliamentary control."[94]

[94] Coombes, *op. cit.*, p. 84.

Chapter Six

# LEGISLATION WITHOUT LEGISLATURES[1]

The full implications of the doctrine of legislative supremacy of Parliament only became apparent during the nineteenth century when numerous and far-reaching changes in the law were introduced in the form of public general Acts. The emphasis placed on parliamentary sovereignty and on specifically parliamentary methods of legislation obscured for many the extent to which legislative methods generally were still developing. The result was that the importance of subordinate or delegated legislation was recognised only belatedly. Even then its legitimacy was accepted in some cases with considerable reluctance. Elements of that reluctance linger, and today there is a similar danger of a failure to assimilate Community legislation, not necessarily because its importance is not recognised, but because it is regarded as too specialised to merit general treatment. Nevertheless it constitutes an important element in the further development of legislative methods and there can be no justification for the failure to recognise the importance of both forms of legislation as sources of law. Within their respective limits they may be as important sources of rights, duties and powers as public general Acts.

There are significant differences in their respective origins. Subordinate legislation is the result of the exercise of law-making powers conferred under Acts of Parliament. It can be thus easily reconciled with the doctrine of the sovereignty of Parliament as law-making carried on with Parliament's express sanction. It is more difficult to accommodate Community legislation within the same framework. It stems from the exercise by the Community institutions of their own law-making powers transferred to them by the Member States (in theory irrevocably) under the Treaties. When made, Community legislation forms part of a separate corpus of law, the "new legal order." As such its validity can only be assessed by the European Court and its content cannot be varied by national legislation.

In both cases, however, the practical results are the same. Both forms of legislation involve the exercise of law-making powers by bodies other than Parliament; in the case of subordinate legislation

[1] The term is taken from Young, "Future of Parliamentary Government" in Campion, *Parliament: A Survey* (1952), p. 285.

by government, and in the case of Community legislation by the Community institutions. When exercising these powers these other bodies are acting every bit as much as legislatures as Parliament. Accordingly their powers represent significant derogations from Parliament's own law-making powers and a diminution in its role in the legislative process overall. Whereas public Bills are considered and approved by Parliament before they become law, Parliament plays no formal part in the Community legislative process and its role in subordinate legislation is severely restricted.

## SUBORDINATE OR DELEGATED LEGISLATION

### *DEFINITION AND FORMS*

The expression subordinate or delegated legislation covers "every exercise of a power to legislate conferred by or under an Act of Parliament."[2] Law-making powers may be conferred on a wide variety of bodes ranging from government departments through local authorities and public corporations to private associations. In this chapter we shall only be concerned with the exercise of law-making powers by government departments.

Law-making powers conferred on government may be expressed to be exercisable in a variety of forms. Orders in Council, statutory instruments, regulations, rules, orders, schemes, warrants and directions are all terms which have been used to describe subordinate legislation. This range of terminology has been criticised as giving rise to unnecessary confusion.[3] Although the terms "regulation" and "rule" tend to be reserved to matters of wide general importance and matters of procedure respectively, little is to be gained from attempts to draw conclusions from the use of one term rather than another. Particular care, however, must be taken with the terms "Order in Council" and "statutory instrument." Orders in Council made under delegated law-making powers must be distinguished from Orders in Council made under the Prerogative.[4] Whereas the latter are a species of primary legislation, the legal

[2] Report from the Joint Committee on Delegated Legislation (1972; H.L. 184; H.C. 475), para. 6.

[3] See *e.g.* Report of the Committee on Minister' Powers, Cmd. 4060 (1932), pp. 16–20; Report from the Select Committee on Delegated Legislation (1953; H.C. 310), vii.

[4] See above, pp. 4–5.

effect of the former is no different from that of any other form of delegated legislation, although they are usually regarded as its most solemn and dignified form.

The expression statutory instrument is a generic term introduced by the Statutory Instruments Act 1946 to describe those forms of subordinate legislation subject to its provisions. In respect of this new class of subordinate legislation the Act introduced a greater degree of uniformity in the procedure for laying them before Parliament and specified rules for their publication.[5] It is important to recognise that the Act does not cover all forms of subordinate legislation.[6] The Act applies to instruments made after January 1, 1948, the date on which it came into force. In respect of those instruments, section 1 of the Act draws a distinction between those made under Acts passed *after* and *before* that date. As regards the former more numerous class of instruments made under Acts passed *after* January 1, 1948, section 1(1) provides that an instrument is a statutory instrument if the parent Act expressly provides that it is to be made by the Queen in Council by way of Order in Council or by a Minister of the Crown by way of statutory instrument. In the absence of such express provision the instrument is not a statutory instrument and the operative provisions of the Statutory Instruments Act do not apply.[7]

The position in relation to subordinate legislation made under Acts passed *before* January 1, 1948, is more complicated. Broadly speaking, every instrument made under an Act of Parliament by the Queen in Council, by a Minister of the Crown, or which relates to any court in the United Kingdom is a statutory instrument, providing it is of a legislative and not an executive character.[8]

In the remainder of this chapter we shall be concerned mainly with those forms of delegated legislation which are equivalent in scope to public general Acts. Where made in the form of statutory instruments they are described as "general" instruments. We shall not be concerned with the various alternatives to private Bill

[5] See below, pp. 154–155.

[6] For criticism of the tendency to depict the Act as being comprehensive in its scope, see Craig, "The Reluctant Executive" [1961] P.L. 45, 52.

[7] Notable examples include the Immigration Rules made under the Immigration Act 1971 and the Highway Code made under the Road Traffic Act 1972.

[8] Statutory Instruments Act 1946, s. 1(2); Statutory Instruments Regulations 1947 (S.I. 1948, No. 1), Reg. 2(1)(*a*). The distinction between legislative and executive instruments is only of significance in relation to the publication of instruments. The distinction is drawn on the basis of expediency: those instruments which it is thought ought to be published are treated as being legislative and so are published. Griffith and Street, *Principles of Administrative Law* (5th ed., 1973), pp. 48–49; Allen, *Law and Order* (3rd ed., 1965), pp. 100–102; and see below, pp. 154–155.

procedure examined in Chapter 1,[9] or with the various rules made by government which do not owe their existence to statute and which, for example, state how powers will be exercised in a given field.[10]

## *HISTORICAL BACKGROUND*

Subordinate legislation in the sense of legislation made by the government alone is not a new phenomenon. During the sixteenth and seventeenth centuries a considerable part of the business of government was carried on by way of administrative regulations made by the Sovereign in Council. However, the limits to the Sovereign's legislative competence—what could be done by way of Prerogative legislation without the consent of Parliament—were never clearly defined.[11] Consequently it is only after Parliament's successful assertion of a monopoly of law-making power that it becomes possible to talk of subordinate legislation in the sense of the exercise by government of legislative powers *conferred by Parliament.*

In its modern form subordinate legislation came into general use during the first half of the nineteenth century as a result of the increased legislative responsibilities of government and the consequent impossibility of deciding all issues of collective choice in the form of primary legislation. Thus the preamble to an Act enacted in 1832 to prevent the spread of cholera stated that:

> "Whereas it has pleased Almighty God to visit the United Kingdom with the disease called the cholera . . . and whereas with a view to prevent as far as may be possible by the Divine Blessing the spreading of the said disease, it may be necessary that rules and regulations may from time to time be established within cities, towns or districts affected with or which may be threatened by the said disease, but it may be impossible to establish such rules and regulations by the authority of Parliament with sufficient promptitude to meet the exigency of any such case as may occur"

—therefore it was enacted that the Privy Council could make such rules and regulations for preventing the spread of the disease, relieving the sufferers and burying the dead.[12] From

[9] See above, pp. 10–11.

[10] For the historical origins of these extra-statutory rules see Parris, *Constitutional Bureaucracy* (1969), pp. 193–196; see further Allen, *op. cit.*, pp. 192–193 and references cited therein.

[11] See especially Carr's discussion of the Statute of Proclamations 1539 (31 Hen. 8, c. 26) in *Delegated Legislation* (1921), pp. 51-53. On the early history of delegation, see Allen, *op.cit.*, pp. 24–29; Seighart, *Government by Decree* (1950), pp. 9–46.

[12] 2 & 3 Wm. 4, c. 10.

these modest beginnings the practice of delegating legislative powers to the Privy Council and to government departments rapidly became widespread in relation to nearly all fields of government activity.

Nineteenth century reaction to the practice was favourable. First, and most obviously, it was seen as a means of easing the growing pressure on the parliamentary timetable. This implicit recognition of the impossibility of deciding all issues of collective choice in the form of primary legislation raised the immediate, but still basic, question of the proper division of law-making responsibilities between Parliament and government. It was in response to this question that the principle was first formulated that Parliament's responsibility was to decide matters of principle, while matters of detail could be left to government. In 1877 Lord Thring wrote:

> "The adoption of the system of confining the attention of Parliament to material provisions only and leaving details to be settled departmentally is probably the only mode in which parliamentary government can as respects its legislative functions, be carried on. The province of Parliament is to decide material questions affecting the public interest; and the more procedure and subordinate matters can be withdrawn from their cognisance, the greater will be the time afforded for the consideration of the more serious questions involved in legislation."[13]

Apart from leaving Parliament free to concentrate on matters of principle by relieving it of the burden of detail, subordinate legislation was seen as having other advantages. The most important of these related to the drafting of Acts of Parliament. Rationalising their content through the exclusion of matters of detail, it was suggested, would lead to an improvement in their drafting. Dicey, for example, considered that: "The cumbersomeness and prolixity of English statute law is due in no small measure to futile endeavours of Parliament to work out the details of large legislative changes." The substance and form of the law, he concluded, "would probably be a good deal improved if the executive could work out the detailed application of general principles embodied in Acts of Parliament."[14] In these terms delegation was consciously and actively pursued by Lord Thring and his successors as First Parliamentary Counsel.[15]

[13] *Practical Legislation* (1877), p. 13.
[14] *An Introduction to the Study of the Law of the Constitution* (10th ed., 1959), pp. 52–53.
[15] Report of the Committee on Ministers' Powers, *op. cit.*, p. 24. The passage quoted from Thring was first drawn up as part of an instruction to draftsmen in the Office, Ilbert, *Legislative Methods and Forms* (1901), p. 99. That neither of the beneficial consequences identified by proponents of the practice has been fully realised is

The outbreak of the First World War saw a massive transfer of law-making powers to the government. Emergencies had previously been accepted as sufficient grounds for delegation,[16] but the extent of the powers delegated under the Defence of the Realm Acts left little room for doubt as to the significance of the new form of legislation.[17] For reasons which have never been altogether satisfactorily explained, post-war reaction—on the part of elements of the judiciary and the legal profession at least—was considerably more hostile. The less extreme form of the criticism made of the practice was that it gave rise to an excessive concentration of law-making power in the hands of government, with none of the safeguards associated with parliamentary methods of legislation.[18] Against a background of growing criticism and mistrust the Donoughmore-Scott Committee was appointed in 1929 "to consider the powers exercised by . . . Ministers of the Crown by way of . . . delegated legislation . . . and to report what safeguards are desirable or necessary to secure the constitutional principles of the sovereignty of Parliament and the supremacy of the law."

Although the constitutional formalism of its terms of reference were widely criticised, the subsequent Report of the Committee was significant for two main reasons.[19] First, it unhesitatingly and unambiguously affirmed the necessity, legitimacy and constitutional desirability of delegated legislation. By doing so it refuted the more extreme criticisms which had been levelled at the practice by its critics. "The truth is that if Parliament were not willing to delegate law-making power, Parliament would be unable to pass the kind and quantity of legislation which modern public opinion requires."[20] Secondly, it attempted to define with a greater degree of

attributable to the continued increase in the volume of legislation and consequent pressure on time. One can only compare the position as it would have been in the absence of delegation. Nevertheless the assumption that time saved will automatically be available for more "worthwhile" proposals remains one of the recurrent fallacies in the reform of parliamentary procedure; see e.g. below, p. 162.

To the arguments examined here there is frequently added the claim that Parliament is in any event an inappropriate forum for the examination of matters of "technical" detail. This argument should be approached with a greater degree of caution than is normally accorded to it. If doubt be had, see Wallace, Wallace and Webb, *Policy-Making in the European Communities* (1977), p. 11.

[16] Carr, *op. cit.*, pp. 23–24.

[17] After the War powers to deal with emergencies were placed on a permanent basis by the Emergency Powers Act 1920.

[18] For a more extreme view, see Hewart, *The New Despotism* (1929). The best survey of the period is contained in Willis, *Parliamentary Powers of English Government Departments* (1933), pp. 38–46.

[19] For a fuller survey see Willis, *op. cit.*, pp. 174–187.

[20] Report of the Committee on Ministers' Powers, *op. cit.*, p. 23.

precision than had been attempted previously the line between proper and improper delegations of legislative power. Drawing on the earlier distinction between matters of principle and matters of detail it argued that "normal" delegated legislation was made under clearly defined powers and largely confined to matters of detail.[21] "Exceptional" delegated legislation, on the other hand, was made under Acts which either conferred powers to legislate on matters of principle, to impose taxation, or to amend Acts of Parliament; or whose provisions excluded the jurisdiction of the courts, or were so wide "that it is almost impossible to know what limits Parliament did intent to impose."[22]

The Committee was not prepared to accept that recourse to these exceptional forms of delegated legislation might never be justified. But it questioned whether "Parliament itself fully realised how extensive the practice of delegation has become, or the extent to which it has surrendered its own functions in the process, or how easily the practice might be abused."[23] To limit the possibility of abuse it recommended the introduction of a number of minor safeguards. These recommendations were not acted upon until the Second World War, when in the wake of a further transfer of law-making powers to government under the Emergency Powers Defence Acts and sustained backbench pressure, a number of reforms were introduced.[24]

## *FUNCTIONS*

In 1921 Cecil Carr drew attention to the increasing extent to which Acts of Parliament were incomplete statements of the law. "Everywhere in our statute book the same process is visible. The action of our Acts of Parliament grows more and more dependent upon subsidiary legislation."[25] At present more than 2,000 instruments are made annually, of which between 1,100 and 1,300 are general instruments. Although the number of instruments made annually has remained roughly constant since the nineteen-fifties their length on occasion has increased markedly. In 1955 the total length of all published statutory instruments was 3,240 pages; by 1974 it had risen to 8,669 pages.[26] In 1979 it fell back to 4,714 pages.

[21] *Ibid.*, p. 30.
[22] *Ibid.*, pp. 31–41.
[23] *Ibid.*, p. 24.
[24] See below, p. 163.
[25] *Op. cit.*, p. 1.
[26] Source: First Report from the Select Committee on Procedure (1978; H.C. 588), para. 3.7, Table 1.

Broadly speaking delegated legislation is used by government in the same way as public general Acts to give legal effect to its policies. As such it has a number of specific applications. First, it may be used in relation to what Carr described as matters of legislative machinery, that is in relation to the commencement, duration or application of Acts.[27] Of these the most important are commencement provisions which are used to bring Acts into operation on appointed days. Provision is frequently made for bringing different parts of Acts into force on different days.[28] Delegated legislation may be used in the same way to revoke Acts or to extend the scope of their application.

Secondly, delegated legislation may be used to adopt or modify the existing law. Thus a reserve power may be taken to make consequential amendments, the need for which was not anticipated or could not have been foreseen at the time the parent Act was introduced. On occasion power may be taken to modify the parent Act itself. The conferral of such a power in the form of what is commonly described as a "Henry VIII clause" has attracted particular criticism.[29] Currently such provisions are used mainly to confer powers to alter financial limits, to bring lists up to date and to make minor amendments.[30]

The most significant delegation of a power to make consequential changes is contained in the European Communities Act 1972. Section 2(2) of the Act confers a power upon government to legislate by way of statutory instrument for the purposes of implementing any Community obligation of the United Kingdom or enabling any such obligation to be implemented, enabling Community rights to be exercised and for dealing with matters arising out of or relating to any such rights or obligations. Such legislation may include "any such provision (of any such extent) as might be made by Act of Parliament."[31] It may thus be used to amend or repeal existing statutory provisions including those contained in Acts of Parliament, or to introduce completely new provisions. The only limitations on this extensive law-making power are that it must be used for the purposes laid down in section 2(2), and that it may not be used to make provisions (a) imposing or increasing taxation, (b)

[27] *Op. cit.*, p. 10.

[28] For the difficulties to which this may give rise see Report of the Statute Law Society Working Party on Commencement of Acts of Parliament [1980] Stat. L.R. 40.

[29] Report of the Committee on Ministers' Powers, *op.cit.*, pp. 36–37 and Appendix II.

[30] Erskine May, *Parliamentary Practice* (19th ed., 1976), p. 574. See, *e.g.* Town and Country Planning Act 1972, s.287; Companies Act 1967, s. 67; *cf.* Remuneration, Charges and Grants Act 1975, s. 1.

[31] European Communities Act 1972, s. 2(4).

having retrospective effect, (c) sub-delegating the power to legislate, with the exception of the power to make rules of procedure for any court or tribunal, or (d) creating new criminal offences punishable with more than two years' imprisonment or, on summary conviction, with more than three months' imprisonment or a fine of more than £400 or £100 a day.[32]

Finally, as the example of section 2(2) of the European Communities Act 1972 illustrates, delegated legislation may be used to lay down rules in the implementation of policies. The scope of such rules depends on the powers conferred by the parent Act. They may be confined to the elaboration of detail or, as in the case of "skeleton" legislation, they may extend to the determination of matters of principle. As we have seen the criterion formulated during the nineteenth century and subsequently affirmed by the Donoughmore-Scott Committee was that subordinate legislation should be confined to the concrete application of principles embodied in the parent Act and of policies discussed during its parliamentary stages. This distinction may be less than easy to draw in practice.[33] However, the key factor is the attitude of the government. It is the government which decides through its parliamentary majority what the Act should contain, including what law-making powers should be reserved in its own hands.

Subordinate legislation has several advantages for the government. First, without recourse to it the government would be unable to enact its legislative programme.[34] Secondly, it allows time for working out the detail of the implementation of policies and for further consultation with affected interests. As Walkland observes there is

> "often a conflict of pace and timing between the stages of major legislative projects. Political and parliamentary considerations may dictate a timetable for gaining agreement on major principles, but scope must be left for lengthy consultations and negotiations at the level of detailed administration."[35]

Treating the enactment of legislation as separable from its implementation has political as well as administrative advantages. By concentrating its initial efforts on securing the enactment of

[32] *Ibid.*, Sched. 2, para. 1(1).

[33] For an attempt to formulate principles upon which the distinction might be drawn see Griffith, "The Place of Parliament in the Legislative Process" (1951) 14 M.L.R. 279, 425, *et. seq.*

[34] Thus the Industrial Expansion Act 1968 began life as five separate Bills for which time could not be found; Crossman, *The Diaries of a Cabinet Minister* (1976), Vol. 2, pp. 243, 455.

[35] *The Legislative Process in Great Britain* (1969), p. 44.

controversial legislation the government may increase its bargaining strength considerably in discussions over its implementation. Finally, subordinate legislation has advantages of speed and flexibility. Provision may be made for unforeseen contingencies and revisions introduced to take account of experience and changing circumstances without the necessity of going back to Parliament for amending legislation.[36]

The government's conception of what should be dealt with by way of subordinate legislation may, of course, be challenged when the parent Act is before Parliament as a Bill. The knowledge that the law-making powers which it seeks will have to be publicly justified and defended during the parliamentary stages of the Bill's progress constitutes an important *a priori* restraint on the nature and scope of the powers delegated to government. Despite the existence of this restraint it is not difficult to discover examples of Acts which contain excessive detail or which confer powers to legislate on matters of principle. As Carr recognised in 1921: "One cannot quite say that all major matters of permanent legislative importance are dealt with by Parliament itself and that all minor matters of temporary importance are delegated."[37]

However, despite the uncertainty of their application and their non-observance in individual cases, the criteria laid down by the Donoughmore-Scott Committee are still widely used as a basis for distinguishing between normal and exceptional instances of delegation.[38] Moreover, there has been a marked reluctance to contemplate the possibility of their revision either on the grounds that they no longer accurately reflect the use made of delegated legislation, or as a means of increasing the scope for its use. When Sir Edward Fellowes, Clerk to the House of Commons, stated in evidence to the 1959 Select Committee on Procedure, in terms not substantially different from those used by Lord Thring nearly a century earlier, that "ultimately the only solution for the amount of legislation and the complexity of legislation in modern times is a vastly extended power of delegation . . . " he felt compelled to add that so little would the House of Commons be prepared to accept such a scheme, that he had not bothered to put it forward.[39] Similarly when the Leader of the House of Commons, Edward Short, canvassed the possibility of increasing the use made of

[36] Report of the Committee on Ministers' Powers, *op. cit.*, p. 51.

[37] *Op. cit.*, p.15; Griffith, *op. cit.*, pp. 295–296; Allen, *op. cit.*, pp. 154–159.

[38] See especially the European Communities Act 1972, Sched. 2, para. 1(1). above, pp. 147–148; and the terms of reference of the Joint Committee on Statutory Instruments, below pp. 163–164.

[39] Crick, *The Reform of Parliament* (2nd ed. 1969), p. 164.

"framework legislation" conferring much wider law-making powers on Ministers,[40] his suggestion was rejected by the 1978 Select Committee on Procedure.[41]

## *MAKING AND PUBLICATION*

Whereas the Cabinet and its committees play the leading role in determining the content and form of primary legislation, the making of subordinate legislation is largely a departmental function. It is difficult to obtain a complete picture of the extent of contemporary Cabinet supervision of the process of making subordinate legislation, but the control exercised appears to be less detailed and continuous than that associated with primary legislation.[42] However, it seems reasonable to assume that the major policy instruments are examined by the appropriate policy committee and by the Legislation Committee.

In addition those instruments which might be objected to on constitutional grounds appear to be referred to the Legislation Committee automatically. According to Morrison the first post-war Labour Government

> "improved the machinery for considering delegated legislation, and the Legislation Committee gave systematic consideration to important Statutory Instruments. When instruments were of importance or likely to be controversial, and certainly when any principles of liberty were involved, we required them to be submitted to the Legislation Committee for examination as if they were bills."[43]

The 1953 Select Committee on Delegated Legislation provided a fuller description of these classes of instruments automatically submitted to the Committee. These included: (a) all Orders in Council under emergency or transitional legislation; (b) all statutory instruments likely to affect a large number of departments whose interests cannot conveniently be ascertained by direct consultation; (c) all statutory instruments likely to give rise to criticism by the Scrutiny Committee; and (d) all statutory instruments involving any departure from precedent, for example, in the type of penalties imposed, in the procedure relating to such matters of appeal, or in encroachments on the liberty of the subject.[44]

[40] H.C. Deb. Vol. 904, ser. 5, col. 968 (February. 2, 1976).
[41] First Report from the Select Committee on Procedure, *op. cit.*, paras. 2.29–2.30.
[42] Walkland, *op. cit.*, p. 45.
[43] *Government and Parliament* (3rd ed., 1964), p. 250.
[44] *Op. cit.*, para. 40.

Practice in making subordinate legislation varies from department to department. In evidence to the Joint Committee on Delegated Legislation, the Civil Service Department stated that: "In general, the practice is for the administrative division concerned with the subject matter of the enabling enactment to take the lead in the preparatory work, undertaking such consultations as are necessary, obtaining ministerial instructions and co-operating with the legal staff in the drafting itself."[45] In some departments a special committee composed of senior officials co-ordinates the preparation of new instruments and keeps existing instruments under review.[46] Whatever the individual arrangements, decisions on the desirability of new instruments will be taken by senior officials, invariably on the basis of discussions within the department, with other interested departments and with affected interests. Where questions of difficulty or importance arise ministerial guidance may be sought and a Minister may decide to remit such matters for the collective consideration of his colleagues.

Consultation is an established feature of the making of delegated legislation. For the government and outside groups it serves the same purposes and has the same advantages as consultation in the preparation of primary legislation.[47] It may take place on the basis of a specific statutory requirement or on the basis of nothing more than the mutual expectations and understandings of the parties.

One of the earliest examples of statutory provision being made for consultation was the *general* requirement of antecedent publication contained in the Rules Publication Act 1893. Section 1 of the Act provided that wherever any statute authorised the making of statutory rules and directed that those rules were to be laid before Parliament, at least forty days' notice had to be given in the *London Gazette* of the proposal to make the rules, and of the place where copies could be obtained. Any interested body could thus obtain copies of the rules and make representations or suggestions in writing which the rule-making authority was obliged to take into consideration before making the rules in their final form. In practice this requirement was of partial application only. The Act excepted certain departments and subsequent statutes tended to exclude the requirement. When the Rules Publication Act was replaced by the Statutory Instruments Act 1946 the requirement was not retained

[45] *Op.cit.*, Appendix 8, para. 8. Detailed guidance and instructions on the making of statutory instruments are contained in the *Handbook on Statutory Instruments Procedure*, compiled by the Statutory Publications Office for the use of departments having the power to make statutory instruments.

[46] Griffith, *op. cit.*, p. 288.

[47] See above, pp. 56–57 and 69–72.

on the grounds that it had been effectively superseded by departmental practice.[48]

In the absence of any general statutory requirements individual Acts often make specific provision for consultation with outside groups, either directly or indirectly through the medium of a specially constituted advisory body composed of representatives of affected interests. Such provisions may be regarded by affected interests as constituting formal procedural guarantees that their views will be given a hearing, if not actually reflected in the content of instruments. Yet they are frequently couched in permissive terms which do not substantially limit the department's discretion in deciding which interests to consult and what action to take after consultation.[49] However, consultation for which statutory provision has been made represents the tip of the iceberg only. Departments invariably consult affected interests as a matter of administrative routine.

Whatever its basis, the timing of consultation, the amount of information provided and its scope may all vary in accordance with the nature of the instrument and the practice of the department. Consultation may take place before or after the preparation of a detailed proposal. It may take place on the basis of a memorandum of proposals for inclusion in the instrument, or on the basis of the instrument itself, or both. Its scope may be confined to the expression of views on the instrument only, or extend to negotiations over its desirability and content.[50]

Reactions generally to consultation have been favourable. The primary emphasis has been on its status as an *a priori* control, the scope of which should be extended wherever practicable and which should not be restricted by unfavourable comparisons with parliamentary controls. By bringing informed opinion to bear at the formative stage it ensures that decisions are taken on the basis of all relevant considerations.[51] Although consultation goes some way towards compensating for the attenuated opportunities for the parliamentary consideration of instruments and may, indeed, render

[48] For a rare expression of discontent at being excluded from the "privileged circle" of consulted bodies, see *The Times*, letters, February 14, 1978.

[49] On the legal significance of such provisions, see further Jergesen, "The Legal Requirements of Consultation" [1978] P.L. 290. On statutory consultation generally see Griffith, "Delegated Legislation—Some Recent Developments" (1949) 12 M.L.R. 297, 306 *et. seq.*; Griffith and Street, *op. cit.*, pp. 123–136 and Garner, "Consultation in Subordinate Legislation" [1964] P.L. 105.

[50] For detailed statements of departmental practice see Report of the Joint Committee on Delegated Legislation, *op.cit.*, Appendix 8; and earlier, Report of the Select Committee on Delegated Legislation, *op.cit.*, Appendix B.

[51] For an early statement, see Report of the Committee on Ministers' Powers, *op.cit.*, p. 66. In a similar vein, see Carr, *op. cit.*, p. 31 and Griffith, "Delegated Legislation—Some Recent Developments", *op. cit.*, p. 306.

these opportunities devoid of purpose, its dangers should not be ignored. An excessive emphasis on consultation may provoke paralysis in government and increase the opportunities for resistance and delay. More significantly, where the principles upon which subordinate legislation is based are not settled independently, or its scope is not confined to matters of detail, the result may be legislation which is the product of negotiation, the content of which has never been exposed to public consideration.

It is exceptional for instruments to be drafted by the Office of Parliamentary Counsel. The drafting of nearly all instruments is undertaken by the legal branches of the various departments by which they are made.[52] On occasion the absence of centralised drafting arrangements has been criticised. The Donoughmore-Scott Committee argued that the main advantages of centralised arrangements lay in the avoidance of illegality and the promotion of increased uniformity of style and clarity of language.[53] Paradoxically, despite the Committee's criticism of the drafting of instruments, subordinate legislation was widely regarded as being inherently superior in form to primary legislation, largely because of the different circumstances and conditions under which it was prepared. In evidence to the Committee, First Parliamentary Counsel, Sir William Graham-Harrison, observed that:

> "In most cases the time available for drafting Bills is inadequate, and their final form when they have passed both Houses is generally unsatisfactory. On the other hand, Statutory Rules can be prepared in comparative leisure and their subject matter can be arranged in a logical and intelligible shape uncontrolled by the exigencies of parliamentary procedure and the necessity for that compression which every Minister (however much in debate he may use the draftsman as a whipping-boy) invariably requires in the case of a Bill."[53]

Whether these advantages have always been realised is debatable.[54] However, the adequacy of the arrangements for drafting subordinate

[52] Report of the Renton Committee, *The Preparation of Legislation,* Cmnd. 6053 (1975), para. 3.2.

[53] *Op. cit.*, pp. 49–50 and 70. As regards the avoidance of illegality, Carr rejected the Committee's implied criticism of the competence of the legal branches of departments. "Parliamentary Control of Delegated Legislation" [1956] P.L. 200, 207, n.2.

[53] *Op. cit.*, Minutes of Evidence, p. 35.

[54] For some of the criticisms which have been made of the drafting of instruments, see Allen, *op.cit.*, pp. 195–202. The Joint Committee and its predecessors have made a considerable indirect contribution to improvements in drafting techniques, see below, pp. 164–166. It goes without saying that the attainment of legal effectiveness may not be consisten with clarity.

legislation has not been seriously challenged since the Report of the Donoughmore-Scott Committee.[55]

Once a draft has been settled a timetable is agreed for the printing, signature, laying, publication and bringing into operation of the instrument. Despite the growth in importance of subordinate legislation during the nineteenth century no official system for its publication was laid down until the Rules Publication Act 1893.[56] Section 3 of the Act stipulated that certain classes of subordinate legislation should be published once they had been made. This requirement shared with section 1 of the Act the defect that it was not comprehensive in its scope. It was eventually replaced by the Statutory Instruments Act 1946, section 2 of which lays down a uniform procedure for the numbering, printing and sale of *statutory instruments* only.

In practice less than half of the instruments made annually are published. The following classes of instruments have been excepted from the requirements of publication and sale by regulations made under the Act: local instruments, that is instruments which are in the nature of local and personal or private Acts; general instruments otherwise printed as a series and made available to the persons affected by them; temporary instruments; bulky schedules and other documents the publication of which is considered unnecessary or undesirable; and instruments whose publication would be "contrary to the public interest."[57] A decision not to publish an instrument on the grounds that it falls within one of these classes must be accompanied by a certificate to that effect issued either by the Minister in whose name it is made or, in the case of Orders in Council, by the Queen in Council. Except in cases where non-publication is justified on the grounds of the public interest, a decision not to publish may be overruled by the Statutory Instruments Reference Committee which is appointed by the Lord Chancellor and the Speaker to decide questions arising in connection with the numbering, classification and printing of instruments.

In setting out the basis upon which section 3 of the Rules Publication Act should be revised, the Donoughmore-Scott Committee had recommended that publication should be made a

[55] The Select Committee on Delegated Legislation considered the existing arrangements to be satisfactory, *op. cit.*, paras. 32–36. The Renton Committee made no comment on their adequacy. *cf.* Bennion, *Statute Law* (1980), pp. 56–57.

[56] Prior to this, important instruments were customarily published in the *London Gazette*. The task of indexing and collating existing subordinate legislation was begun in 1889 when work started on the preparation of the first annual volume of Statutory Rules and Orders.

[57] Statutory Instruments Regulations 1947 (S.I. 1948 No. 1), regs. 4–8.

condition precedent of subordinate legislation being brought into operation.[58] When that Act was replaced in 1946, backbench attempts to insert an amendment implementing this recommendation failed. The Government was prepared to go no further than to provide that, with exceptions, instruments should be *laid* before Parliament before they become operative.[59] However, section 3(2) of the Act makes it a defence to proceedings for contravention of an instrument to prove that it should have been published and that it was not published at the date of the alleged contravention. Reliance on this defence is precluded where it can be proved that at that date "reasonable steps had been taken for the purpose of bringing the purport of the instrument to the notice of the public, or of persons likely to be affected by it, or of the person charged."[60]

## *CONTROLS*

Linked to the question of the division of law-making powers between Parliament and government is the question of the control of their exercise. As Aneurin Bevan observed in evidence to the Select Committee on Delegated Legislation: "There is now general agreement about the necessity for delegated legislation; the real problem is how this legislation can be reconciled with the processes of democratic consultation, scrutiny and control."[61] The controls exercisable over subordinate legislation operate at a number of levels and assume a variety of forms. As we have seen there are arrangements at Cabinet and departmental level for vetting not only the content and form of subordinate legislation but also its legality. These internal controls are supplemented by external control over its content through consultation with affected interests. In addition both Parliament and the courts exercise a continuing responsibility in relation to subordinate legislation. In this section we examine the respective roles of these last two.

### THE ROLE OF PARLIAMENT

As we have seen the conferral of statutory law-making powers upon government requires the consent of Parliament. Although the

[58] Report of the Committee on Ministers' Powers, *op. cit.*, p. 67.

[59] Statutory Instruments Act 1946, s. 4(1), below p. 156. By s. 4(2) every statutory instrument must bear on its face a statement showing the date on which it came or will come into operation.

[60] Proviso to s. 3(2). *Simmonds* v. *Newell* [1953] 1 W.L.R. 826; *R.* v. *Sheer Metalcraft Ltd.* [1954] 1 Q.B. 586.

[61] *Op. cit.*, Minutes of Evidence, p. 144.

granting of that consent is seldom in doubt its necessity does provide an opportunity for parliamentary consideration of the powers sought when the parent Act is before Parliament as a Bill. Clearly the purpose of delegation would be defeated were the exercise of these powers to be subject in all cases to the same degree of consideration as parliamentary legislation. Both historically and in their present form the arrangements which have been made are directed towards two aspects of subordinate legislation: its content or political merits and, secondly, what are commonly described as its technical merits, that is, its formal and constitutional aspects.

## Political Merits

In addition to determining the extent of the legislative powers reserved in its own hands, the government also decides initially whether there should be any statutory provision for subsequent parliamentary consideration of their exercise, or proposed exercise. Apart from the possibility that no provision may be made for the consideration of instruments, there are currently three possibilities.

First, the parent Act may stipulate that once the instrument has been made it should be *laid* before both Houses, or the House of Commons only in the case of financial instruments. All that this requirement involves is the delivery of complete copies of instruments to the Votes and Proceedings Office of the House of Commons, and, where necessary, to the Office of the Clerk of the Parliaments in the case of the House of Lords.[62] By itself this does not entail any formal opportunity for subsequent parliamentary discussion or action. Section 4(1) of the Statutory Instruments Act 1946 provides that any statutory instrument which has to be laid before Parliament after being made "shall be so laid *before* the instrument comes into operation." As we have seen this provision was included in response to pressure for the operation of instruments to be made conditional upon their publication.[63] Clearly, laying and publication are not the same thing; but whatever the relationship between them an instrument may be brought into force at an earlier date under section 4(1), provided that the Lord Chancellor and the

[62] H.C. S.O. No. 120; H.L. S.O. No. 66. Both Houses control their own laying procedures: Laying of Documents Before Parliament (Interpretation) Act 1948, an Act passed for the "removal of doubt." *R.* v. *Immigration Appeal Tribunals* [1972] 1 W.L.R. 1390.

[63] See above, pp. 154–155.

Speaker of the House of Commons are notified with reasons immediately.[64]

Secondly, the parent Act may stipulate that the instrument should be subject to *affirmative* resolution procedure. There are two variants of this procedure. Under the first the instrument comes into operation immediately, but its continued operation depends on its being subsequently approved by resolution of both Houses, or the House of Commons only in the case of financial instruments. This combination of immediate operation and subsequent parliamentary approval is commonly used to alter taxes or duties where prior notice would be prejudicial.[65] The period within which the affirmative resolution must be secured if the instrument is to remain in force is laid down in the parent Act. Usually a period of twenty-eight or forty days is specified. Under the second alternative, the instrument is laid in draft subject to affirmative resolution prior to coming into effect.[66]

Procedure by way of affirmative resolution is used infrequently. It comes closest to parliamentary methods of legislation in that the making or continued operation of the instrument depends upon Parliament's express approval. Apart from this, its main practical significance lies in the fact that the government must find time for discussion and approval of the instrument if it is to be made or remain in force. Where the approval of both Houses is required their powers are co-extensive. The provisions of the Parliament Acts do not apply.[67]

[64] Statutory Instruments Act 1946, s. 4(1). Opinions differ on the legal effects of a failure to lay. The Statutory Instruments Act 1946 left the question open. In the absence of express provision to the contrary, one view is that failure to lay will *not* invalidate the instrument: *Bailey* v. *Williamson* (1873) L.R. 8 Q.B. 118; Allen *op. cit.*, pp. 144–147. *Cf.* de Smith's *Judicial Review of Administrative Action* (4th ed.,1980), p. 148. Failures to lay have been dealt with by statute and statutory instrument. The National Fire Service (Regulations) Indemnity Act 1944, the Price Control and Other Orders (Indemnity) Act 1951, and the Town and Country Planning Regulations (London) Indemnity Act 1971 declared that instruments not laid should be deemed to have been laid. S.I. 1965, No. 1116 and S.I. 1974, No. 1955 revoked and re-enacted instruments not laid which ought to have been laid.

[65] See *e.g.* Import Duties Act 1958, s. 13(4).

[66] A variation of this procedure involves the instrument being laid with its operation deferred until approved by resolution; see *e.g.* Legal Advice and Assistance Act 1972, s. 11(2). There are no significant differences between these two procedures and the government has agreed in normal circumstances to avoid its use in future enactments; Second Report from the Joint Committee on Delegated Legislation (1972, H.L. 204, H.C. 468), p. 49.

[67] On June 18, 1968 the House of Lords rejected the Southern Rhodesia (United Nations Sanctions) Order made under the Southern Rhodesia Act 1965. On July 18 the Order was re-introduced and approved, see Crossman, *op. cit.*, Vol. 3, pp. 99–102.

The final possibility is that the instrument may be made subject to *negative* resolution procedure. Again this procedure may take two forms. The instrument may be laid with immediate effect subject to annulment in pursuance of a resolution of either House or, in appropriate cases, of the House of Commons only. A motion for annulment of an instrument is known as a "prayer." If a prayer is successful the instrument is revoked by Order in Council without prejudice to the validity of anything done under the instrument when it was in force. Alternatively, the instrument may be laid in draft subject to annulment. In this case it will only be implemented if a motion to annul the instrument is not passed. Such a motion does not prevent a fresh draft being laid. Prior to the Statutory Instruments Act 1946 there was an almost total lack of uniformity in the periods specified in enabling Acts during which prayers for annulment could be moved. Periods ranged from as little as twenty days to as much as one hundred days. Section 5 of the Act lays down a uniform procedure of forty days during which prayers may be moved.[68] The same period applies to instruments laid in draft subject to annulment.[69]

Whereas recourse to affirmative resolution procedure is exceptional, provisions for instruments to be made subject to annulment are common. The key differences between the two procedures are, first, that under negative resolution procedure Parliament retains a right of veto only. It is not required to formally approve the instrument. As Kersell observes, the contrast is between "explicitly assenting, often prior to the effective date of the instrument, and refraining from dissenting, invariably *ex post facto* and frequently before particular grievances emerge."[70] More importantly the contrast is between those occasions upon which the government has to find time for discussion and those occasions when, as in the case of prayers, it does not. As we shall see, the lack of time for the discussion of prayers on the floor of the House has rapidly emerged as the major problem confronting this procedure.[71]

The absence of any clear principles governing the choice between the two procedures has consistently attracted criticism.[72] Governments for their part have denied the possibility of formulating any hard and fast rules which might be treated as limiting their

[68] On the calculation of the period see Statutory Instruments Act 1946, s. 7(1).
[69] *Ibid.*, s. 6.
[70] *Parliamentary Supervision of Delegated Legislation* (1960), p. 86.
[71] See below, pp. 160–162.
[72] See *e.g.* Report of the Committee on Ministers' Powers, *op.cit.*, p. 42.

discretion.[73] This lack of principle is taken to its ultimate lengths in the unique provision made for the consideration of instruments made under section 2(2) of the European Communities Act 1972. Schedule 2(2) of the Act provides that instruments shall be subject to annulment by resolution of either House unless a draft has been approved by each House before it was made. The government is therefore free to choose the procedure to which instruments shall be subject. Little use has been made of affirmative resolution procedure, and the Joint Committee on Statutory Instruments has criticised the use of negative resolution procedure for instruments involving considerable sums of expenditure or which substantially amend Acts of Parliament.[74]

During the nineteenth century Parliament appears to have been largely unconcerned with the political merits of subordinate legislation.[75] This is reflected in the fact that these procedures originated as part of a gradual and ad hoc response to the practice rather than as an integral feature of it. When the delegation of legislative powers became controversial after the First World War, the proposition that Parliament nevertheless controlled the merits of their exercise was largely based on the further development and refinement of these procedures. In assessing their contemporary significance three general points should be borne in mind.

First, as controls they are, and always have been, directed more towards the general aspects rather than the details of subordinate legislation. This is so if only because instruments must be approved or rejected in their entirety. Although instruments may be withdrawn and revised in response to points made before being re-laid, there is no provision for their formal amendment. The introduction of anything like a committee stage has always been resisted on the grounds that it would extend debate and defeat the purpose of delegation.[76]

Secondly, they parallel and to a considerable extent are replaced by consultation. This is seen most clearly in the case of prayers. Although they may be used to seek explanations or clarifications and

[73] For an outline of those categories of instrument normally made subject to affirmative resolution procedure, see the evidence of First Parliamentary Counsel to the Select Committee on Delegated Legislation, *op. cit.*, pp. 31–34, and more recently, Report of the Joint Committee on Delegated Legislation, *op. cit.*, paras. 194–195.

[74] First Special Report from the Joint Committee on Statutory Instruments (1978; H.C. 169, H.L. 51), para. 36.

[75] Willis, *op. cit.*, pp. 20–21.

[76] See most recently, First Report from the Select Committee on Procedure, *op. cit.*, paras. 3.19–3.21.

to express grievances, prayers are used mainly by the Opposition for the purpose of criticising government policies.[77] Thus they may be used to initiate general debates loosely linked to instruments, without necessarily any intention of pressing them to a division, or to issue a straight-forward challenge to the government ending in a division. Barring mishaps, the government is unlikely to be defeated on a division. Even if it is, its power to move a new instrument is not circumscribed.[78]

Thirdly, it has become increasingly difficult to find time for the discussion of prayers. Originally there were no limits: as exempted business prayers were taken after 10 p.m. and discussion could, in theory, last indefinitely. Between 1950 and 1952 this possibility was exploited by both Conservative and Labour Oppositions to exhaust the Government through the constant threat of divisions. The use of prayers as a tactic in party warfare came to a head in late 1952, and in January 1953 a Select Committee on Delegated Legislation was appointed "to consider in what respects the existing procedures by which the control of this House over delegated legislation is exercised need to be improved or supplemented and by what means this can best be achieved." However, as Carr observed later, the real issue "was not so much the control of delegated legislation as the control of attacks on delegation."[79] In its Report the Committee recommended that it should no longer be possible to move prayers after 11.30 p.m. and that discussion should normally end at that time. The "11.30 rule" was agreed to in the form of a sessional order in March 1954 and made permanent in 1958. Its result was to limit the time available for their discussion on any one day to a theoretical maximum of one and a half hours.[80]

During the 1960s the available time was squeezed further by the increase in government business, including debates on affirmative resolutions, taken after 10 p.m. Consequently it became impossible

[77] Eaves, *Emergency Powers and the Parliamentary Watchdog: Parliament and the Executive in Great Britain, 1939–1951* (1957), p. 181.

[78] The Conservative Government was defeated in November 1972 on a new set of immigration rules. Modified orders were subsequently approved in February 1973. In November 1978 an instrument was defeated by mistake when a Government Whip voted in favour of a prayer moved by the Opposition without any intention of pressing it to division.

[79] "Parliamentary Control of Delegated Legislation", *op. cit.*, p. 215.

[80] Since 1967 debates on affirmative resolutions have been subject to the same time-limit of one and a half hours for each instrument. The "11.30 rule" was relaxed in 1973 to allow discussion of instruments on a "take-note" motion at any time subject to the same time-limit.

to find time for the discussion of all prayers. In the 1970–71 session only eleven of the forty-eight prayers moved were discussed within the statutory forty day period.[81] Increasingly it became the case that the only ones discussed were those "major" prayers which had the strong support of the Opposition, though even here the pressure of business was such that time could not be found for the discussion of all of them.

One response to this problem was to discuss prayers on motions to "take note" of them or calling for their withdrawal *after* the expiry of the forty day period. Five were discussed on such motions during the 1970–71 session.[82] Given that the period had expired the outcome of these debates could not affect the validity of instruments. More significantly, in a development similar to that which had taken place earlier in relation to public Bill procedure, active consideration was given to the possibility of discussing instruments off the floor of the House. This idea had been favoured by both the 1967 and 1971 Select Committees on Procedure.[83] The 1971 Committee had recommended that the time available for the consideration of instruments should be increased and that non-contentious prayers and resolutions should be referred to a specially constituted standing committee.[84] Its proposals were referred to the Joint Committee on Delegated Legislation for further consideration.

In its Report the Joint Committee emphasised the importance of finding sufficient time for the consideration of instruments on the floor of the House. "It is essential that there should be sufficient time available in the Commons for the debating of *all* legislative instruments which it is desired to debate, *if Parliamentary control over delegated legislation is to be a reality*."[85] With a view to increasing the time available for their discussion the Committee examined the suggestion that certain classes of instruments might be considered off the floor of the House. It concluded that existing procedures should be revised to enable instruments subject to prayers, and those affirmative instruments which were "too technical or too narrow to require debate" to be referred to a standing committee on the motion of a Minister, unless twenty or more Members objected.[86]

[81] Report of the Joint Committee on Delegated Legislation, *op. cit.*, para. 95.
[82] *Ibid.*
[83] *Public Bill Procedure Etc.*, Sixth Report from the Select Committee on Procedure (1967; H.C. 539), para. 56; *The Process of Legislation*, Second Report from the Select Committee on Procedure (1971; H.C. 538), paras. 20–21.
[84] *Ibid.*
[85] *Op. cit.*, para. 107, emphasis added.
[86] *Ibid.*, paras. 110–111.

The Committee's recommendation was implemented in 1973. Under Standing Order No. 73A one or more standing committees on Statutory Instruments etc. may be appointed to consider instruments or draft instruments referred to them. Committees normally consist of 17 Members, although any Member may attend and speak, but not vote. They do not discuss or vote upon the prayer or the resolution, but simply discuss the instrument itself on a neutral motion. No recommendation may be made to the House, and discussion is limited to one and a half hours except on instruments relating to Northern Ireland where it may last for two and a half hours. At the end of this period or earlier the chairman reports to the House that the instrument has been considered and the question is put without further discussion. Although this reform has increased the time available for the consideration of instruments it has reduced the number of effective voting opportunities on the floor of the House. In practice affirmative resolutions are taken late at night and prayers are seldom voted upon after they have been considered in standing committee.

The Joint Committee had envisaged standing committee procedure as supplementing rather than supplanting existing parliamentary procedures.[87] However, the system has worked mainly to the advantage of the government who have used it as a means of off-loading business from the floor of the House. "The government have not hesitated to utilise this useful method of saving time on the floor of the House by transferring some of their responsibilities to Committee scrutiny; there has not, however, been any noticeable increase in the time available for prayers."[88] The assumption that the time available for the consideration of instruments on the floor of the House would be increased has proved largely unfounded, and the problem of finding time for their discussion has been left effectively unresolved. In evidence to the 1978 Select Committee on Procedure, the Chairman of the Joint Committee described the system as "an unsatisfactory procedural device which has failed to meet the real needs of the House."[89]

## Technical Merits

Parliamentary interest in the technical merits of subordinate legislation is of more recent origin. In 1925 the House of Lords

[87] *Op. cit.*, paras. 127–128.

[88] Byrne, "Parliamentary Control of Delegated Legislation" (1976) 29 *Parliamentary Affairs*, 366, 373.

[89] Report, *op. cit.*, para. 3.10. The Committee made a number of recommendations at paras. 3.15–3.21. These have not been implemented.

established a Special Orders Committee to examine instruments subject to affirmative resolution procedure prior to their consideration by the House. Similar arrangements were only established by the House of Commons in 1944, and only then against a background of a massive increase in subordinate legislation and in response to concerted backbench pressure.

The Donoughmore-Scott Committee had drawn attention to the weaknesses of a system of supervision based on the awareness and interest of individual MPs. It argued that these weaknesses could only be overcome by the provision of automatic machinery for the scrutiny of subordinate legislation laid before Parliament, and it recommended the establishment of a committee in each House charged with this responsibility.[90] During the war this recommendation was taken up by backbench MPs.[91] Their pressure was resisted initially by the Government on the grounds that it would be inconvenient and that it would interfere with the obligation of every MP to "make himself reasonably skilled in these matters."[92] However, the Government's interest in increasing its own opportunities to legislate could not be pursued in isolation from parliamentary pressures for greater control over subordinate legislation. The issue was referred to the internal Machinery of Government Committee and the Government brought forward its own proposals in May 1944. The House of Commons Select Committee on Statutory Rules and Orders was set up in June 1944.[93] Following the enactment of the Statutory Instruments Act it was renamed the Select Committee on Statutory Instruments in 1947.

The existence of separate arrangements in each House led to unnecessary duplication of effort and produced defects and anomalies in the overall system for the parliamentary scrutiny of the technical merits of subordinate legislation. In 1973, following the recommendation of the Joint Committee on Delegated Legislation, these arrangements were replaced by a Joint Committee of both

[90] Report of the Committee on Ministers' Powers, *op. cit.*, pp. 62–64, 67–70. It also recommended that the Committee should examine every Bill containing proposals for conferring legislative powers on Ministers. This recommendation was never implemented.

[91] The best account is contained in Eaves, *op. cit., passim.*

[92] Herbert Morrison, H.C. Deb., Vol. 386, ser. 5, col. 158 (July 15, 1943).

[93] See further, Lee, *Reviewing the Machinery of Government 1942–1952* (1977) pp. 123–125. Kersell suggests that the Government's concession may have had the more immediate consequence of defusing backbench demands for greater use of affirmative resolution procedure, *op. cit.*, p. 46.

Houses on Statutory Instruments.[94] The Committee consists of seven Members of each House, chaired by a Member of the House of Commons. Instruments laid before the House of Commons only, are examined by the Commons Members sitting separately as a Commons' Select Committee.

Apart from examining all instruments laid before Parliament,[95] the Joint Committee also examines those *general* instruments in respect of which there is no laying requirement. By its terms of reference it is required to determine whether the special attention of either House should be drawn to an instrument on any of the following grounds:

(i) that it imposes a tax or charge;
(ii) that it is made under an Act excluding the instrument from challenge in the courts;
(iii) that it purports to have retrospective effect despite the absence of express provision in the parent Act;
(iv) that there appears to have been unjustifiable delay in its publication or laying;
(v) that it has come into operation before being laid and there appears to have been unjustifiable delay in notifying the Lord Chancellor and Speaker in accordance with section 4(1) of the Statutory Instruments Act 1946;
(vi) that there appears to be a doubt whether it is *intra vires* or that it appears to make some unusual or unexpected use of the powers conferred by the parent Act;
(vii) that for any special reason its form or purport requires elucidation;
(viii) that its drafting appears to be defective;

or on any other ground which does not impinge on its merits or on the policy behind it. Before drawing the attention of either House to an instrument the Committee is obliged to seek an explanation from the department concerned.

Indirectly the impact of the Joint and Select Committees and their predecessors has been considerable. The knowledge that instruments will be examined undoubtedly reduces the likelihood of the criteria contained in their terms of reference being intentionally or accidentally ignored. "The very existence of the Committee must

[94] Report of the Joint Committee on Delegated Legislation, *op. cit.*, paras. 68–90. The House of Lords Special Orders Committee was retained for the purpose of examining "hybrid" instruments. It was replaced by a Hybrid Instruments Committee in 1975.

[95] Excluding instruments made under the Northern Ireland Act 1974, Sched. 1, para. 1.

prevent more shortcomings than the Committee detects. . . . "[96] Moreover, they have had considerable unanticipated success in the establishment of some canons of good law-making through the preparation of special reports and through discussions with departments. Between 1944 and 1973 the Select Committee on Statutory Instruments issued a number of special reports covering matters as diverse as the consolidation of instruments, their drafting, clarity of language, the form and importance of explanatory notes and sub-delegation as well as more technical details.[97] The necessity of seeking the views of departments before making an adverse report ensures that the views of departments are taken into account, and criticisms made by the Committee may be drawn to the attention of departments in the form of circulars or amendments to the *Handbook on Statutory Instruments Procedure.*

So far as their direct impact is concerned the Joint and Select Committees examine upwards of 1,000 instruments each year. Of these less than one per cent. are formally drawn to the attention of either House. Other instruments may be withdrawn and modified in response to criticisms or, as is more common, the department concerned may undertake to ensure that defects are not repeated in subsequent instruments. Where the Committee remain unsatisfied and an adverse report is made the outcome depends upon whether any further action is taken by Parliament. In practice such action is rare. Little formal notice is taken of the work of the Joint Committee[98] and the likelihood of a defeat on an affirmative resolution or of a successful prayer is further diminished by the decrease in the time available for the consideration of instruments. Moreover, in the House of Commons it has always proved difficult to ensure that votes are not taken on instruments before the Committee has completed its consideration of them.[99] Increasingly

[96] Griffith, "Delegated Legislation—Some Recent Developments", *op. cit.*, p. 305; Wheare, *Government by Committee* (1957), pp. 234–235.

[97] The First Special Report of the House of Commons Committee in October 1944 led to the enactment of the Statutory Instruments Act 1946, Lee, *op. cit.*, pp. 125–128. More recently, see the highly critical First Special Report from the Joint Committee on Statutory Instruments, *op. cit.*

[98] First Report from the Select Committee on Procedure, *op. cit.*, para. 3.8.

[99] This problem does not arise to the same extent in the House of Lords where under S.O. No. 68 instruments subject to affirmative resolution procedure may not be brought before the House until they have been considered by the Committee. The 1978 Select Committee on Procedure recommended the adoption of a similar procedure in the House of Commons and that where the Committee has made an adverse report a further ten days should be allowed for prayers. It also recommended that consideration should be given to the possibility of making instruments drawn to the attention of the House automatically subject to

the work of the Joint Committee appears to be treated as a largely separate undertaking which relies for its impact on the status of the Committee and the outcome of discussions with departments, rather than effective voting in Parliament.

## THE ROLE OF THE COURTS

Unlike primary legislation the validity of subordinate legislation may be challenged in judicial proceedings on the grounds that it is *ultra vires* either the powers conferred by the parent Act or the procedural requirements laid down in it.[1] Originally governments attempted to overcome the uncertainty caused by the possibility that instruments might be held invalid by excluding the jurisdiction of the courts. One device by which this was done was by including in the parent Act a stipulation that regulations made under it "shall have effect as if enacted in this Act," thereby attempting to invest subordinate legislation with the same status as Acts of Parliament.[2] This and similar devices were strongly criticised by the Donoughmore-Scott Committee. It affirmed the importance of judicial review in securing the legality of subordinate legislation. "The rule of law requires that all regulations should be open to challenge in the courts except where Parliament deliberately comes to the conclusion that it is essential in the public interest to create an exception and to confer on a Minister the power of legislating with immunity from challenge."[3]

Despite these strictures the impact of judicial review has been limited. It was partly because of the perceived failure of the courts to exercise any sustained control over the exercise of emergency powers during the war that so much emphasis was placed on the assertion of parliamentary controls.[4] More importantly, however, its effect has been limited because the government itself determines through its parliamentary majority the scope for judicial review, and hence, indirectly, the legality of its own legislative actions. Although attempts to exclude the jurisdiction of the courts directly and totally

affirmative resolution procedure, *op. cit.*, paras. 3.13–3.14. No action has been taken on these proposals.

[1] See *e.g. Commissioners of Customs and Excise* v. *Cure and Deeley* [1962] 1 Q.B. 340; *cf. McEldowney* v. *Forde* [1971] A.C. 632.

[2] *Institute of Patent Agents* v. *Lockwood* [1894] A.C. 347; on the duty of the courts see the dissenting remarks of Lord Morris at 365. The effect of such provisions was cut down by the House of Lords in *Minister of Health* v. *R., ex p. Yaffe* [1931] A.C. 494.

[3] *Op. cit.*, pp. 61–62, 65.

[4] Eaves, *op. cit.*, pp. 103–105.

have now been abandoned, the scope for judicial review has been indirectly cut down by the assumption of legislative powers in wide and subjective terms. This, coupled with the care exercised by departmental lawyers in the preparation of subordinate legislation, has to a considerable extent pre-empted the possibility of the exercise of legislative powers being held invalid.[5]

## COMMUNITY LEGISLATION

One of the distinctive features of the Communities is that they possess their own law-making powers. This feature is most marked in the EEC Treaty where the task of laying down rules for the attainment of the Community's objectives is, subject to the principles contained in the Treaty, left to the institutions. However, the Communities do not possess any general law-making competence of their own but only a plurality of specific powers conferred upon them by individual articles of the Treaties.

In Chapter 1 we briefly examined the impact Community legislation has had on the legislative competence of the Queen in Parliament. In this section we are primarily concerned with the parliamentary response to the Communities' legislative capacity in the form of the arrangements which have been established for the scrutiny and consideration of Community legislation. Before doing so, however, we may usefully outline the main forms of Community legislation and some salient features of the legislative process within the Communities.

### *FORMS AND PUBLICATION*

Under the EEC Treaty legislative acts take the form of Regulations, Directives and Decisions. Regulations are of general application, binding in their entirety, and directly applicable in all Member States. Directives are binding upon the Member States to which they are addressed as to the result to be achieved, but they leave to national authorities the choice of the form and methods by which that result is to be achieved. Decisions, finally, are binding in their

[5] Carr, "Parliamentary Control of Delegated Legislation", *op. cit.*, p. 207. For a recent affirmation of the applicability of the *ultra vires* doctrine to subordinate legislation see *Hoffman-la Roche (F.) & Co. A.G.* v. *Secretary of State for Trade and Industry* [1975] A.C. 295, especially at 349 *per* Lord Morris of Borth-y-Gest 354 *per* Lord Wilberforce and 365, *per* Lord Diplock.

entirety upon those to whom they are addressed.[6] Once made, acts are published in the Official Journal of the European Communities.[7]

## *THE LEGISLATIVE PROCESS*

Under the EEC Treaty law-making powers are conferred upon both the Council of Ministers and the Commission, but typically the Treaty envisages their exercise by the Council of Ministers on a proposal from the Commission and after consultation with the Assembly. Under this procedure the guarantee and furtherance of the Community interest (conceived of as an interest distinct and separable from that of the Member States) was sought through vesting an almost exclusive right of initiative in the Commission as the institution representative of that Community interest. Consequently the Council of Ministers, the institution in which the governments of Member States participate in the activities of the Communities, was denied any power to act except on a proposal from the Commission, and the Commission's right of initiative was buttressed further by the provision that its proposals could only be amended by a unanimous vote of the Council, contrary to the normal practice of majority voting envisaged by the Treaty.[8] The vesting of the power to decide in the Council of Ministers, on the other hand, recognised that any increase in the powers of the Community could only be achieved at the expense, and thus with the consent, of Member States.

In the absence of agreement among national governments over the future direction and development of the Communities, the reconciliation of these principles has proved difficult and the modifications and accommodations effected have materially altered the nature of the legislative process. The decline in the ability of the Commission to exercise any independent form of leadership and the exhaustion of the mandate it derived from the Treaty as its immediate objectives were achieved, have meant that, although the procedural forms have in the main been preserved, the centre of initiative as well as decision-making has shifted increasingly to the member governments.

Although the Commission retains the right to initiate proposals that right is not exercised in isolation. The detailed preparation of proposals by its own departments or services involving new

[6] EEC Treaty, Art. 189. Decisions may be both legislative and executive in character.
[7] EEC Treaty, Art. 191.
[8] EEC Treaty, Arts. 148 and 149.

departures in policy is usually embarked upon either at the initiative of national governments or after extensive consultation with national politicians and senior civil servants as well as with representatives of interest groups. Where the proposal concerns the implementation of previously agreed policies there is less need for consultation although the views of national civil servants and experts are normally sought by the Commission. As originally conceived the purpose of this consultation was to assist the Commission in the preparation of proposals designed to further the Community interest rather than simply the immediate short-term interests of the Member States. Consequently outsiders were to participate in the preparation of proposals on the basis of their expertise rather than representativeness. They were not to act as agents or to have the power to commit their national governments. Experience has forced the revision of this highly technocratic conception of the legislative process. Confronted with the reality of a Community dominated by the Member States, the Commission has had to formulate proposals with an eye to what is likely to command their support and agreement. It has, however, been criticised for going too far in this direction; in particular for its failure to formulate proposals in a more independent manner and for its tendency to become involved in negotiations at this initial stage.[9]

Once the draft proposal has been prepared it is submitted to the Council of Ministers which then refers it, if this is required by the Treaty article under which it has been prepared, to the Assembly for its opinion.[10] The penultimate stage of the process involves the preparation of the Council's decision on the basis of the Commission's proposal and the opinions received. This is not normally undertaken by the Council itself but by working groups specially set up for this purpose. These groups consist of senior civil servants who, in contrast to the preparatory stage, participate as representatives of their national governments. Their primary function is to negotiate an agreed response rather than to bring their expertise to bear. The work of these groups is co-ordinated by the Committee of Permanent Representatives (COREPER) consisting of the heads of Member States' permanent delegations to the Communities.

Under the Treaties COREPER is charged with preparing the work of the Council and carrying out the tasks assigned to it by the

[9] *Report on European Institutions* (1979), pp. 71–72.

[10] See *e.g.* EEC Treaty, Art. 100. It is difficult to avoid the conclusion that the Assembly was added as an afterthought. Although the Assembly has the right to be consulted it has no right to have its views taken into account; see further case 138/79, *Roquette Freres* v. *Council of the European Communities* and case 139/79, *Maizena Gesellschaft mbH* v. *Council of the European Communities* [1980] E.C.R. 3333, 3393.

Council,[11] but this description conveys little of the importance of the position which it occupies in the legislative process. In fact it is the institution through which the reactions of national governments are first expressed and co-ordinated, and negotiations are carried on. Representatives of the Commission are in constant attendance throughout the deliberations of working groups. This enables the Commission not only to explain its proposal but also to gauge Member States' reactions. Where the reaction is unfavourable or where amendments are submitted the Commission may exercise its discretion to withdraw a proposal with a view to submitting an amended proposal, or successive drafts may be worked out within the group. COREPER's deliberations are concluded by a decision to submit the amended or unamended proposal to the Council to which are attached any further amendments sought by the national governments and the opinions of the institutions consulted. The final stage takes place within the Council of Ministers. If agreement has been reached the draft proposal is put on the agenda as an "A point" which means that it will be accepted without discussion unless objection is raised, in which case the proposal is deferred to be discussed as a "B point." Draft proposals are also placed on the agenda as "B points" where agreement has not been reached but the outstanding issues may be resolved by further discussions at ministerial level.

## *THE ROLE OF PARLIAMENT*

The main feature which stands out from this brief exposition is that national parliaments do not play any formal role in the enactment of Community legislation. Only the institutions of the Communities, representatives of the party and permanent elements in national governments and of interest groups participate directly or are consulted in its formulation and enactment. In addition, as we have seen, Community legislation does not depend for its domestic legal effects on the sanction of national parliaments. It may give rise to implementing legislation at the national level, but its validity as law is not conditional upon the existence of such legislation. In the United Kingdom the method of implementation chosen, for example, by way of administrative circular or subordinate legislation made under section 2(2) of the European Communities Act 1972, may in any event preclude or substantially restrict the opportunities for its parliamentary consideration, and even where recourse is had to primary legislation the scope for discussion and

[11] Merger Treaty, Art. 4.

amendment will be limited by the binding and inescapable nature of the obligation assumed. As the House of Commons Select Committee on European Secondary Legislation observed: " . . . whilst the semblance of parliamentary control remains, it would in practice be extremely difficult to assert (much more difficult even than in the case of domestic delegated legislation)."[12] Although we were concerned in Chapter 1 to outline the legal restraints imposed on the legislative supremacy of Parliament, one of the major political consequences of membership of the Communities has been to increase government's freedom to act (in conjunction with the governments of the other Member States) without the domestic consequences of that action being subject to the need for parliamentary approval or the degree of scrutiny and discussion formerly associated with the legislative process. " . . . the Executive itself by agreeing with the other Member governments to a proposal for legislation makes the law *i.e.* has assumed the constitutional function and power of Parliament. . . . "[13]

Before examining the parliamentary response to this development two general points may be made. First, this consequence was inherent in membership and in particular in the ideas of direct applicability and direct effect.[14] Secondly, it is possible to over-emphasise its practical significance. Domestic legislation is as we have seen a function of government and one of the criticisms made of the arrangements discussed below was that they "stifled the rights of Ministers." Not only were attempts made to discuss matters which ministerially if not constitutionally were regarded as being within the domestic prerogative of Ministers, such as negotiations over agricultural prices, but those attempts were made *in advance* of decisions being taken.[15] Nevertheless the break with the principle that the government cannot legislate without the consent of Parliament was so marked as to call into question the previously accepted view of the constitutional position of Parliament as the institution through which government is carried on.

The obligations assumed on membership, and the existing procedures for the enactment of Community legislation, severely restricted the scope for reducing this disparity between practice and previously accepted theory. Given the impossibility of providing Parliament with any direct say in the Community legislative process

[12] (1973; H.C. 463), para. 34. [13] *Ibid.*

[14] Recognising this the Labour Government apparently discussed the possibility of seeking the amendment of EEC Treaty, Art. 189 (which embodies the idea of direct applicability) so as to subject decisions of the Council of Ministers to the need for parliamentary approval. Castle, *The Castle Diaries 1974–76* (1980), pp. 301–302.

[15] *Ibid.*, and see pp. 331–332.

or of subjecting Community legislation to the need for subsequent parliamentary approval, the emphasis has been on the adaptation of traditional methods of calling Ministers to account, such as questions and debates, and the institution of new proceedings, largely based on those developed earlier in response to subordinate legislation, whereby Parliament can be informed of proposed Community legislation and express its opinion to government on those proposals before their consideration by the Council of Ministers. Shortly before accession, Select Committees of both Houses were appointed to consider possible procedures for the scrutiny of proposals for Community legislation. In its two reports the House of Commons' Select Commitee recommended various methods by which the House should be informed of and be enabled to discuss Community issues, including legislative proposals. These included the preparation by the government of explanatory memoranda on proposals; the provision of forecasts of the agenda for meetings of the Council of Ministers; ministerial statements after meetings; twice yearly reports on Community matters and the provision of time for their debate. To assist the House in formulating and arriving at conclusions on legislative proposals it recommended the establishment of a committee to identify those of political importance and those which would change the law or require its amendment, with a view to their consideration by the House before any decision was taken by the Council of Ministers.[16]

## THE HOUSE OF COMMONS' SELECT COMMITTEE

The House of Commons' Select Committee on European Legislation and Etc. was appointed in May 1974, nearly eighteen months after accession. By its terms of reference it is required:

> "To consider draft proposals by the Commission for legislation and other documents published for submission to the Council of Ministers or to the European Council whether or not such documents originate from the Commission, and to report their opinion as to whether such proposals or other documents raise questions of legal or political importance, to give their reasons for their opinions, and to report what matters of principle or policy may be affected thereby, and to what extent they may affect the law of the United Kingdom, and to make recommendations for the further consideration of such proposals and other documents by the House."

[16] (1973; H.C. 143 and 463), and see Kolinsky, "Parliamentary Scrutiny of European Legislation" (1975) 10 *Government and Opposition* 46.

The Committee consists of sixteen Members drawn from all shades of opinion on membership within the House, assisted by Speaker's Second Counsel and three full time advisers. It is empowered to appoint Sub-Committees but the difference in views among its Members has restricted the scope for effective delegation. Proposals and other documents are referred to the Committee by the government together with memoranda providing information on their background, contents and economic, legal and policy implications. Before arriving at a conclusion the Committee may seek further evidence from government departments, as well as outside bodies and individuals. In practice it has relied most heavily on government departments for the evidence upon which its conclusions are based. The Committee's conclusions are embodied in regular reports to the House in which proposals are classified in terms of their legal and political importance. In its reports the Committee has strictly observed its terms of reference in refraining from expressing any view on the merits of the proposals; it simply outlines the matters of principle or policy raised by the proposals, its reasons for its conclusions and recommends whether or not they should be considered further by the House.[17] The practical significance of the Select Committee's recommendations derives from the commitments of successive governments that where the Committee has recommended that any legislative proposal should be considered by the House, agreement in the Council of Ministers should *normally* be withheld until after the House has had the opportunity to consider the proposal.[18] Not surprisingly in view of the pressure of domestic business on the parliamentary timetable, finding parliamentary time for consideration of proposals on the floor of the House has proved difficult, particularly during the period immediately after the establishment of the Committee when a considerable backlog of proposals awaited consideration.[19] Following the recommendations of the 1975 Select Committee on Procedure[20] provision was made for the referral of proposals on the motion of a Minister, unless twenty or more Members objected, to the Standing Committee on Statutory Instruments. This proved unpopular partly because objection was taken in principle to the false analogy with statutory instruments and, more materially, because the time for debate was restricted to one and a half hours (the time available on the floor of the House is

[17] The extent to which this distinction between the substance of proposals and their merits can be maintained is questionable, see further Bates, "The Scrutiny of European Secondary Legislation at Westminster" (1976) 1 E.L. Rev. 27, 30.

[18] H.C. Deb., Vol. 991, ser. 5, col. 838 (October 30, 1980).

[19] For the difficulties which emerged see Castle, *op. cit.*, pp. 301–302.

[20] First Report from the Select Committee on Procedure (1975; H.C. 294).

similarly restricted unless the debate begins before 10 p.m.) and partly because the rules of debate prevented the amendment or rejection of the motion that "the Committee has considered the document."[21] In 1980 provision was made for the referral of documents to a new Standing Committee on European Community Documents and at the same time the Government accepted that debates could be on substantive motions and that the time available for their consideration should be increased to two and a half hours.

Apart from the problem of time other difficulties have been experienced. In part these stem from the fact that the Committee has found it difficult to harmonise its deliberations with those of a separate legislature with its own procedure, timetable and momentum. Thus it has found it difficult to adjust to the differing speeds at which proposals may be enacted. "Some proposals are extremely fast moving and are adopted within a few days; others may take years."[22] Its task is further complicated by the fact that proposals may be revised after their submission to the Council of Ministers. Although the government has undertaken to inform the Committee of amendments made to proposals, the Committee may have no opportunity to consider whether the proposals as revised should be considered by the House of Commons. Other difficulties which have been experienced, such as those of obtaining information about the negotiating position to be adopted by the government or the government's attitude to proposals have their origins in the wider question of the relationship between the government and the House of Commons. Although both the fact that the procedures are designed to provide a measure of pre-legislative scrutiny and the fact that the government is committed to providing time for debate represent significant departures from previous practice it seems clear that government does not regard them as a device whereby the House can encroach on its monopoly in the formulation of policy. Rather they are treated as extraordinary devices which are justifiable by reference to the fundamental nature of the change which took place through which some semblance of parliamentary control, however slight, can be maintained,[23] and which provide an additional mechanism for sounding backbench opinion.

[21] Only 15 proposals were referred to Standing Committees in 1975–76 and 5 in 1976–77; First Report from the Select Committee on Procedure (1978; H.C. 588), para. 4.16.

[22] Bates, "British Government and the EEC" *Most*, No. 21, October 1979, p. 26.

[23] The alternative would have been for the government itself to decide what should be discussed. This was rejected by the Labour Government on the grounds that it involved the explicit admission of the impossibility of maintaining any form of parliamentary control over Community legislation; Castle, *op. cit.*, p. 296.

## THE HOUSE OF LORDS' SELECT COMMITTEE

Whereas the House of Commons' Select Committee acts as a political filter through which contentious measures are referred to the House for further consideration, the House of Lords' Select Committee on the European Communities has concentrated on the evaluation of Community policies and legislative proposals and in doing so has expressed its views on their merits. The Committee was set up in 1974 in accordance with the recommendations of the Select Committee on Procedure.[24] Under its terms of reference it is required

> "to consider Community proposals, whether in draft or otherwise, to obtain all necessary information about them, and to make reports on those which in the opinion of the Committee, raise important questions of policy or principle, and on other questions to which the Committee consider the special attention of the House should be drawn."

The Committee is chaired by the Deputy Chairman of Committees and it is assisted in its deliberations by the Second Counsel to the Chairman of Committees. In addition any member of the House may be co-opted to assist in its deliberations, a power which has been extensively exercised as has the power to appoint specialist advisers. In contrast to the House of Commons' Select Committee the main work of the Committee is undertaken through special Sub-Committees. Six Sub-Committees have been appointed: A, Finance, Economics and Regional Policy; B, Trade and Treaties; C, Health, Employment, Education and Social Affairs; D, Agriculture and Consumer Affairs; E, Law; and F, Energy, Transport, Research and Environment. It has also made much greater use of its power to take oral and written evidence from outside bodies as well as government. The Committee issues regular reports in which it expresses its opinion on the merits of proposals. Although the government has similarly undertaken to provide time in the House for debates, these are recommended sparingly and its reports are treated as an expression of opinion and a source of detailed information in their own right.[25]

[24] First and Second Reports from the Select Committee on Procedure for Scrutiny of Proposals for European Instruments (1973; H.L. 67 and 194).

[25] Coombes, "Parliament and the European Community" in *The Commons Today* (Walkland and Ryle ed., 1981), p. 243.

## CHAPTER SEVEN

# INTERPRETATION

## INTERPRETATION AND APPLICATION

Modern legislation is concerned primarily to determine the structure and powers of public authorities and to a lesser extent to regulate the conduct of citizens and of private organisations. It is implemented, that is, put into practice, by a wide variety of individuals: for example, civil servants in government departments responsible for the collection of income tax, value added tax and other revenues; local authority officials responsible for education, highways, planning and housing; officials of administrative agencies such as the Equal Opportunities Commission, the Health and Safety at Work Executive and the Gaming Board, and of administrative tribunals such as the Employment Appeal Tribunal and the Lands Tribunal; legal and other consultants to public and private companies and to trade unions; judges, barristers and solicitors. For most of these individuals, the implementation of a statutory provision in a given instance will usually be a routine and simple matter, involving firstly a finding that the factual circumstances specified in it have occurred and secondly the application of the appropriate legal consequences. An everyday example of this process is a policeman booking a car parked on a double yellow line.

Authorities which deal on a routine basis with the public, particularly those collecting revenues and distributing benefits, frequently issue booklets, pamphlets and other publications designed to indicate how specific provisions will be applied in individual cases. Common examples of such publications are those issued by the Department of Health and Social Security concerning pensions, maternity benefits, supplementary benefits and national insurance contributions; those issued by local authorities concerning rent and rate rebates and those issued by the Inland Revenue concerning the extra-statutory concessions it makes in relation to taxes. Sometimes an authority will be under a duty to issue such publications[1], or to consult those which are issued by another body

[1] *e.g.* the duty imposed on the Director-General of Fair Trading under s. 4 of the Consumer Credit Act 1974 to publish information and advice about credit facilities available to the public and about the operation of the Act.

such as a government department[2]; sometimes, as we have seen, such publications will be promulgated as subordinate legislation,[3] on other occasions they will take the form of a simple leaflet. Moreover, many public authorities, such as the police, and many non-government organisations, such as insurance companies, finance houses and credit agencies prepare guidelines concerning the application of statutory provisions which are intended for internal use only.

However, not every application of a statutory provision is either routine or simple: among other things an individual may be in doubt about its meaning or scope, or about its relationship with other provisions. The process of resolving such doubts is frequently called interpretation.[4] In deciding upon a particular interpretation, these various publications may have an effect which is little short of legislation. In many cases they will in practice constitute an official, final and authoritative interpretation of a provision, both for those implementing it, and for those subject to it. The views of professional advisers may also have a similar effect:

> "Although we like to pretend that only Parliament and the judges make law, the fact is that the legal and accountancy professions, by their interpretation (or misinterpretation) of it and by their practices and standards, do so too. So much so that when these occasional misinterpretations are exposed by the judiciary the legislature may step in and whitewash them."[5]

In giving advice, however, these advisers endeavour to reach an interpretation which satisfies at least two potentially conflicting conditions: first, that it should, if possible, be favourable to their clients' interests; and secondly, that it should, if challenged in a court of law, receive judicial approval.

In this chapter, we examine four aspects of the judicial

[2] *e.g.* the duty imposed on a local authority under s. 12 of the Housing (Homeless Persons) Act 1977 to take into account the Code of Guidance published by the Department of the Environment when deciding whether a person is homeless. The nature of the duty was discussed in *De Falco* v. *Crawley B.C.* [1980] 1 All E.R. 913.

[3] See above, pp. 148–149.

[4] This process is also sometimes referred to as the construction of statutes. Some writers argue that an analytical distinction exists between interpretation and construction: "All statutes must be 'construed,' and only when there is some ambiguity, obscurity or inconsistency in a statute is the term 'interpret' fitting," Driedger, *The Construction of Statutes* (1974), p. ix. For the most part, however, the terms are used interchangeability by academic writers, practitioners and the judiciary.

[5] Gower, *Review of Investor Protection: A Discussion Document* (1982), pp. 47–48, citing *Shearer* v. *Bercain Ltd.* [1980] 3 All E.R. 295 and the Companies Act 1981, s. 39.

interpretation of statutes[6]: first, its significance; secondly, the constitutional theory of judicial interpretation; thirdly, the characteristic forms of argument used; and finally some of the suggestions which have been made for reform.

## THE SIGNIFICANCE OF JUDICIAL INTERPRETATION

Sometimes the interpretation placed on a statutory provision by a public official or a private individual will be challenged in a court of law, either directly by calling in question the merits of the interpretation or indirectly by calling in question the procedures by which the interpretation was reached. As we have suggested, judicial interpretation comprises only a very small proportion of the countless number of occasions on which statutory provisions are applied to particular sets of circumstances. Nevertheless, it displays two characteristics which give it a special significance setting it apart from all other instances of interpretation: it is formally authoritative and it purports to be disinterested. Thus, leaving aside the possibility of further legislative intervention, the decision which a court reaches concerning the meaning or scope of a provision, or its relationship with other provisions, has legal priority over all other interpretations. This subordination to judicial interpretation applies as much to competing interpretations held by officers of the Crown or local authorities regarding the exercise of their statutory powers[7]

[6] The interpretation of subordinate legislation differs in one fundamental respect from the interpretation of primary legislation, in that a court may determine its validity, see above, pp. 166–167. However, "it seems clear that the courts when dealing with such legislation apply the same general common law principles which they apply to statutes;" The Law Commissions, *The Interpretation of Statutes*, (1969) Law Com. No. 21, Scot. Law Com. No. 11, para. 77. Section 11 of the Interpretation Act 1978 more specifically provides that "where an Act confers power to make subordinate legislation, expressions used in that legislation have, unless the contrary intention appears, the meaning which they bear in the Act." It was the intention both of the Law Commissions, and of their sponsors, that the Interpretation of Legislation Bills 1980 and 1981 should apply to the interpretation of subordinate legislation; see *ibid.*, and Appendix A, and below, n. 85. On the use of subordinate legislation as an aid to the interpretation of statutes, see *Hanlon* v. *Law Society* [1980] 2 W.L.R. 765, 821–822, *per* Lord Lowry.

[7] In addition to those occasions on which specific decisions made by public authorities in pursuance of their interpretation of particular statutory provisions are subject to judicial review, the judiciary are sometimes called upon to decide the lawfulness of such interpretations as expressed in policy documents or guidelines published by the authority; *e.g.* *Vestey* v. *I.R.C.* [1980] A.C. 1148 on Inland Revenue concessions; *R.* v. *Metropolitan Police Commissioner, ex p. Blackburn* [1968] 2 Q.B. 118 and *R.* v. *Metropolitan Police Commissioner, ex. p. Blackburn* (No. 3) [1973] Q.B. 241 on police directives concerning prosecutorial discretion; and *Buckoke* v. *G.L.C.* [1971] Ch. 655 on fire brigade directives contemplating breaches of the Road Traffic Acts.

as it does to individuals' interpretations of the scope of their rights and duties. Only those applications of statutory provisions which comply with the interpretation placed on them by the courts will be lawful. A court's interpretation has therefore a legally compelling quality which may be duly enforced by those having an interest in its subject matter. Secondly, judicial interpretation is in theory impartial. By his oath, a judge is bound to "do right to all manner of people after the laws and usages of this realm,"[8] and this means that he is expected to interpret statutory provisions from a position of disinterestedness. Thus although a legal advisor will seek an interpretation which best serves his client's interests, whether the client be a private individual or a government department, he will have to reconcile this with the need to seek an interpretation which would appeal to a disinterested judge.

It is for these reasons that the government's primary expectation of the draftsman, that he will draft a Bill which is legally effective, includes the requirement that should it come before a court, there will be as little opportunity as possible for it to be interpreted in any way other than the government wishes. Should it do so, the key issue for the government is whether the disputed section bears the meaning which the government intended it to have. If a disinterested judge arrives at the same interpretation of the section as that placed upon it by the interested department, the draftsman has done exactly what was required of him. Thus, as the Law Commissions recognised when they drew attention to the interaction between judicial approaches to legislation and the drafting of Acts of Parliament, the judiciary play a key role in the implementation of legislation.[9] For government departments and public authorities, judicial interpretation (or the prospect of it) provides the acid test of their own interpretation of a statutory provision. To this end they attempt to forecast what a court would decide, and sometimes treat actions against them as offering the opportunity to clarify the scope of their powers and duties.[10] The costs to a department or an authority of a decision contrary to its own interpretation may be quite devastating.[11] Sometimes the challenge which an individual brings against such an interpretation results in the adoption by the

[8] Promissory Oaths Act 1868, s. 4.

[9] Law Commissions, *The Interpretation of Statutes, op. cit.*, para. 5.

[10] *e.g.* in areas such as social security: *R.* v. *Sheffield Supplementary Appeal Tribunal, ex. p. Shine* [1975] 1 W.L.R. 624; discrimination in employment: *Jenkins* v. *Kingsgate* [1981] 1 W.L.R. 972; the powers of nationalised industry: *Roberts* v. *British Railways Board* [1975] 1 W.L.R. 396 and taxation: *Vestey* v. *I.R.C.* [1980] A.C. 1148.

[11] *e.g.* the House of Lords' decision that the G.L.C.'s cheap fares policy was unlawful; *Bromley L.B.C.* v. *Greater London Council* [1982] 1 All E.R. 129.

department or authority of a different interpretation even in the absence of a judicial decision on the point, if it is felt by those implementing the provision that judicial proceedings would in fact support the challenge. The attitudes and practices of the judiciary thus provide a *model* of authoritative interpretation which for many officials constitutes a standard to be complied with. In this sense, although judicial interpretation is confined to a few hundred cases a year, it has a normative significance for interpretation generally. For example, even though a solicitor has no intention of pursuing litigation, he will *inter alia* present arguments to the other party's solicitor which he believes either have received, or would receive, judicial approval. This is hardly surprising, for solicitors, like all others who offer legal advice, rely for authority on legal text books; and these, for the most part, attempt to present, in a systematic way, judicial interpretations of particular areas of law.

Judicial interpretation therefore casts a long shadow over the interpretation of statutes generally. In the absence of further statutory definition, a judicial decision is *the* authoritative answer to a particular question of interpretation, and for some questions is the acid test of their interpretation. Where there is no decision directly in point, judicial interpretation may provide useful analogies; and even where there is no possibility of a particular interpretation being challenged in a court of law, judicial practices provide a model to be emulated.

## THE CONSTITUTIONAL THEORY OF JUDICIAL INTERPRETATION

As we saw in Chapter 1, the doctrine of the sovereignty of Parliament has been traditionally understood to include the proposition that the judicial function in relation to legislation is confined to its interpretation and application.[12] In approaching these tasks, the primary constitutional duty of a judge is to give effect to the intention of Parliament *as expressed in the words of the statute*. This duty in turn imposes in theory two fundamental constraints on judicial interpretation. The first is that where a statutory provision clearly applies to the facts of a case, a court must give effect to them, no matter how unpalatable it considers the result to be. This was emphatically reasserted by the House of Lords in *Duport Steel* v. *Sirs:*

> "My Lords, at a time when more and more cases involving the application of legislation which gives effect to policies that are

[12] See above, p. 19.

> the subject of bitter public and parliamentary controversy, it cannot be too strongly emphasised that the British Constitution, though largely unwritten, is firmly based on the separation of powers: Parliament makes the laws, the judiciary interpret them. When Parliament legislates to remedy what the majority of its members at the time perceive to be a defect or a lacuna in the existing law (whether it be the written law enacted by existing statutes or the unwritten common law as it has been expounded by the judges in decided cases), the role of the judiciary is confined to ascertaining from the words that Parliament has approved as expressing its intention what that intention was, and to giving effect to it. Where the meaning of the statutory words is plain and unambiguous it is not for the judges to invent fancied ambiguities as an excuse for failing to give effect to its plain meaning because they themselves consider that the consequences of doing so would be inexpedient, or even unjust or immoral. In controversial matters such as are involved in industrial relations there is room for differences of opinion as to what is expedient, what is just and what is morally justifiable. Under our Constitution it is Parliament's opinion on these matters that is paramount."[13]

The second constraint is that a judge must reject an interpretation which the words of the statute cannot sustain, even where it seems to him that such an interpretation would give effect to what he understands to be Parliament's intention in passing the Act. In applying statutory words to a particular set of facts, judges are expected to elucidate their meaning and scope, but where the words as elucidated do not cover the facts at hand, it is not the judge's function to devise interpretations based upon what he thinks the draftsman would have said in such circumstances. A judge should give effect to "the meaning of what Parliament has said and not what Parliament meant to say."[14] This is in reality only another way of saying that a judge should not re-write the legislation, for this is the exclusive right of the legislature.

The application of the law on the one hand and the "naked usurpation of the legislative function under the thin disguise of interpretation"[15] on the other, are thus extreme points on a continuum of adjudicative behaviour, and it is impossible to say,

[13] *Per* Lord Diplock, [1980] 1 W.L.R. 142, 157.

[14] *Per* Lord Simon, *Black-Clawson International Ltd.* v. *Papierwerke Waldhof-Aschaffenburg* [1975] A.C. 591, 645.

[15] *Per* Lord Simonds, *Magor and St. Mellons R.D.C.* v. *Newport Corporation* [1952] A.C. 189, 191.

according to any objective measure, where the line between acceptable and unacceptable adaptation of statutory words falls in any given case. This does not mean that judges themselves do not argue about where the line should be drawn, indeed some of the most acrimonious judicial exchanges, such as that between Lord Denning and Lord Simonds in the early fifties,[16] concern precisely this issue; but it is still the case that wherever they do draw the line on a particular occasion, their decision is typically sustained by the rhetoric of what they conceive to be their constitutional duty.

The constitutional duty of the judiciary to give effect to the intention of Parliament does not however indicate *how* they are to resolve those disputes in which the statutory words can reasonably sustain more than one interpretation, each of which may arguably be considered to give effect to the legislature's intention in the case at hand. A judge has to "choose the construction which in his judgment best meets the legislative purpose of the enactment."[17] This inevitably allows for the possibility of a divergence between his interpretation and someone else's, including that of another judge, or of the legislature. Disagreements about what are the appropriate criteria for deciding a particular question of statutory interpretation are legion. For example, if a court decided that

> "it was the intention of Parliament to exclude Conservative clubs or dockers' clubs from the operation of the Race Relations Act 1968, some critics will say that so widespread an exception, applying to clubs with such extensive membership, is wholly contrary to the spirit and the intention of that statute. And they will go on to say that the courts are showing a restrictive attitude on a matter of social policy and politics.
>
> "On the other hand there will be those who say that the Race Relations Acts mark a serious intervention and a considerable regulation of personal relationships. Therefore, they will argue, such regulation should be kept to a minimum and Parliament should be assumed to have intended that the intervention should not be extended beyond the most explicit provision."[18]

[16] In *Seaford Estates* v. *Asher* [1949] 2 K.B. 481, 499 Denning L.J. said: "We do not sit here to pull the language of Parliament to pieces and make nonsense of it. That is an easy thing to do and it is a thing to which lawyers are too often prone. We sit here to find out the intention of Parliament and of ministers and carry it out, and we do this better by filling in the gap and making sense of the enactment than by opening it up to destructive analysis." Lord Simonds' response in *Magor and St. Mellons R.D.C.* v. *Newport Corporation, ibid.* is quoted in the text, above p. 181, and see n. 15.

[17] *Per* Lord Scarman, *Duport Steel* v. *Sirs, op.cit.,* 168.

[18] Griffith, *The Politics of the Judiciary* (1977), pp. 175–176.

Such disagreements are not of course *just* about the intention of Parliament, but are also about the values that are appropriate in the context. Some of the more critical accounts of judicial behaviour argue that the values which are likely to be preferred by judges will, in many instances, be antithetical to those to which the government intended to give expression in the legislation.

In one such account, Griffith examines the way in which the judiciary have interpreted statutes dealing with, for example, industrial and race relations, and police powers. As we noted earlier, judges are supposed to decide cases from a position of disinterestedness: "Everyone agrees that impartiality is the first essential in any judge. And that means not only that he must not appear to favour either party. It also means that he must not take sides on political issues."[19] Griffith's argument is that such traditional accounts are quite inadequate descriptions of what judges do, largely because they fail to explain the basis on which judges in fact determine these political issues. In his view, this basis can be seen in the way in which the judiciary conceive of "the public interest" in such cases: "It concerns, first, the interests of the State (including its moral welfare) and the preservation of law and order, broadly interpreted; secondly, the protection of property rights; and thirdly the promotion of certain political views normally associated with the Conservative party."[20]

Whether or not Griffith is right, it is clear that the traditional constitutional theory cannot account for judicial practice because that theory is frequently unable to furnish any guidelines as to which of two conflicting readings of a statute should be preferred. In a dispute over statutory interpretation, each side can generally argue with some measure of plausibility that its interpretation reflects the intention of the legislature as expressed in the statutory words. Yet on some basis or other, the judge must make his choice.

## THE CHARACTERISTIC FORMS OF ARGUMENT IN INTERPRETATION

It is a judge's duty to give effect to the intention of Parliament as expressed in the words of the statute.[21] These words therefore

[19] Lord Reid, "The Judge as Law-Maker" (1972) 12 J.S.P.T.L. 22, 23.

[20] *The Politics of the Judiciary*, *op.cit.*, p. 195.

[21] Besides the constitutional and political aspects of this duty, there are also significant conceptual problems associated with the expression, "the intention of Parliament"; see *e.g.* MacCallum, "Legislative Intent" 75 Y.L.J. 754 and Twining and Miers, *How To Do Things With Rules* (2nd ed., 1982), Chap. 5.

constitute the natural and proper starting place for interpretation.[22] The question that immediately arises is, what forms of argument do judges use to justify the interpretations they have reached? As in the interpretation of case law rules, judges rely on a variety of arguments, but our concern is with those that have particular, or in some instances, exclusive relevance to statutory interpretation. Three such forms of argument may be distinguished: those based on the language and purpose of the statute; those based on certain kinds of interpretative guidelines and those based on earlier judicial decisions.

Like the interpretation of case-law rules, there are few criteria determining the weight and priority to be attached to these arguments. Indeed one of the primary characteristics of the interpretation of statutes is that the judiciary have not developed any systematic methodological principles specifying how their interpretative tasks are to be performed. As we shall see, the arguments that are characteristically relied upon to justify an interpretation vary considerably in the degree to which they are determinative of the issue being decided.

## *THE LANGUAGE AND PURPOSE OF THE ACT*

Arguments based upon the express words of the statute, or more broadly on its purposes, or both, have traditionally been primary justifications for particular interpretations of statutory provisions. Purposive, or teleological, arguments have been employed for centuries, certainly since the celebrated formulation of the mischief rule in Heydon's case in 1584:

> "That for the sure and true interpretation of all statutes in general (be they penal or beneficial, restrictive or enlarging of the common law) four things are to be discerned and considered: (1) what was the common law before the passing of the Act, (2) what was the mischief and defect for which the common law did not provide; (3) what remedy the Parliament hath resolved and appointed to cure the disease of the commonwealth; (4) the true reason of the remedy. And then the office of all the judges is always to make such construction as

[22] Although the words of a statutory rule are in fixed verbal form, this is not to say that there is no leeway for reformulating the rule by formal re-arrangement of its parts, or by the occasional substitution, inclusion or deletion of words; see *e.g.* Twining and Miers, *How To Do Things With Rules*, *op. cit.*, Appendix 1, Bennion, *Statute Law* (1980), Chap. 27 and Appendix B; *Federal Steam Navigation* v. *D.T.I.* [1974] 1 W.L.R. 505 and *Re Beaumont* [1980] 1 All E.R. 266, 270–271.

> shall suppress the mischief and advance the remedy, and to suppress subtle intentions and evasions for the continuance of the mischief and *pro privato commodo*, and to add force and life to the cure and remedy according to the true intent of the makers of the Act *pro bono publico*."[23]

It should be emphasised that as originally conceived, the mischief argument was a "four corners" argument; that is, the defect and its remedy were to be ascertained from the text of the Act as a whole, but not beyond it.[24] This may be distinguished from the present conception of a purposive argument, in which evidence of Parliament's intention may be ascertained from material extraneous to the Act, although as we shall see, there are both limitations on, and controversy about, the kinds of material that may be used and the inferences that may be drawn from them.

Arguments based upon the mischief dealt with by the Act gradually gave way to those based upon the actual words used in it. This shift began following the emergence of the doctrine of the legislative supremacy of Parliament, and was considerably hastened by the development of more exact drafting styles in the nineteenth century. The judiciary's insistence on interpreting Acts of Parliament according to the precise words used has two historically important aspects. The first is, as we noted in Chapter 4, that it reflected the judiciary's preference for the common law and their consequent hostility to legislation as a source of law.[25] These attitudes found expression in the presumption that changes in the law must, if they were to be enforced by the courts, be expressed in the clearest possible terms, and are neatly captured in Lord Diplock's remark, though spoken in a different context, that "Parliament is sovereign only in respect of what it expresses by the words used in the legislation it has passed."[26] One of the main consequences of these attitudes was the unwillingness of the courts to extend the statutory words to cover the *casus omissus* – "the inexplicable and probably inadvertant failure of the draftsman to use words entirely apt to cover the instant case."[27] As we have seen, the draftsman's response was to draft Bills with ever greater degrees of specificity, a response which further encouraged literal interpretation.

[23] 3 Co. Rep. 7a; 76 E.R. 637, 638.
[24] See Lord Diplock, *Black-Clawson International Ltd.* v. *Papierwerke Waldhof-Aschaffenburg*, *op.cit.*, 637–638.
[25] See above, pp. 94–97.
[26] *Black-Clawson International Ltd.* v. *Papierwerke Waldhof-Aschaffenburg*, *op.cit.*, 638.
[27] Cross, *Statutory Interpretation* (1976), p. 10.

Secondly, the entrenchment of literal interpretation reflected the judiciary's conception of their role as interpreters:

> "The only rule for the construction of Acts of Parliament, is that they should be construed according to the intent of the Parliament which passed the Act. If the words of the statute are in themselves precise and unambiguous, then no more can be necessary than to expound those words in that natural and ordinary sense. The words themselves alone do, in such a case, best declare the intention of the lawgiver."[28]

•Although this rule was subject to the qualification that where a literal interpretation led to a result that was absurd or inconsistent with the rest of the statute, the ordinary meaning of the words could be modified so as to avoid such a result,[29] the primary obligation on a court was to give effect to their plain meaning.-The mischief rule was subordinated to interpretations based on the plain meaning of the words in issue, and indeed until recently, arguments based upon it have been typically presented as being appropriate only where the words of the statute do not clearly apply to the facts of the case at hand.[30] While there is obvious value in interpreting words in their ordinary sense in context, it is generally recognised that in the past the judiciary did place too great an emphasis upon textual interpretation at the expense of purposive interpretation.

[28] *Per* Tindal C.J., *Sussex Peerage Claim* (1844) 11 Cl. & Fin. 85, 143; 8 E.R. 1034, 1057.

[29] It has traditionally, but wrongly, been asserted that the "golden" rule is an alternative to the "literal" rule of interpretation which operates in cases where a literal interpretation would lead to an absurdity or anomaly. The *locus classicus* of the "golden" rule is Lord Wensleydale's *dictum* in *Grey* v. *Pearson* (1857) 6 H.L.C. 61, 106:

> "I have been long and deeply impressed with the wisdom of the rule, now, I believe, universally adopted, at least in the Courts of Law in Westminster Hall, that in construing wills and indeed statutes, and all written instruments, the grammatical and ordinary sense of the words is to be adhered to, unless that would lead to some absurdity, or some repugnance or inconsistency with the rest of the instrument, in which case the grammatical and ordinary sense of the words may be modified, so as to avoid that absurdity and inconsistency, but no farther";

(explicitly approved by Lord Blackburn in *River Wear Commissioners* v. *Adamson* (1877) 2 App. Cas. 743, 764). It is clear, however, to follow Driedger; "that only the words down to 'unless' constitute the 'rule'; the remainder is a qualification;" *The Construction of Statutes, op.cit.*, p. 27. See also Lord Simon's modern formulation of the golden or primary rule of interpretation in *Maunsell* v. *Olins* [1975] A.C. 373, 391 and his discussion of the circumstances under which it is permissible for a court to remedy what it perceives to be an anomaly: *Stock* v. *Frank Jones (Tipton) Ltd.* [1978] 1 W.L.R. 231, 235–237.

[30] *e.g.* the formulation of the relationship between the literal and the mischief rules in Maxwell, *The Interpretation of Statutes* (12th ed., 1969), Chap. 2; Craies, *Statute Law* (7th ed., 1971), pp. 65 and 96 and Odgers, *The Construction of Deeds and Statutes* (5th ed., 1967), p. 297.

However, both the preponderance of academic writers and some senior judges now argue that current judicial practice incorporates both literal and purposive interpretation, and is better expressed as a series of questions: "What was the statute trying to do? Will the proposed interpretation give effect to that object? Is the interpretation ruled out by the language?"[31] Two points about this characterisation deserve emphasis: first, that it presents the two aspects of purpose and language as complementary parts of a whole enterprise; and secondly, that the interpretative process begins with an examination of the statute's purposes. This is well exemplified by Driedger's formulation:

> "1. The Act as a whole is to be read in its entire context so as to ascertain the intention of Parliament (the law as expressly or impliedly enacted by the words), the object of the Act (the ends sought to be achieved), and the scheme of the Act (the relation between the individual provisions of the Act).
> 2. The words of the individual provisions to be applied to the particular case under consideration are then to be read in their grammatical and ordinary sense in the light of the intention of Parliament embodied in the Act, and if they are clear and unambiguous and in harmony with that intention, object and scheme and with the general body of the law, that is the end.
> 3. If the words are apparently obscure or ambiguous, then a meaning that best accords with the intention of Parliament, the object of the Act and the scheme of the Act, but one that the words are reasonably capable of bearing, is to be given them."[32]

Although it includes references to arguments based on considerations other than the language of the Act, Lord Simon's more specific set of prescriptions for ascertaining the intention of Parliament succinctly captures contemporary judicial practice:

> "The courts have five principal avenues of approach to the ascertainment of the legislative intention: (1) examination of

[31] Williams, "The Meaning of Literal Interpretation" (1981) N.L.J. 1128 and 1149, 1150. Although there is some variation between them, the view that there is essentially only one rule of interpretation is maintained by Lloyd, *Introduction to Jurisprudence* (4th ed., 1979), p. 865; Cross, *Statutory Interpretation, op.cit.*, pp. 43–52 and Driedger, *op.cit.*, pp. 67 and 81. They all rely on the *dicta* of a few senior judges, notably Lords Diplock and Simon, who have attempted to systematise the basic judicial practices; see *e.g. Maunsell* v. *Olins, op.cit.; Stock* v. *Frank Jones (Tipton) Ltd., op.cit.; Ealing L.B.C.* v. *Race Relations Board* [1972] A.C. 342 and *Hanlon* v. *Law Society, op.cit.*, 804, *per* Lord Scarman.

[32] Driedger, *op.cit.*, p. 81.

> the social background, as specifically proved if not within common knowledge, in order to identify the social or juristic defect which is the likely subject of remedy; (2) a conspectus of the entire relevant body of the law for the same purpose; (3) particular regard to the long title of the statute to be interpreted (and, where available, the preamble), in which the general legislative objectives will be stated; (4) scrutiny of the actual words to be interpreted in the light of the established canons of interpretation; (5) examination of the other provisions of the statute in question (or of other statutes *in pari materia*) for the light which they throw on the particular words which are the subject of interpretation."[33]

Nevertheless, the lengths to which a judge may think it proper to go in exploring these five avenues, and the nature of the inferences about the intention of Parliament that he draws from them, in particular in holding that the language of a provision does sustain the interpretation which an argument based upon the purpose of the Act requires, remain a matter for his discretion.

This indeterminacy which exists as to the manner in which that discretion should be exercised may be seen also in the judicial approach to the use to be made of policy documents to ascertain the purpose and meaning of statutory provisions. In Chapters 2 and 3 we discussed the role of bodies such as the Law Commissions, Royal Commissions and parliamentary select committees in the formulation of legislative proposals. The reports which these bodies publish upon which legislation is based may be relevant to ascertaining why a statute was enacted, and will in some cases be relevant to determining the meaning of particular provisions in it. These considerations extend to policy documents prepared by international agencies. A judge is at liberty to read whatever policy documents he likes in order to arrive at a *private* understanding of the legal effect of a statutory provision; the question is whether, and in what circumstances, it is permissible for him to refer *explicitly* to such resources when giving judgment. The answer has been recently substantially clarified, although as Ormrod L.J. said in *Firman* v. *Ellis*, "leaving aside the propriety of looking at such material (an interim report of the Law Reform Committee) when construing a provision in an Act of Parliament, the practical question is whether it is of any assistance."[34] The present position may be briefly stated as follows.

[33] *Ealing L.B.C.* v. *Race Relations Board, op.cit.*, 361.
[34] [1978] 3 W.L.R. 1, 17.

### DOMESTIC PRE-LEGISLATIVE DOCUMENTS

This category includes reports of Royal Commissions, the Law Commissions, the Criminal Law Revision Committee, the Law Reform Committee, departmental inquiries and of parliamentary select committees. These "may be used as an aid to identify the mischief which the legislation is intended to remedy; but not for the purpose of construing the enacting words in such a way as to conform with recommendations made in the report as to the form the remedy should take."[35]

### DOMESTIC PARLIAMENTARY DOCUMENTS

The explanatory memoranda and notes of clauses prepared by the department to accompany the parliamentary stages of a Bill may not be referred to by a judge when interpreting an Act. More importantly, it has recently been "emphatically and unanimously" affirmed that "recourse to the reports of proceedings in either House of Parliament [Hansard] during the passage of a Bill . . . is not permissible as an aid to [the Act's] construction."[36]

### DOCUMENTS PREPARED BY INTERNATIONAL AGENCIES

The words of a treaty to which the United Kingdom is a signatory, but which have not been incorporated into domestic law by statute cannot override the meaning of a United Kingdom statute even though there may be conflict between them.[37] Where the treaty is however incorporated into domestic law (usually in the form of a Schedule to the Act),

> " . . . it is a legitimate aid to the construction of any provisions of the Act that are ambiguous or vague to have recourse to the terms of the treaty in order to see what was the obligation in international law that Parliament intended that this country should be enabled to assume."[38]

[35] *Per* Lord Diplock, *Davis* v. *Johnson* [1979] A.C. 264, 330. See also, *Black-Clawson International Ltd.* v. *Papierwerke Waldhof-Aschaffenberg, op.cit.*, 629, *per* Lord Wilberforce.

[36] *Per* Lord Diplock, *Hadmor Productions* v. *Hamilton* [1982] 1 All E.R. 1042, 1055; and see *Davis* v. *Johnson, op. cit.*, 337 *per* Viscount Dilhorne.

[37] *R.* v. *Chief Immigration Officer, ex. p. Bibi* [1976] 3 All E.R. 843; *Surjit Kaur* v. *The Lord Advocate* [1981] S.L.T. 322.

[38] *Per* Lord Diplock, *Quazi* v. *Quazi* [1979] 3 W.L.R. 833, 840. See also *James Buchanan* v. *Babco Forwarding and Shipping* [1978] A.C. 141 and *Fothergill* v. *Monarch Airlines* [1980] 3 W.L.R. 209.

Frequently treaties are accompanied by *travaux preparatoires,* that is, "materials used in the preparation of, and having a formative influence on, the ultimately adopted form"[39] of the treaty; and where the treaty has been incorporated into domestic law, they may be referred to when two conditions are fulfilled: "first, that the material involved is public and accessible, and, secondly, that the travaux preparatoires clearly and indisputably point to a definite legislative intention."[40]

Thus arguments based upon the purpose of an Act may be derived from some kinds of policy document, but the weight to be attached to such arguments varies with the characteristics of the relevant document: its age, the extent of its research, the nature of its recommendations and their proximity to the Act in issue, the cogency of its reasoning and so on. As we shall see later, these considerations are relevant to the issue of reform in the process of interpretation.

## *GUIDELINES TO INTERPRETATION*

In addition to those arguments based upon the language and purpose of the Act, an interpretation may gain support from a variety of interpretative guidelines, some of which are statutory in origin, but most of which have been developed by the judiciary to deal with particular issues of interpretation. Despite this formal difference in their origins, these guidelines function in a broadly similar way, offering a variable degree of support for a proposed interpretation. In some instances this support may be conclusive of an issue of interpretation, but for the most part these guidelines are of persuasive value only. For the purposes of exposition we may differentiate between those guidelines that are directed to the language of the statute and those that relate more generally to the purpose of Parliament.

### LINGUISTIC GUIDELINES

To a limited extent, the interpretation of statutes is regulated by the Interpretation Act 1978. This Act, which consolidated the Interpretation Act 1889 and a number of other enactments, specifies the manner in which certain references in statutes are to be interpreted, for example, references to gender, number, distance, time of day and other enactments, and defines certain words in common use in

[39] Walker, *The Oxford Companion to Law* (1980), p. 1231.
[40] *Per* Lord Wilberforce, *Fothergill* v. *Monarch Airlines, op.cit.*, 220.

statutes, such as "Bank of England," "County Court," "Secretary of State" and "United Kingdom." However, many of its provisions are expressed to apply "unless the contrary intention appears," and it can be a matter of some judgment whether such intention is indeed expressed in a particular statute.[41] In addition to these statutory rules which apply to the interpretation of all statutes, unless the contrary intention appears, the judiciary have developed recognisably distinct approaches to the interpretation of particular classes of legislation, notably penal, fiscal and consolidating statutes; but here too there may be room for disagreement. For example, judges may disagree as to whether a penal statute is expressed in sufficiently clear terms as to pre-empt the presumption of *mens rea*[42]; or as to whether there is indeed a distinct approach to fiscal statutes or merely that in cases involving such legislation, the courts have applied the normal principles to different effect[43]; or as to whether the different kinds of consolidating Acts require different interpretative techniques.[44]

Indeterminacy also exists with regard to arguments derived from the statute within which the disputed words appear, and from statutes *in pari materia*. As Cross has written:

> "It is scarcely necessary to cite authority for the proposition that Acts must be construed as a whole. Guidance with regard to the meaning of a particular word or phrase may be found in other words and phrases in the same section or in other sections although the utility of an extensive consideration of other parts of the same statute will actually vary from case to case."[45]

A similar conclusion applies to arguments based upon such parts of a statute as the long and short titles, the preamble, cross-headings, side-notes and punctuation. Although some of the indeterminacy with regard to the appropriateness of using these as aids to interpretation has been removed as a result of recent judicial pronouncements,[46] the compelling nature of arguments based upon them remains a matter for the judgment of the deciding court.

[41] See *e.g.* Leitch, "Interpretation and the Interpretation Act 1978" [1980] Stat. L.R. 5, 9.

[42] See *e.g.* Maxwell, *The Interpretation of Statutes*, *op.cit.*, pp. 123–134.

[43] See Williams, "Taxing Statutes are Taxing Statutes" (1978) 41 M.L.R. 404 and *per contra*, Vinelott J. "The Interpretation of Fiscal Statutes" [1982] Stat. L.R.

[44] *e.g. Maunsell* v. *Olins*, *op.cit.*, 392, 393; *Farrell* v. *Alexander* [1977] A.C. 59, 82; and Newhouse, "Constructing and Consolidating" [1980] B.T.R. 102.

[45] *Statutory Interpretation*, *op.cit.*, p. 99.

[46] On the long and short titles and the preamble, see *A.G.* v. *Prince Augustus of Hanover* [1957] A.C. 436, 460–467, *per* Viscount Simonds, and *The Norwhale* [1975] 2 All E.R. 501, 507, *per* Brandon J.; on cross-headings and side (or marginal) notes, see

Sometimes a statute will provide that it is to be construed as one with an earlier statute, but even in the absence of such a provision reference may be made to statutes which are *in pari materia,* that is, which deal with the same person, thing or class as the one in issue. It is, however, impossible to generalise the circumstances under which a statute may be held firstly to be sufficiently *in pari materia,* (since similarity is a question of degree) and secondly to be specifically relevant to the interpretation of the word or phrase in the later statute.

Persuasive arguments may also be derived from the immediate statutory context of the disputed word(s). "The principles of language applicable to all written instruments apply to statutes as well. Many of the so called rules of interpretation or canons of construction are but ordinary principles of language."[47] At its most general, the implication of this observation is that statutes are to be read subject to the same principles of composition, syntax and grammar as a novel or a biography. English law has however developed a number of "rules" concerned with the interpretation of associated words, class words and excluded words.[48] Although it has been suggested that the first two of these rules are not needed for the interpretation of modern legislation, "since a modern draftsman ought not to draft in so sloppy a fashion as to make [them] applicable,"[49] they continue to figure in judicial interpretation. One example should indicate both the nature of these rules of linguistic methodology, and their open-endedness.

The *eiusdem generis* rule provides that where a section contains two or more expressions having specific meanings which share some characteristic from which it is possible to recognise them as being species of a single genus, any general words following those specific expressions are to be interpreted so as to include only those additional objects or persons which do not go beyond that genus.[50] This rule is no more than a particular application of the general

*D.P.P.* v. *Schildkamp* [1971] A.C. 1 and *R.* v. *Kelt* [1977] 3 All E.R. 1099, 1101–1102, *per* Scarman L.J.; and on punctuation see *Hanlon* v. *Law Society, op.cit.*, 815, *per* Lord Lowry.

[47] Driedger, *The Construction of Statutes, op.cit.*, p. 85.

[48] These guidelines are, like many others, artificially elevated by being rendered into Latin; respectively *noscitur a sociis, eiusdem generis* and *expressio unius est exclusio alterius.* Their indeterminate scope can be readily seen in any of the standard textbooks on the interpretation of statutes; *e.g.* Maxwell, *The Interpretation of Statutes, op.cit.*, pp. 289–306; Craies, *Statute Law, op.cit.*, pp. 178–186 and Odgers, *The Construction of Deeds and Statutes, op.cit.*, pp. 268–272.

[49] Bennion, *Statute Law, op.cit.*, pp. 83–84.

[50] A modern authoritative definition of the *eiusdem generis* guideline is contained in Lord Diplock's speech in *Quazi* v. *Quazi, op.cit.*, 839.

principles that words are read in context, and "derive colour from those which surrounded them"[51]; but the primary difficulty with the *eiusdem generis* rule is deciding whether the specific words belong to a class, and what that class might be.[52] For example, in *Derrick* v. *Commissioners of Customs and Excise*[53] the question arose whether reels of 35mm film which were admittedly pornographic could be forfeited under section 42 of the Customs Consolidation Act 1876 which prohibited the importation of "[I]ndecent or obscene prints, paintings, photographs, books, cards, lithographic and other engravings, or any other indecent or obscene articles." The importer argued that the words "or any other . . . articles" should be read *eiusdem generis* the preceding items and thus be restricted to articles whose indecent or obscene character could be discovered by visual inspection, which he thought was the element common to them. This interpretation would thus exclude the 35mm film, which was too small to be inspected visually without mechanical aid. The Divisional Court decided that the specific items were not members of any one class; the obscene character of a book could not be discovered "from a short and brief survey of its pages,"[54] unlike a print or a photograph. Accordingly there was no restriction and the film was correctly forfeited. Commenting on this and other cases involving the *eiusdem generis* rule, Lloyd remarks:

> "It should not be thought that this rule involves a purely rational process. The legislature intends other *like* instances to be covered by their general categorising clause, but what is a 'like' case may involve considerations of policy."[55]

Finally, an interpretation may be justified by an argument based on the authority of a definition or interpretation section in the statute. Most modern statutes contain such specific statutory guidelines; their primary function is to clarify words and phrases by assigning specific meanings to them, or by setting limits upon their normal meaning. A secondary function is to shorten statutes.[56]

So far as the interpretation of definition sections is concerned,

[51] *Per* Stamp L.J., *Bourne* v. *Norwich Crematorium Ltd.* [1967] 2 All E.R. 576, 578.

[52] The same difficulty arises in connection with the guideline relating to associated words, as Diplock L.J. observed in *Letang* v. *Cooper* [1965] 1 Q.B. 232, 247; "the maxim *noscitur a sociis* is always a treacherous one unless you know the *societas* to which the *socii* belong."

[53] [1972] 3 All E.R. 993.

[54] *Ibid.*, 995, *per* Lord Widgery L.J.

[55] *Introduction to Jurisprudence*, *op.cit.*, p. 867, n. 90.

[56] On the functions and types of definition commonly used in statutes, see Thornton, *Legislative Drafting* (2nd ed., 1979), pp. 165–170; Dickerson, *The Fundamentals of Legal Drafting* (1965), pp. 98–100 and Wilson, "The Complexity of Statutes" (1974) 37 M.L.R. 497.

they are part of the enactment in which they appear and must be treated as any other enacting part of it; but they do not

> "require you bodily to substitute the definitions for the words defined so as to enable you as a matter of grammar to treat words in the definitions as being antecedents of words, actually appearing later in the statutory provision. The definitions explain what the expressions mean in the statutory provision, but they remain outside that provision and for grammatical purposes leave unchanged in the provision the actual words that are there, even though they have become freighted with their statutory meanings."[57]

Moreover, many definitions are subject to the qualification, variously expressed, that they apply "unless the context otherwise requires."[58] Definitions may indeed complicate matters for interpreters, in particular where they specify novel or unusual meanings, and like the provisions which they qualify, they use language which "like all language, is capable of an almost infinite gradation of 'register',"[59] which in turn may pose further problems of interpretation.

## Guidelines as to the Purpose of Parliament

Statutes are not enacted in a legal vacuum. The draftsmen and the legislature take for granted a background of established legal principle and doctrine, and do not seek to formulate these in the text of an Act. This reliance (real or assumed) is acknowledged by the courts in a series of presumptions. We noted in Chapter 1 that some writers argue that legislation ought to meet certain conditions, such as generality or non-retroactivity. A classic exposition of such an argument is to be found in Fuller's notion of "the inner morality of law,"[60] where some of these conditions are expressed negatively, for example that statutory provisions should be neither self-contradictory, nor retroactive, nor require the impossible; others positively, for example that legislation should be clearly written and be constant through time. While we rejected such conditions as supplying adequate criteria upon which to define legislation, it should be observed that they find expression as presumptions of interpretation: the legislature, it is presumed, does not intend to

[57] *Per* Megarry J., *Number 20 Cannon Street Ltd.* v. *Singer & Friedlander Ltd.* [1974] 2 All E.R. 577, 586.

[58] See Jamieson, "The Doctrine of Free Expression in Legislative Drafting" [1981] Stat. L.R. 4, 6–16.

[59] *Per* Lord Simon, *Maunsell* v. *Olins, op.cit.*, 391.

[60] *The Morality of Law* (1969), Chap. 2; and see above, pp. 2–3.

enact conflicting provisions, but in that event the later takes precedence; statutes are presumed not to operate retrospectively; the legislature is presumed not to intend to enact what is inconvenient or unreasonable; words are to be used in their ordinary sense; and the legislature is presumed not to intend to change the law beyond that which it expressly declares.

It is important to stress that these guidelines are based upon the various role expectations of the institutions involved in the formulation and enactment of legislation: "they are expressions of fundamental principles governing the relations between Parliament, the executive and the courts."[61] We have already seen how the doctrine of parliamentary supremacy requires courts to interpret and not to "make" laws. But the courts also operate a number of presumptions which are based upon their expectations of the legislature. In addition to those mentioned in the previous paragraph, Parliament is presumed to know the law, to respect vested rights, to act in accordance with the principles of international law, and not to oust the jurisdiction of the courts. But like the other arguments described above, such guidelines are seldom conclusive; either the statute may expressly indicate that the presumption is inapplicable, or another guideline, or some other kind of argument, may conflict in a particular case.

## *ARGUMENTS BASED ON JUDICIAL AUTHORITY*

A judicial decision interpreting a word or phrase in a statute will in many cases constitute a conclusive argument when that same word or phrase is in issue on a subsequent occasion: "in our system the stare decisis rule applies as firmly to statute law as it does to the formulation of common law and equitable principles."[62] Nevertheless, because the statutory words are themselves of greater authority than the judicial gloss that is placed upon them, judicial interpretations cannot be regarded as *direct* substitutions for them.[63] Clearly, if a court misinterprets a word or phrase, its interpretation cannot be relied upon subsequently, but even where Parliament re-enacts a statutory provision which has been the subject of judicial interpretation, there is at best a presumption which a later court may make, that Parliament has also endorsed that interpretation.[64]

[61] Cross, *Statutory Interpretation, op.cit.*, p. 143.

[62] *Per* Lord Scarman, *Duport Steel* v. *Sirs, op.cit.*, 169; and see also Lord Diplock's speech in *Carter* v. *Bradbeer* [1975] 1 W.L.R. 1204, 1205–1207.

[63] See Lord Upjohn, *Ogden Industries Property Ltd.* v. *Lucas* [1970] A.C. 113, 127.

[64] *Per* Salmon L.J., *R.* v. *Bow Road Domestic Proceedings Court, ex. p. Adedigba* [1968] 2 Q.B. 572, 583.

An important limitation of arguments based on judicial authority is that a decision on the interpretation of one statute cannot generally be regarded as being applicable to the same word or phrase in a different statute.

> "A question of statutory construction is one in which the strict doctrine of precedent can only be of narrow application. The ratio decidendi of a judgment as to the meaning of particular words or combinations of words used in a particular statutory provision can have no more than a persuasive influence on a court which is called on to interpret the same word or combination of words appearing in some other statutory provision. It is not determinative of the meaning of that other provision. This is because the inherent flexibility of the English language may make it necessary for the interpreter to have recourse to a variety of aids or canons of construction, which are not merely lexicographical, in order to select from what may be a number of different meanings which the words as a matter of language are capable of bearing, the precise meaning in which the legislature intended them to be understood."[65]

## REFORM OF JUDICIAL INTERPRETATION

Apart from the fact that all of these forms of argument must be subordinated to the actual words of the statute, a commonly remarked feature of many of them, in particular the various guidelines to interpretation, is that they frequently offer conflicting advice. This dimension of normative ambiguity may permit judges, and other interpreters, to reach contradictory interpretations in a given case. On the other hand, the conventions may sometimes jointly support a particular interpretation, in which event they come close to having a dispositive effect. An apparently striking example of this effect is to be found in the judgment of Lord Simon of Glaisdale in *R.* v. *Governor of Pentonville Prison, ex p. Cheng.*[66] Cheng had been convicted in New York of the attempted murder of the Taiwanese vice-premier. He had escaped to London while on bail pending sentence, and the United States' government requested his extradition. Cheng's activities were aimed at in the overthrow of the Taiwan government, and were in no way directed against the government of the United States. He argued that his offence was "one of a political character" within section 3(1) of the Extradition

[65] *Per* Lord Diplock, *Carter* v. *Bradbeer, op.cit.,* 1206.
[66] [1973] A.C. 931 (Lord Wilberforce, conc.).

Act 1870, and was thus non-extraditable. The issue therefore concerned the scope of this statutory phrase; in particular whether it extended to cover criminal acts directed against the political control or government of a state other than that of the requesting state. In deciding that it did, Lord Simon relied upon a number of conventions of interpretation:

> "English law provides a number of guides to interpretation or 'canons of construction.' A difficulty arises that various canons could return conflicting answers, since English law has not yet authoritatively established any complete hierarchy among the canons. Fortunately, this presents no difficulty in the instant case, because all the many relevant canons of construction in question here return the same answer—in favour of the appellant's construction."[67]

His Lordship then invoked successively the primary or golden rule of construction, a construction according to historical setting and the mischief rule, and three presumptions—that against changes in the common law, that in favour of conformity with international law, and that against anomaly or absurdity. He concluded that "it must be rare for so many canons of statutory construction . . . to concur in pointing to a particular interpretation."[68] Lord Simon was however in the minority; a majority of the House, relying on the decision in *R.* v. *Governor of Brixton Prison, ex p. Schtraks*,[69] and on a more restricted view of the history of the Extradition Act, held that the words "of a political character" connoted opposition to the government or political control of the requesting state, and Cheng's appeal failed.

It is such stark variations in the authority and weight ascribed to the conventions of interpretation by individual judges, and in the results obtained in individual cases, that prompted Willis to write in 1938 that a court invokes "whichever of the rules produces a result which satisfies its sense of justice in the case before it"[70] and C.K. Allen to conclude that "[O]n the whole, it cannot be pretended that the principles of statutory interpretation form the most stable, consistent or logically satisfying part of our jurisprudence."[71] Attempts to systematise such principles as do exist have been, and

[67] *Ibid.*, 949–950.

[68] *Ibid.*, 959.

[69] [1964] A.C. 556.

[70] "Statutory Interpretation in a Nutshell" (1938) 16 Can. Bar. Rev. 1, 16. Not only do judges use different interpretative methods and arrive at different interpretations,

[71] *Law in the Making* (1964), p. 526.

continue to be, generally unsuccessful. This is so because the courts have for the most part, and notwithstanding some recent *dicta*, chosen neither to formulate the conditions under which the various forms of argument will be authoritative, nor to formulate priority rules in the event of conflict between them. This persistent characteristic of judicial practice has not however deterred writers from arguing that the judiciary ought to set about such formulations. Many suggestions for reform have been made, but the issue whether judicial practice ought to change is not a simple one. Two aspects of it may be identified, which have not always been sufficiently distinguished: *why* should judicial practice be different and *how* could it be different? These questions raise more general issues concerning the function of interpretation, the role of the judiciary and their relationship with the legislature.

## *WHY SHOULD JUDICIAL PRACTICE BE DIFFERENT?*

For the argument to be sustained that judicial practice ought to be different, it has to be shown that the changes advocated would in some way lead to better results than are encouraged by current practice. This in turn raises the question, *who* defines the criteria for improvement. Three groups who have an interest in the interpretation of statutes may be broadly differentiated: the government, the users and the judiciary themselves.

In Chapter 4 we saw that one of the principal obstacles to achieving legal effectiveness has been the "narrowly semantic approach to statutory construction" adopted by the judiciary "until the last decade or so."[72] It is thus commonly argued that the adoption of more systematically elaborated techniques of interpretation, coupled with a generally purposive approach, would make it easier for the draftsman to fulfil the expectations which the government has of him, so increasing the likelihood of its intentions being given legal effect. Leaving aside the question whether these prescriptions would in fact have their predicted consequences, it should be observed that despite public expressions by successive governments of dissatisfaction with particular judicial interpretations, their response has typically been to seek the enactment of further legislation intended to neutralise or to qualify the offending decision,[73] or more radically to remove the subject matter altogether

[72] *Per* Lord Diplock, *Fothergill* v. *Monarch Airlines*, *op.cit.*, 222.

[73] *e.g. Burmah Oil* v. *The Lord Advocate* [1965] A.C. 75 and the War Damage Act 1965; *Fisher* v. *Bell* [1961] 1 Q.B. 394 and the Restriction of Offensive Weapons Act 1961; and *Rookes* v. *Barnard* [1964] A.C. 1129 and the Trade Disputes Act 1965.

from the jurisdiction of the courts. It has not normally taken the form of attempts to impose rules regulating how statutes should be interpreted. Such attempts have been confined to the relatively limited compass of the Interpretation Acts.

Nor does it seem as though government wishes to modify the traditional understanding that it is part of the judiciary's function to develop such guidelines as they deem appropriate to the task of fulfilling their constitutional duty to interpret and give effect to Acts of Parliament, without further legislative intervention. Thus, whatever the substantive criticisms that could be levelled against the Interpretation of Legislation Bill which Lord Scarman sponsored in the 1980–81 session,[74] the Government, like its predecessors, did not appear to be overly enthusiastic about the principles behind such an initiative. This response may be contrasted with the widespread adoption in other common law jurisdictions, such as Canada,[75] New Zealand,[76] and more recently, Australia,[77] of statutory provisions advocating a purposive approach to the interpretation of statutes generally. Whether such provisions result in "better" interpretation, meaning, from the government's point of view, increased legal effectiveness, is a moot point; but the government in this country

[74] In the 1979–80 session Lord Scarman sponsored the Interpretation of Legislation Bill (H.L., Bill No. 141) which was entirely based on the draft Bill prepared by the Law Commissions in their report *The Interpretation of Statutes*, *op.cit.*, Appendix A. The Bill thus took no account of the criticisms in the Report of the Renton Committee, *The Preparation of Legislation*, Cmnd. 6053 (1975), Chap. 19 and was unfavourably received; see H.L. Deb., Vol. 405, ser. 5, cols. 276–306 (February 13, 1980). In the following session Lord Scarman introduced a similar measure which took account of some of the criticisms made the previous year; see below, n. 85.

[75] "The law shall be considered as always speaking, and whenever a matter or thing is expressed in the present tense, it shall be applied to the circumstances as they arise, so that effect may be given to the enactment and every part thereof according to its true spirit, intent and meaning." "Every enactment shall be deemed remedial, and shall be given such fair and liberal construction and interpretation as best ensures the attainment of its objects." Interpretation Act 1967–9 c.7, ss. 10 and 11.

[76] "Every Act, and every provision or enactment thereof, shall be deemed remedial, whether its immediate purport is to direct the doing of anything Parliament deems to be for the public good, or to prevent or punish the doing of anything it deems contrary to the public good, and shall accordingly receive such fair, large, and liberal construction and interpretation as will best ensure the attainment of the object of the Act and of such provisions according to its true intent, meaning and spirit." Acts Interpretation Act 1924, s. 5(*j*).

[77] "In the interpretation of a provision of an Act, a construction that would promote the purpose or object underlying the Act (whether that purpose or object is expressly stated in the Act or not) shall be preferred to a construction that would not promote that purpose or object." Acts Interpretation Act 1901, s. 15AA (1) as introduced by the Statute Law Revision Act 1981. See the commentary "Guidelines for Interpretation in Australia" [1981] Stat. L.R. 181.

appears to take the view that legal effectiveness is best ensured through its continued control over the preparation of legislation.

From the user's point of view, it is argued that if the judiciary employed more determinate and systematic interpretative methods, their decisions would be better informed and hence more predictable. Such consequences would obviously be beneficial to most of those giving or relying on legal advice. However, all of the proposals which have been made for reform along these lines suffer from the same flaw. The few hundred cases which reach the higher courts are almost always atypical; they are precisely those cases in which reasonable men may genuinely disagree about the outcome. The test of the interpretative methods employed by the judiciary is not whether they can reduce the number of atypical cases to nil, but whether, in the vast majority of disputes, litigated or not, the relevant interpreters share an understanding about the cogency and validity of particular arguments and acknowledge the results to which they lead. In open systems of reasoning, whether concerned with case-law or statutory rules, no comprehensive methodology could be devised which would be dispositive of all issues of interpretation. Although hard cases exemplify the limitations of interpretative practices, they do not provide the most fruitful starting place for devising a methodology which is to be of general application. Thus, "better" interpretative methods might, from the user's perspective, commence with a diagnosis of *issues* of interpretation; of their nature and their aetiology.[78] It is not especially helpful to ask for better interpretative practices until one has some idea of the nature of particular problems of interpretation which these practices are designed to resolve. In this respect, there is one obvious difficulty in relying on judicial pronouncements; that is, that there is no reason to suppose that it will be any easier for the user to derive clear rules concerning the diagnosis and resolution of problems of statutory interpretation from judicial decisions any more than it is easy to derive clear *rationes decidendi* concerning judge-made rules of law.

For the judiciary, a more systematic approach to interpretation would arguably have two kinds of effects. The more immediate is that under a well-articulated regime, they would be able to make better informed decisions, for example as to the admissibility, relevance and weight of policy documents and other statements of purpose and intended impact, since they would be in a position to determine more accurately why and in what circumstances recourse

[78] *e.g.* Twining and Miers, *How to Do Things with Rules*, *op.cit.*, Chap. 6 and Bennion, *op.cit.*, pp. 92 *et seq.*

to such material would be valuable. Of more importance, however may be the possible enhancement of their image, particularly in the eyes of the government, as interpreters. Although we conclude this chapter by predicting very little significant change in interpretative practices, this is not to say that they are beyond criticism, or that some improvement is not possible.[79]

## *HOW COULD JUDICIAL PRACTICE BE DIFFERENT?*

As we argued in the previous section, a key issue in the consideration of why judicial practice should be different is the identification of those who define the criteria of improvement. Similarly, in considering what options are available to improve judicial interpretation, it is important to focus on those who have the power to effect change. In this respect it must be recognised that the ultimate users are not, for the most part, in a position directly to influence the practices and methods of judicial interpretation; only the government and the judiciary themselves can do this.

### GOVERNMENT OPTIONS

By virtue of its almost complete control over the initiation, preparation and enactment of legislation, the government has a wide range of options which would arguably make the task of interpretation easier to perform. It could, for example, remove some of the pressure on the draftsman by planning more modest legislative programmes or by increasing the establishment and supporting services of the Office of Parliamentary Counsel. These initiatives would give the draftsmen more time to prepare a Bill and, possibly improve its intelligibility.[80] Secondly, the parliamentary stages could be utilised so as to allow more informed discussion with those principally affected by a Bill and thus to anticipate difficulties in interpretation, for example as was suggested by the 1978 Select Committee on Procedure,[81] or to permit scrutiny of the form and drafting of Bills.[82] Thirdly, the government could provide authoritative explanatory material to accompany the Act, possibly based upon the explanatory memoranda and notes of clauses which are

[79] See *e.g.* the criticisms developed in Murphy and Rawlings, "After the Ancien Regime: The Writing of Judgments in the House of Lords 1979/80" (1981) 44 M.L.R. 617, and (1982) 45 M.L.R. 34.

[80] See above, p. 93.

[81] See above, pp. 122–123.

[82] See above, pp. 134–136.

already provided to accompany the Bill through its parliamentary stages.[83] Finally, it could devote increased resources to consolidation, statute law revision and the publication of revised statutes.[84] As we have seen these various remedies have been proposed to deal with problems not directly concerned with the interpretation and implementation of statutes, and face practical and policy objections. Of more immediate relevance however is the suggestion that the government should support legislation establishing rules of interpretation of general application. In this connection, the criticisms of the Interpretation of Legislation Bill 1981 are of some importance, in that they raise issues which go beyond the particular proposals against which they were directed. Two objectives of Lord Scarman's Bill which received particular attention were the authorisation of explicit reliance on pre-legislative policy documents to ascertain the meaning of the provision in issue, and the establishment of the purposive approach as the main principle of interpretation.[85]

**Formal reliance on policy documents**

The first of these proposals goes some way beyond the present law, which confines explicit reliance upon such documents to the ascertainment of the *purpose* of the Act, expressly precluding their use to ascertain the *meaning* of specific provisions. Nevertheless, such an extension has some judicial support. So where the statutory provision being interpreted is a *verbatim* reproduction of the draft Bill prepared by a specially appointed committee, it may seem artificial to maintain a rule which precludes explicit consideration of the views which that committee expressed as to the provision's meaning.[86] As the Law Commissions recognised, however, such documents are always available to a judge if he chooses to consult them privately, so that the issue is not one of forbidding *any* use of them, but of controlling their formal and specific use as aids to interpretation.[87]

There were four main objections to the proposal to permit formal reliance on policy documents. The first was essentially pragmatic. As the Bill was not confined to judicial interpreters, it was argued

[83] See the proposals put forward by the Law Commissions, *op.cit.*, Chap. 6 and commented upon by the Report of the Renton Committee, *op.cit.*, Chap. 15.

[84] See above, pp. 93–94.

[85] The Interpretation of Legislation Bill 1981 (H.L., Bill No. 67). The Bill is set out in an Appendix, below pp. 245–246.

[86] *e.g.* Viscount Dilhorne and Lord Simon in *Black-Clawson International Ltd.* v. *Papierwerke Waldhof-Aschaffenburg*, *op.cit.*, 662–623 and 646–647.

[87] *The Interpretation of Statutes*, *op.cit.*, paras. 46–48.

that legal practitioners would feel obliged to obtain access to such documents in case they offered support for alternative interpretations. This in turn would increase their work load, which would ultimately be translated into lengthier proceedings and higher fees.[88] The second objection concerned the value to be obtained from such documents. Although reading a committee report may encourage an informed conception of the scheme of the Act which is based upon it, there are unlikely to be many occasions on which such a report will be directly relevant to specific problems of interpretation. This lack of direct relevance has traditionally been a factor relied upon to justify the limited formal consultation permitted by judicial practice, and is seen most forcefully in the recent reaffirmation of the formal exclusion of parliamentary debates from forensic settings. In the past judges have occasionally explicitly relied on Hansard,[89] and it is arguable that there are a few cases in which reference to debates would have prevented a court from arriving at an interpretation at odds with the legislature's intentions,[90] but such cases of obvious relevance will be rare. Parliamentary debate is seldom concerned, even in committee, with precise problems of interpretation, and is an unreliable indicator of the government's intentions. These conditions apply, though with less force, to pre-legislative policy documents. However, the limited reliance which may, under current practice, be placed upon such documents, raises the question, more starkly posed by the 1981 Bill, of what weight is to be attached to them. The Bill's answer, that this should be "no more than is appropriate in the circumstances"[91] was thought to introduce too great a degree of indeterminacy into an already uncertain exercise.[92]

[88] See H.L. Deb., Vol. 418, ser. 5, cols. 1341–4 (March 26, 1981): Lord Bledisloe, representing the views of the Law Society and the Bar Council.

[89] *e.g.* Lord Upjohn in *Beswick* v. *Beswick* [1968] A.C. 58, 105; Lord Denning M.R. in *Sagnata Investments Ltd.* v. *Norwich Corporation* [1971] 2 Q.B. 614, 624, *R.* v. *Local Commissioner for Administration, ex p. Bradford Metropolitan City Council* [1972] 2 W.L.R. 1, 26, and *Hadmor Productions Ltd.* v. *Hamilton* [1981] 2 All E.R. 724, 731 and 733, criticised on appeal to the House of Lords, see above, n. 36; and H.L. Deb., Vol. 405, ser. 5 cols. 303–304 (February 13, 1980).

[90] Cretney, "Judicial Blinkers" (1969) 119 N.L.J. 301.

[91] *Op.cit.*, clause 1(2).

[92] See H.L. Deb., Vol. 418, ser. 5, col. 69 (March 9, 1981) and cols. 1341–1344 (March 26, 1981). Of the equivalent clause in the 1980 Bill, Lord Elwyn-Jones said, "the task is to strike a balance between the advantages for a limited number of cases from enabling the courts to refer to material which might be relevant in a question of interpretation and the price to be paid for a change which might impose additional uncertainties on those who are concerned with the effect of legislation and with litigation and which would lead to extra work in the machinery of government;" H.L. Deb., Vol 405, ser. 5, col. 284 (February 13, 1980).

The third objection was that the proposal trespassed upon and confused the respective functions of the legislature and the judiciary. Although reports of Royal Commissions and other bodies may be discussed in Parliament, they cannot be amended and thus do not formally represent, as statutes do, the uniquely authoritative expression of the will of the legislature. The judiciary's function is to give effect to Acts of Parliament, not to some other documents which purport to explain their meaning[93]; and as we have seen, in the absence of further legislative intervention, judicial interpretation is uniquely authoritative, taking precedence over any interpretations preferred by other agencies.

These three objections were mainly voiced by representatives of certain users' groups, and by the judiciary; the final objection was more concerned with the implications of this proposal for the government. These were that the drafting process would be made very much more difficult as the draftsman would have to prepare a Bill knowing that those interpreting it would also be construing other documents with the statutory text to arrive at an understanding of it; that in consequence of this difficulty the completion of the legislative programme might be delayed; that difficulties would be created during the parliamentary stages of a Bill's progress, for reference would presumably be made to those documents which could be used as aids to interpretation, but with whose conclusions the government might not wholly agree, a difficulty compounded by the fact that there would be no opportunity to amend them; and finally that formal reliance on these documents might at best lead to increased uncertainty in interpretation and at worst frustrate the government's objective of achieving legal effectiveness.[94]

## Purposive interpretation

The second proposal, that in the event that two interpretations of a provision are reasonably possible, "a construction which would promote the general legislative purpose underlying the provision is to be preferred to a construction which would not,"[95] took its inspiration from similar provisions in New Zealand and Canada, but again raises more questions than it answers.[96] In the first place it

[93] *e.g.* Lords Reid and Wilberforce in *Black-Clawson International Ltd.* v. *Papierwerke Waldhof-Aschaffenburg, op.cit.*, 613–614 and 629–630; and Viscount Dilhorne, H.L. Deb., Vol. 405, ser. 5, col. 298 (February 13, 1980).

[94] See Lord Elwyn-Jones, H.L. Deb., *ibid.*, col. 286.

[95] Interpretation of Legislation Bill 1981, *op.cit.*, clause 2(1).

[96] Bennion, "Another reverse for the Law Commissions' Interpretation Bill" (1981) 131 N.L.J. 840.

may be objected that the proposition is either obvious, in that judges should and do endeavour to give effect to a statute according to its apparent purpose, or begs the question, when would a court *not* interpret a provision in such a way? One answer to this question appears to be: when the phraseology is such that it cannot reasonably sustain an interpretation based on the statute's purpose without some substantial addition, deletion or substitution of words or phrases. What is implicit in purposive interpretation is a shift in the conception of the judiciary's role. Co-operation is certainly one aspect of the traditional relationship between the judiciary and the legislature, but it is by no means the only one. The judiciary have taken their role to include restricting the application of statutory provisions, even where their apparent purpose is clear, if the words cannot sustain the interpretation necessary to give effect to that purpose. The question thus arises, in what circumstances, and to what extent, should judges reformulate such provisions to give effect to what they understand to be their purpose? Judges make law interstitially, within the limits of existing rules, precedents and doctrine; but it is of course notoriously difficult to define what these limits are in particular cases. As we saw earlier, what constitutes an appropriate line of reasoning for one judge will constitute "a naked usurpation of the legislative function" for another.[97] What should be recognised, however, is that a consciously pursued purposive approach entails some re-alignment of the relationship between the judiciary and the legislature, and so of the permissible limits of judicial action.

Secondly, the notion of "purpose" is itself problematic: a statutory provision and its purpose(s) should not be confused, for there are many instances in which they are not co-extensive; a provision may have a number of purposes, some direct, some indirect and some of which conflict; purposes may be as uncertain as the provision whose scope or meaning, or whose relationship with other provisions, they are hoped to clarify; and lastly, evidence of purposes may be difficult to ascertain. At the very least, if the principle of purposive interpretation were to become a more prominent feature of the judiciary's interpretative methods, some changes are arguably required in the rules governing access to evidence of such purpose.

Finally, it may be asked whether such a principle would make any appreciable difference to judicial practice and to its results; would it make interpretation "better"? At one level the answer must be in the affirmative: explicit discussion in courtrooms of the values, goals

[97] Above p. 181.

and policies being pursued by the legislature and expressed in the statute must surely generate more informed and more thoughtful interpretation. On the other hand, experience in New Zealand, where a statutory provision requiring such interpretation has been operative for well over fifty years, does not suggest that the outcome in individual cases has been especially consistent with the purpose of the provisions being interpreted.[98] The difficulty with such conclusions is that as evaluators of judicial decisions, we have no clear criteria by which we can judge whether *this* particular case *was* intended to fall within, or without, the apparent purpose of the provision. Like the judges who decided the case, we can only make an informed guess; and like them, we may disagree over the outcome.

Some of the arguments concerning the Interpretation of Legislation Bill thus raise basic questions concerning the role of the judiciary and their relationship with the legislature which have a significance beyond their immediate context. Essentially there is little which the government can do to direct judicial interpretation to its desired interpretation beyond constraining them by the words of the individial statute. So far as the Government was concerned the Bill held out little prospect of permanent advantage and in the short term arguably would have run counter to its continued interest in completing the legislative programme and achieving legal effectiveness. The Law Commissions' report, from which the 1980 Bill was drawn, "got across the departments and aroused the antagonism of the Parliamentary draftsmen,"[99] and even with some of the "offensive" clauses[1] omitted from the 1981 version, the Government's official position was one of neutrality.[2] In these circumstances the failure of the Bill was virtually inevitable.

## JUDICIAL OPTIONS

The judiciary obviously have far fewer options available to them to effect systematic changes in interpretative practices, although given the freedom that they enjoy under the present regime, it is difficult to see why they should want to initiate radical changes in them. Nevertheless, some senior members of the judiciary have attempted to synthesise the practices currently in use, but these attempts have

[98] See the Law Commissions, *The Interpretation of Statutes, op.cit.*, para. 33.

[99] H.L. Deb., Vol. 405, ser. 5, col. 300 (February 13, 1980).

[1] These were clauses 1(1)(*d*) and (*e*) and 4 of the 1980 Bill, see H.L. Deb., Vol. 405, ser. 5, col. 298 (February 13, 1980) and *ibid.*, Vol. 418, ser. 5, col. 75 (March 26, 1981).

[2] H.L. Deb., Vol. 418, ser. 5., col. 79 (March 9, 1981).

fallen short of the systematic and comprehensive code of interpretation which some writers have thought desirable. For example, Friedmann suggested in 1951 that statutes should be classified in an appropriate way and that different forms of argument be devised for each class.[3] The rudiments of such an approach exist in the differing approaches that the judiciary take towards some kind of statutes, and in such presumptions as those in favour of a strict construction of penal statutes, or of the interpretation of provisions consistent with international obligations, but the suggestion faces formidable difficulties. It would be virtually impossible to agree an appropriate basis for the purposes of classification. As we have seen, the 137 titles adopted by *Statutes in Force*, which classifies statutes by subject-matter, are not uncontroversial.[4] In addition, there are other bases upon which to classify statutes: such as the type of legal prescription, that is whether a provision confers a right or power or imposes a duty or liability, or in terms of what Summers has called the five basic "techniques of social management," namely penal, facultative, administrative – regulatory, remedial and public benefit conferral.[5] None of these classificatory devices is analytically, or in reality, water-tight. Even if it were possible to agree a basis for classification, it would not be possible to prescribe categorically that all cases falling within a particular class should always be treated according to the same interpretative methods. In the first place, there would always be some room for disagreement about how the facts of a particular case should be classified, and secondly, as we discussed in Chapter 4, our relative ignorance of fact makes it impossible to foresee, and hence to provide for, every future combination of circumstances. Moreover any system of interpretation along these lines would require changes in government practices with regard to the planning and implementation of the legislative programme and in the authoritative publication of statutes, and would require government approval of the interpretative methods devised.

A more popular option which has been increasingly canvassed since the United Kingdom's accession to the European Communities is that the courts should, of their own volition, generally adopt a purposive approach to interpretation. This argument is based upon the premise that the interpretation of Community law (and of statutes within the civil law tradition generally) is qualitatively

[3] See above, p. 8.
[4] *Ibid.*
[5] "The Technique Element in Law" (1971) 59 Calif. L.R. 733.

different from that to which courts in England and Wales, at least, are accustomed. This premise should be treated with some care.[6]

The European Court of Justice is uniquely entitled to give authoritative and final rulings on the interpretation of Community law. Accordingly, its interpretative methods and practices are likely to be regarded as models for domestic courts. The predominant, but by no means the only, interpretative methods it has employed are teleological—purposive—and schematic:

> "It is rare for an important judgment, settling a point of economic law, not to mention the opening Articles of the Treaty, which always enables the Court to view the case before it and the technical provision applying to it from a distance, and to elucidate facts and texts in the light of the objectives of the Community."[7]

The Court's "basic" methods of interpretation are thus firstly to ascertain the general objectives which the authors of the Treaty set for the matter under consideration, and secondly to establish the legislative scheme which they devised for the implementation of those objectives, both of which may involve consideration of the effectiveness of alternative interpretations.[8] These methods do not however exclude exegetical, or text-based analysis of Community legislation. The Court has always had recourse to such methods and in addition may justify its rulings by reference to the *ratio legis*, that is, to the proposition that individual provisions must be interpreted so as to be mutually consistent within the framework of the Treaty.

In view of the way in which judges of the European Court have themselves characterised its interpretative methods,[9] Lord Denning M.R.'s description in *H.P. Bulmer Ltd.* v. *Bollinger*, although widely cited, must be treated with some reservation:

> "The treaty is quite unlike any of the enactments to which we have become accustomed. . . . It lays down general principles. It expresses its aims and purposes. All in sentences of moderate length and commendable style. But it lacks precision. It uses words and phrases without defining what they mean. An

[6] *e.g.* Lord Wilberforce in *James Buchanan* v. *Babco Forwarding and Shipping* [1978] A.C. 141, 153; and H.L. Deb., Vol. 418, ser. 5, col. 74 (March 9, 1981). See generally, Herman, "A Study of the English Reaction to Continental Interpretive Techniques" (1981) 1 *Legal Studies* 165.

[7] Chevallier, "Methods and Reasoning of the European Court in its Interpretation of Community Law" (19641–5) 2 C.M.L.R. 21, 30. See also Bredimas, *Methods of Interpretation and Community Law* (1978).

[8] *Ibid.*

[9] Court of Justice of the European Communities, Judicial and Academic Conference 27–28 September 1976 (Luxembourg 1976).

> English lawyer would look for an interpretation clause, but he would look in vain. There is none. All the way through the treaty there are gaps and lacunae. These have to be filled in by the judges, or by regulations or directives. It is the European way. . . . Seeing these differences, what are the English courts to do when they are faced with a problem of interpretation? They must follow the European pattern. No longer must they examine the words in meticulous detail. No longer must they argue about the precise grammatical sense. They must look to the purpose or intent. To quote the words of the European Court in the *Da Costa* case; they must limit themselves to deducing from 'the wording and he spirit of the treaty the meaning of the Community rules . . . ' They must not confine themselves to the English text. . . . They must divine the spirit of the treaty and gain inspiration from it. If they find a gap, they must fill it as best they can. They must do what the framers of the instrument would have done if they had thought about it. So we must do the same."[10]

From this characterisation of the interpretation of Community legislation, a "dramatic contrast" with domestic methods which "is probably more impressive than exact,"[11] it is urged that teleological or purposive methods could in general be profitably employed. Apart from the difficulties mentioned earlier concerning the theory and practice of purposive interpretation, the analogy between the European Court and the courts in the United Kingdom is not complete. First, as Dagtoglou observes,[12] it is as misleading to think of judges in the European Court as enjoying unfettered freedom as it is to think of the judiciary in this country as being completely constrained to pedantic interpretation. Secondly, to reiterate a point made earlier in this chapter, drafting and interpretation may be seen as being intrinsically interrelated aspects of the communication of legislative policy, and as the drafting of the Treaties is generally of a different order from that typically to be found in Acts of Parliament, the scope for judicial enterprise is considerably limited.[13] The conclusion to which we are inevitably drawn is that, as with suggestions for reforming the drafting process, there is little likelihood of significant change in judicial practices unless changes

[10] [1974] 2 All E.R. 1226, 1237.

[11] Dagtoglou, "The English Judges and European Community Law" (1978) 37 C.L.J. 76, 78.

[12] *Ibid.*, p. 78.

[13] On the differences between English and European drafting techniques, see Smith, "Legislative Drafting: English and Continental" [1980] Stat.L.R. 14 and Warner, "European Community Legislation" [1982] Stat.L.R.

are also made to other stages of the legislative enterprise, in particular the preparation of Bills. Such changes are ultimately dependent on the government's perception that they will help to make its legislative initiatives legally more effective.

CHAPTER EIGHT

# THE IMPACT OF LEGISLATION

In this book we have so far adopted a formal approach to the concept of legislation; we have described the primary characteristics of the preparation, enactment and interpretation of those forms of legislation applicable in the United Kingdom. In this formal sense legislation may be seen as an authoritative and compelling definition of that which is lawful or unlawful. We have also seen that legislation is of primary significance in the management of the country's economic, political, social, administrative and legal affairs: government is carried on largely by virtue of statutory powers granted to Ministers and public authorities, and there are few aspects of the individual's life, or of the affairs of private organisations, which are not regulated by statute. In so far as legislation is principally addressed to public bodies, what we may call "government talking to itself," it defines and gives legitimacy to the structure, composition, powers, obligations and financing of such institutions as nationalised industries, other public corporations and administrative agencies. In so far as legislation is principally addressed to individuals and to private organisations, it defines or alters the legal significance of their actions, or of their legal relationships with one another or with the state.

Legislation thus creates, or gives legitimacy to, certain kinds of arrangements within, and between, these three groups, and may do so in a variety of ways. A statute may first give powers directly to individuals or to private organisations to make legally enforceable arrangements such as wills, contracts, conveyances of land, incorporation and trusts. Secondly, legislation may be enacted which confers powers on the government to regulate and control aspects of their behaviour, such as trading practices, the discharge of pollutants or the management of public houses, and to distribute benefits to them, such as the national insurance system or the procedures for giving grants to industry. Finally, legislation may be enacted to establish machinery for the settlement of disputes and the enforcement of rights and duties. Thus a primary aspect of legislation, for the government as well as for individuals and private organisations, is that it legitimates and facilitates their attempts to enforce the rights and duties arising from these substantive arrangements. Legislation can be coercive, and its selective use gives these groups the ability to coerce others.

Legislation is not, however, only concerned with *defining* the legal significance of actions: it is almost always intended by its sponsors to affect the way in which the activities of public bodies, individuals and private organisations are conducted, to affect the attitudes of those groups towards their conduct or their relationships with others, or both. The enactment of legislation is thus a purposeful activity, typically an aspect of the wider implementation of government policy which is intended to have an impact in the real world. Thus the question, with which this chapter is concerned, inevitably arises: under what conditions, and how, do people react to legislative rules and conform to or make use of them? In discussing this question we will consider first the distinction between the impact and the efficacy of legislation and the main reasons why these are difficult to measure; and secondly the principal variables which influence the impact of legislation.

## THE IMPACT AND THE EFFICACY OF LEGISLATION

Although there are many empirical studies which examine variously the impact and efficacy (or effectiveness) of particular laws in terms of their effects upon the target population, or upon other groups, including those implementing the law, and in terms of their production of consequences which may or may not have been foreseen, and which may or may not be desirable,[1] it is important to distinguish clearly between these two expressions. By *impact* we mean those consequences which the legislation brings about in practice. More fully, a "legal impact study" involves "an attempt to ascertain how a particular law affects the conduct and attitudes of those individuals, groups or other relevant units located in jurisdictions where that law is in force."[2]

Two features of impact studies deserve emphasis. First, they are concerned with *all* the consequences of the enactment of the legislation, a focus which is considerably broader than is to be found, for example, in compliance studies. These examine the extent to which a target population complies with or conforms to legal norms, typically those backed by criminal or analogous sanctions. As we have seen not all statutory provisions are of this kind; many confer powers to be exercised at the option of the individual. While it

[1] See further Tomasic, "The Sociology of Legislation" and Beerworth, "The Evaluation of Legislation" in *Legislation and Society in Australia* (Tomasic ed., 1980), pp. 35–90 and 67–87.

[2] Lempert, "Strategies of Research Design in the Legal Impact Study" (1966) 1 Law and Society Rev. 111.

is not particularly meaningful to talk of compliance with such facultative norms, this does not mean that provisions such as those empowering individuals to marry, to vote at local and national elections or to enter into hire-purchase agreements are devoid of significance for those individuals or for the community at large. Impact, in other words, is more than the degree of obedience; it is the total effect of the legislation on behaviour and attitudes, positive and negative.[3] Secondly, in so far as impact studies seek to show a causal connection between a legislative enactment and the subsequent behaviour of some individual(s), they are primarily descriptive exercises, although some evaluation of behaviour is necessarily involved.[4] Essentially, an examination of the impact of legislation describes the variables which condition individual responses to particular statutory provisions. Such an examination may be contrasted with the primarily evaluative exercise which is involved in the determination of the efficacy of legislation.

By *efficacy* we mean the extent to which the legislation brings about in practice the results which its sponsors—usually the government—intended or may be supposed to have intended. A statutory provision may be said to be efficacious when the behaviour or attitudes in question move in the desired direction.[5] Efficacy is thus a composite notion, depending in part on the measurement of the impact of the legislation and in part upon the identification of the real or supposed purposes for which the legislation was enacted. A statutory provision may have an impact on the behaviour of individuals, in the sense that they comply with, or make use of it, but such behaviour, though causally connected to the legislation will be judged inefficacious if it does not in practice realise the intended results. Thus the answer to the question, does the legislation work? is in part predicated on an answer to the question, how does the legislation affect behaviour and attitudes? Both questions raise difficult conceptual and methodological issues. In the following sections we deal with these issues firstly as they affect the measurement of the impact of legislation, before considering their relevance to the evaluation of its efficacy.

[3] This is adapted from Friedman, *The Legal System* (1975), p. 46.

[4] This is not to suggest that all such studies are descriptive; some may be concerned with testing hypotheses about the impact of legislative provisions.

[5] Friedman, *op.cit.*, p. 45. The *degree* of movement is obviously also a relevant factor.

## *THE MEASUREMENT OF IMPACT*

### CONCEPTUAL ISSUES

It is notoriously difficult to measure the impact of legislation. This is so because behavioural or attitudinal change following the enactment of legislation may be as much caused by the social conditions which prompted the legislation as by the legislation itself. Even where the impact of the legislation can be identified, that impact will be dependent upon the operation of other social variables such as the occupational grouping or class of those implementing or complying with the law, and the distribution of wealth and power among these groups. Accordingly it is neither possible to treat the implementation of legislation or the fact of compliance with it, as being uninfluenced by these variables, nor possible to describe the impact of legislation without also taking them into account.[6] Moreover, legislation frequently forms only one part of the implementation of policy. Many other institutional, financial and procedural arrangements may be made which will have a bearing upon the impact of the law. For example, the impact of the legislation may be affected by the existence and amount of publicity given to its provisions.

Thirdly, most of these studies have had a restricted focus. For the most part they have sought to describe the impact of laws backed by criminal sanctions, such as those proscribing murder, drinking and driving or writing bad cheques.[7] We hardly need to repeat the point that the criminal law paradigm by no means represents the whole range of legal forms. Among others, statutory provisions define public offices, facilitate private arrangements, confer benefits, distribute selective incentives, and establish remedies for injuries. However,

> "[C]hanges brought about by such laws are not likely to be formally stated, clearly identified or even widely acknowledged. Neither are they likely to be immediately obvious to the outside observer and at times even to *all* their sponsors. Further, in contrast to the bluntness of most command-type laws, these facilitative types of law are likely to pursue their ends by

[6] *e.g.* Griffiths, "Is Law Important?" (1979) 54 New York U.L.R. 339.

[7] *e.g.* Sellin, *The Death Penalty* (1959); Campbell and Ross "The Connecticut Crackdown on Speeding" (1968) 3 Law and Society Rev. 373; Ross, "Law, Science and Accidents: The British Road Safety Act of 1967" (1973) 2 J. Legal Studies 1; Brentel, *Some Potentialities of Experimental Jurisprudence as a New Branch of Social Science* (1957); and see generally Tomasic, *op.cit.*, p. 43, n.2.

altering the rates of activity rather than flatly prohibiting or requiring a prescribed pattern of behaviour."[8]

Research has focused on negative sanctions *inter alia* because it is relatively easier to measure the impact of a penalty such as a fine or a term of imprisonment than it is to measure the impact of positive sanctions, and because power-conferring rules are frequently directed to corporate institutions which are unwilling or unable to identify those who made the decision to use the law. Moreover the impact of these provisions is likely to be diffuse, long-term, susceptible to the influence of other legal and extra-legal variables and not otherwise methodologically easy to ascertain. This focus has an unfortunate effect. It obscures the occasions on which such rules are instrumental in encouraging behaviour, and it undervalues what is probably a more subtle means of control. Thus, notwithstanding the low visibility of some of the behaviour encouraged and permitted by these kinds of statutory provisions, they may be of considerable political, economic or social significance. This is so, for example, in the case of those provisions which define and give legitimacy to the decisions of public officials in central and local government, in nationalised industries and in administrative agencies. Similarly, in the management of trade and industry, "[P]rovisions which selectively and strategically distribute incentives . . . [are] an important feature of legal policy-making, especially in a market economy and contract-oriented society where so much of government action takes the form of exerting marginal influence and control over activities nominally within the 'private' sector."[9]

## METHODOLOGICAL ISSUES

The ideal research design would be one in which it is possible to hold constant all those variables which have potential impact upon the behaviour and attitudes in question, save the enactment of the legislation; for only in this way could an unambiguous measure of the causal connection, if any, between the legislation and any subsequent changes in the target population be derived. Such a design is manifestly not possible, and thus research which does attempt to measure impact has to be very carefully constructed so as

[8] Feeley, "The Concept of Laws in Social Science" (1976) 11 Law and Society Rev. 497, 508.

[9] *Ibid.*, p. 507. There is a growing body of literature that deals especially with regulatory legislation, some instances of which we refer to later in this chapter; see also Kagan, *Regulatory Justice* (1978); Diver, "A Theory of Regulatory Enforcement" (1980) 28 *Public Policy* 257; Wilson, "The Politics of Regulation" in *The Politics of Regulation* (Wilson, ed., 1980), p. 357; and Tomasic, *op.cit.*, p. 43, n.3.

to minimise the likelihood of "rival explanations which can explain away experimental effects and which can be used to rebut the presumption that the experimental variable caused any genuine change in individuals or groups."[10]

Undertaking research into the impact of legislation thus poses a number of problems. First, the behaviour may be of low visibility and so it is difficult to identify and to measure any variations in it. It is accordingly essential to be able to separate *this* behaviour from what would have happened if the legislation had not been enacted. Would there for example, have been any variation in incestuous behaviour if the Punishment of Incest Act 1908 had not been passed?[11] Where legislation is enacted as much to bring about changes in attitudes as changes in behaviour, for example in the case of sexual and racial discrimination, it will be necessary to devise instruments for measuring each change separately, and care will obviously have to be taken not to confuse behavioural with attitudinal change. Other factors that may threaten the internal validity of an impact study are that natural changes occur in individuals and groups over time; that the mere fact of being tested often produces a change in the behaviour of individuals or groups; that changes in data may result from changes in the way in which they are measured and recorded; and that other historical events may have been significant.[12]

Measuring the impact of legislation presupposes that we understand what particular forms of behaviour a provision describes. Accordingly, where it has been subject to interpretation which is formally or in practice authoritative, it is the impact of the provision *as interpreted* which should be measured, not just the original statutory formulation. This is of particular importance where the implementation of a statutory scheme is in the hands of officials who may, in time, place their own gloss upon the legislative text. As we shall see later, the attitudes and behaviour of the officials who implement legislation are important variables in influencing its impact.

## *THE EVALUATION OF EFFICACY*

As we have seen, a statutory provision may be judged efficacious if the consequences which it brings about in practice realise the purposes for which it was enacted. In so far as this evaluation

[10] Beerworth, *op.cit.*, p. 72.
[11] Lempert, *op.cit.*, p. 120.
[12] These factors are succinctly discussed by Beerworth, *op. cit.*, pp. 71–84.

depends initially on the measurement of the impact of the legislation, it raises the conceptual and methodological issues discussed above. There are, however, further difficulties. Before we discuss these it is pertinent to consider why research into the efficacy of legislation may be thought desirable.

The answer to this question is not, perhaps, surprising. Legislation is relied upon by government to assist in the implementation of complex policies which are intended to have far-reaching political, social and economic consequences. For example, legislation is intended to be instrumental in shaping behaviour and attitudes in such matters as town and country planning, health and safety at work, the dissemination of pornography and the sale of second-hand motor-vehicles. Therefore, "it is important that efforts be made to understand the reasons why legislation is enacted and once enacted, the reasons for its success or failure."[13] This knowledge in turn may be relied upon by government departments to avoid the enactment of costly and ineffective legislation, or to amend existing legislation so that it becomes more efficacious. Efficacy studies therefore, have a programmatic quality: they are designed to inform policy-makers of the consequences of the enactment of legislation so that they may make appropriate adjustments to the manner in which their policies are being, or will be, implemented.

The evaluation of efficacy is therefore in the first instance dependent upon the possibility that the purposes for which the statute was enacted can be clearly identified, and herein lies a major difficulty. A distinguishing feature of efficacy studies is that they characterise the focus of their research as the gap between "the law in the books" and "the law in action."[14] Their approach "is to posit the *ideal* or *goal* of a law as a benchmark and then measure the extent to which it is or is not being met. . . . Implicit in such an approach is the assumption that it is possible to identify, operationalise and measure the goals of the law."[15]

As we saw in Chapter 7, the idea that an understanding of the purpose of a statute can help to resolve issues of interpretation is problematic.[16] This is so because legislation is typically enacted to serve a number of purposes which may be formulated at varying levels of generality, be short or long term in conception, be more or less clearly stated, or in the case of older legislation, difficult to

[13] Tomasic, *op.cit.*, p. 9.

[14] These phrases were coined by Pound (1910) 44 American L.R. 12, but are now standard features of the vocabulary of efficacy.

[15] Feeley, *op.cit.*, pp. 498–499.

[16] See above, pp. 204–206.

ascertain. A serious criticism which has been made of efficacy studies is that they generally do not treat the identification of purposes as problematic. "Typically legal goals tend to be viewed as self-evident or easily identified and are posited without much ado."[17] Accordingly there is likely to be substantial variation in the way in which research studies formulate their conception of "the" purpose(s) of the legislation. Nor do these considerations exhaust the problem of identifying purposes. Where legislation has been in force for some time, and especially where its implementation is the responsibility of an official agency, it is likely that its original purposes will have undergone modification, or will have been subordinated to other purposes which the agency considers important. For example, a standard way of coping with failure is to modify one's goals, and so an agency which perceives that the legislation for which it is responsible is inefficacious may reformulate its purposes in more modest terms.

Implicit in this discussion of purpose is an instrumental view of legislation. It is of course the case that particular statutes or statutory provisions, for example, those concerning the consumption of alcoholic liquor[18] or the provision of compensation to individuals made redundant as a result of a closed-shop agreement,[19] may be enacted as much to reaffirm values held by their sponsors as to affect the conduct of the target populations. Such symbolic effect need not depend upon implementation; rather the mere fact of enactment realises this purpose. Although it is important to recognise that legislation may have symbolic as well as instrumental purposes, care must be taken not to present these two as independent aspects of the legislative enterprise. Such an approach "neglects the vital possibility of dynamic interplay between them. Instrumental objectives may be recosted when their realisation comes to entail an inflated symbolic price, and vice versa; there is no *a priori* reason to assume that attitudes towards the instrumental and symbolic ramifications of projected legislation will always run in the same direction."[20] The difficulty which the recognition of interplay between symbolic and instrumental purposes raises relates to the evaluation of efficacy.[21]

[17] Feeley, *op.cit.*, p. 499.

[18] Gusfield, *Symbolic Crusade, Status Politics and the American Temperance Movement* (1963) and "Moral Passage; The Symbolic Process in Public Designations of Deviance" (1967) 15 Social Problems 175 are standard works. See also Duster, *The Legislation of Morality* (1970).

[19] Employment Act 1981, s. 1 and Sched. 1.

[20] Carson, "Symbolic and Instrumental Dimensions of Early Factory Legislation" in *Crime, Criminology and Public Policy* (Hood ed., 1975), p. 107, 136.

[21] *e.g.* Abel, "Redirecting Social Studies of Law" (1980) 14 Law and Society Rev. 805, and Black, "The Boundaries of Legal Sociology" (1972) 81 Y.L.J. 1086.

Assuming that analysis could disentangle these two aspects of the enactment of a particular statute, and further, specify the nature of their relationship, no criteria exist for evaluating the symbolic efficacy of legislation.

Evaluating the instrumental efficacy of legislation is also problematic. Since efficacy is usually posited in terms of the extent to which the impact of legislation realises its purposes, a number of tasks present themselves. First it is necessary, though as we have seen inherently difficult, to develop a relatively precise conception of what those purposes may be. Secondly, it is necessary to agree on criteria for determining whether the consequences which are brought about by the legislation were intended or unintended; if intended the degree to which they realise its purposes; and if unintended whether they are good or bad. The judgment that legislation is efficacious is thus a complex one; for it depends also on what is considered to be an acceptable balance between the realisation of its purposes on the one hand and the quantity and quality of unintended consequences on the other.[22]

Legislation which realises its purposes and at the same time produces a few beneficial consequences will probably be judged a success; *a fortiori*, if it produces many beneficial, though unintended, consequences. Conversely, legislation which fails to realise its purposes and at the same time produces many bad consequences will almost invariably be judged a failure. In between these extremes lies a range of permutations, in which the judgment that a statutory provision is (in)efficacious will depend on a complex set of criteria, many of which will necessarily involve conceptions of value which are not amenable to empirical study.[23] This is not to deny that there are provisions defining recognisably hard and fast behaviour which are amenable to empirical testing, for example those specifying particular procedures or expressing the conditions of legal action in terms of external and quantifiable characteristics such as age, income, expenditure or marital status. It is much less easy to assess the efficacy of legislation controlling such matters as industrial relations, trade practices or agreements between landlords and tenants, as these typically rely, as we saw in Chapter 4, on open-ended expressions such as "reasonableness" "good faith" or "fairness."[24] However, the fact that it may not be possible to

[22] Examples of studies that have analysed the efficacy of legislation in terms which include the production of unintended consequences are Barnett, *The Politics of Legislation – The Rent Act 1957* (1969); Gunningham, *Pollution, Social Interest and the Law* (1974); and Paulus, *The Search for Pure Food* (1974).

[23] See in particular Black, "The Boundaries of Legal Sociology," *op.cit.*

[24] See above, pp. 91–92.

evaluate the efficacy of legislation *exactly* does not prevent us from identifying either the principal variables that influence the impact of legislation on behaviour and attitudes, or the gross outcome patterns that may be generally characterised as success or failure.

## PRINCIPAL VARIABLES INFLUENCING THE IMPACT OF LEGISLATION

Given the great range of conceptual and empirical literature concerned with this matter, it would be impossible in a short space to give even a resumé of the major contributions.[25] This section instead aims to identify, and to give some examples of, the principal variables which influence the impact of legislation. Thus it is not directly concerned with efficacy, although many of these variables will necessarily influence the extent to which the consequences which are brought about in practice realise the purposes of the legislation. We consider these variables under two broad headings; the characteristics of the legislation itself, and the characteristics of those to whom it is addressed.

### *THE CHARACTERISTICS OF THE LEGISLATION*

The legal prescriptions defined in legislation may be expressed in many ways varying from the simple prohibition of conduct, such as theft or speeding, to the complex regulatory mechanisms governing such matters as consumer credit or the management of casinos. Direct prohibitions and regulatory controls are but two examples of a wide range of legal forms that includes, as we have seen, those facilitating the making of legally enforceable private arrangements, those conferring benefits upon groups and individuals, and those establishing institutions and procedures whereby grievances may be remedied. Any one or more of these forms may be used in a given statute, but the key issues so far as the impact of legislation is concerned are first, whether the primary form that is selected is appropriate to the behaviour or attitudes being addressed; secondly, whether, and what kind of, incentives or disincentives are formally

[25] Many of these are, however, discussed or reproduced in books which, in addition to addressing questions of impact, consider the broader questions of the impact of law on society, and vice versa; *e.g.* Simon, *The Sociology of Law* (1968); Friedman and Macaulay (eds.), *Law and the Behavioural Sciences* (2nd ed., 1977); Schwartz and Skolnick (eds.), *Society and the Legal Order* (1970); Black and Mileski (eds.), *The Social Organisation of Law* (1973); Akers and Hawkins, *Law and Control in Society* (1975); and Aubert (ed.), *Sociology of Law* (1969).

provided by the legislation to encourage implementation or compliance; and thirdly, whether where relevant, some means of enforcement is provided. We shall consider each of these general issues in turn.

## THE FORM OF THE LEGISLATION

As we noted in Chapter 1, a primary feature of the form of a public general Act is its extreme elasticity[26]; it may accommodate many different kinds of legal prescription upon an infinite variety of subjects. In some cases the same policy objective may be approached in a variety of ways; and as we have indicated, a key issue is whether the approach chosen is appropriate to realising the statute's purposes. For example, although it is relatively easy to formulate direct prohibitions where the intention is to suppress or limit an aspect of individual behaviour, the criminal law is, for many purposes, a blunt instrument. This is particularly so in the case of consensual acts, or victimless crime, such as prostitution, drug abuse or the supply of pornography. It is difficult for law enforcement agencies to obtain direct evidence of the commission of such offences, since they will normally occur in private, and it is unlikely that any of the participants will inform upon the others. This difficulty may in turn lead to the adoption of enforcement practices which are themselves potentially unlawful.

Some of the problems associated with formulating effective prohibitions on conduct are illustrated by the difficulties that are predicted in the implementation of the Indecent Displays (Control) Act 1981.[27] The Act makes the public display of indecent matter a criminal offence. In common with other statutes directed to the suppression of obscene or indecent publications, the Act seeks to identify some matter whose offensive aspects are not capable of being expressed in objective terms. Whereas the offensive aspects of other "environmental pollutants" such as chemical waste can be quantified, and thus clearly identifiable standards can be specified in the legislation or regulations made under it, the primary and secondary enforcers of this Act—the police, and magistrates, judges and juries—will have to rely on subjective criteria, such as that which they find "shocking, disgusting and revolting."[28] It is hardly

[26] See above, p. 7.

[27] *e.g.* Stone, "Out of Sight, Out of Mind. The Indecent Displays (Control) Act 1981" (1982) 45 M.L.R. 62.

[28] *Per* Lord Reid, *R.* v. *Knuller (Publishing etc.)* [1973] A.C. 435, 458; criteria which were repeatedly quoted with approval during the debates on the Bill; H.C. Deb., Vol. 997, ser. 5, cols. 1165–1209 (January 30, 1981).

necessary to point out the relativity of judgments such as these, and the consequent difficulties that are created for those trying to establish in criminal proceedings that the matter complained of was indecent. From the point of view of shop-keepers too, the indeterminacy of this expression creates difficulties. Suppose a newsagent wishes to avail himself of that provision in the Act which permits indecent displays to be maintained in a "part of the shop to which the public can only gain access by passing beyond an adequate warning notice" which must, and only, read:

> "WARNING
> Persons passing beyond this notice will find material on display which they may consider indecent. No admittance to persons under 18 years of age."[29]

Although some publications may be "obviously" indecent, there will inevitably be marginal cases in which a shopkeeper will be uncertain how the police, or, since a prosecution under the Act may be brought by anyone, one of his customers, might react.

A principal motivation behind the Act was to suppress "cinema club posters, bookshop and sex shop window displays that people cannot avoid seeing as they walk along the pavement."[30] Viewed as a matter of environmental control, there are other legal forms which might be thought more appropriate to the purpose. One such, which was tabled by the Government as an amendment to the Local Government (Miscellaneous Provisions) Act 1982 is to give local authorities the power to licence sex shops and cinemas; their decision whether to grant or refuse a licence being based upon conditions specified in the legislation.[31] For many people this form of control is unwelcome even if it is potentially more efficacious than the criminal law, for it gives legitimacy to some manifestations of what they perceive as undesirable. In this sense the symbolic

[29] ss. 1(3)(*b*) and (6).

[30] H.C. Deb., Vol. 997, ser. 5, col. 1167 (January 30, 1981).

[31] See s. 1 of the Act. In considering whether to grant a licence, a local authority may take into account the character of the locality, the number of sex shops and cinemas within it and the use to be made of the premises. In granting a licence the authority may specify the hours of opening, and impose conditions on advertising, displays, and the visibility of the interior from the street. The Government also supported a private Member's Bill that sought to bring cinema "clubs" within the provisions of the Cinematograph Acts, which specify that films may be exhibited to the public only if the premises are licensed by the local authority. Under the Cinematograph (Amendment) Bill 1981, those provisions apply to all exhibitions for *private gain*, which it is hoped will cover all apparently "private" clubs; H.C. Deb., Vol. 17, ser. 6, cols. 1215–1261 (February 12, 1982).

purposes of the direct prohibition of indecent displays may have been more important to the Act's sponsors than its possible instrumental effects.

Efforts at social control range from such explicit commands envisaging particular kinds of behaviour by individuals to more diffuse regulation of corporate behaviour. Here, as Cranston has argued,

> "broad statutory standards, backed by criminal sanctions, are generally an unsophisticated instrument of regulation and not always a satisfactory method of controlling the undesirable features of modern business practices . . . Broad standards prohibit all forms of a particular activity, including what may be desirable, on the assumption that the latter is outweighed by what is objectionable. Not only does economic analysis often seriously undermine this argument, but the fact that many more law-abiding people than evildoers are thus affected dictates a policy of relatively low maximum penalties which clearly lessens the deterrent effect."[32]

More common forms of prescription for controlling corporate behaviour are administrative regulation and licensing. Through administrative regulation, companies can be required to disclose information about their processes, products and practices; to adhere to and maintain specific standards of quality, performance or durability; and to refrain from certain kinds of trade practice such as unfair competition, monopoly, fraud or price-fixing. The impact of such prescriptions will vary not only according to their appropriateness to the behaviour in question. For example, information on food labels must be accurate and thus will in many cases use technical expressions not familiar to the ordinary consumer. Setting realistic standards of quality and performance may be problematic, and like the regulation of trade practices, these will require expert enforcement which may be costly in terms of technology and manpower.

Licensing is a powerful tool frequently used by modern government to control a wide variety of activities. For example, licensing may be used to develop natural resources such as oil, gas or minerals; to allocate scarce resources such as airline routes, radio and television frequencies; to authorise occupational practices such

[32] "Reform through Legislation: the Dimension of Legislative Technique" (1979) 73 Northwestern University L.R. 873; reprinted in Tomasic, *op.cit.*, p. 88, 93–94. We draw on Cranston's analysis in the following two paragraphs. See also his study, *Regulating Business: Law and Consumer Agencies* (1979); and Kadish, "Some Observations on the Use of Criminal Sanctions in Enforcing Economic Regulations" (1963) 30 U. Chi. L.R. 423.

as dentistry, medicine and pharmacy; and for sumptuary purposes, such as the management of public houses, restaurants and cinemas. "The theory is that prior approval permits beneficial activity but at the same time prevents its harmful consequences . . . [C]losely related is the consideration that it is frequently easier to prevent an activity than to undo the undesirable consequences associated with it."[33] Thus, when establishing a licensing system, the government may specify: the kind of person (corporate or otherwise) who may hold a licence; the criteria which have to be met in the condition of the premises or equipment used in the activity; the quality of the processes, products and practices of the activity; and some of its financial aspects. The primary threat in the event of non-compliance is that the licence will be revoked and thus the holder will be denied the right to continue the activity at all.

## INCENTIVES AND DISINCENTIVES

Although they may take a variety of forms, the legal consequences which attach to behaviour may be broadly distinguished in terms of those which encourage and those which discourage the target population from continuing it. The most obvious example of a disincentive is the penalty which attaches to a conviction for a criminal offence, usually of a financial nature, though it may equally entail deprivation of liberty or some other restriction on freedom of movement. Financial punishments also attach to some breaches of the civil law, for example, under the income tax legislation, and the award of damages is a more general instance of such a sanction. Sometimes both criminal and civil sanctions may be used to penalise behaviour; for example, a person who deliberately misrepresents some material fact in the formation of a contract may be liable both to a criminal fine or imprisonment, and to a civil action for damages. Other, less obvious, negative sanctions will be provided in legislation which establishes a system of licensing or registration, typically disqualification, licence revocation or deregistration for single or repeated instances of non-compliance.

Like negative sanctions, positive sanctions assume a variety of forms and serve a variety of purposes. Sometimes they are enacted simply as ends in themselves, for example, the provision of compensation for industrial injury and disease or the security given to a statutory tenant; on other occasions they may be intended to serve some further purpose, for example, the provision of grants or development subsidies specifically linked to the relocation of industry. These benefits may be available as of right or at the

[33] Cranston, *ibid.*, p. 100.

discretion of officials; further, some of them may be subject to conditions which the beneficiary must subsequently fulfill. Occasionally, the threat of their refusal may be made to induce compliance with desired patterns of behaviour, as in the enforcement by the Labour Government between 1975 and 1979 of its "voluntary" pay policy. "During this period, an undertaking to comply with the policy was a prerequisite for the award of almost all government contracts and of some government industrial assistance; a known breach of the policy disqualified from consideration for such contracts and assistance; compliance with the policy was secured for the future as a legally enforceable term thereof."[34]

The impact of incentives and disincentives, which may in addition to their instrumental effects also have a symbolic dimension, for example being married or not being a bankrupt, may alternatively be analysed in terms of the audience to whom they are addressed. Thus on the one hand there are those primarily addressed to the exercise of individual choice, such as the prohibitions against the use of personal violence, the licensing of firearms or motor vehicles, personal taxation, social security benefits and rent and rate rebates. On the other hand are those which aim at an aggregate response, for example in the commercial and professional behaviour of estate agents, solicitors or credit agencies, or in the safety practices of industry. The incentives and disincentives contained in the legislation dealing with these matters "is analogous to raising and lowering prices to affect demand, consumption and substitution."[35]

## THE MEANS OF, AND PROCEDURES FOR, ENFORCEMENT

A fundamental aspect of the impact of legislation is that

> "*the law is most often set in motion by people who apply it to themselves and to each other without benefit of explicit mobilization of legal institutions*. The basic aspect of law and social control is found in the unheralded response and anticipations to abstract sets of rules which intrude in the lives of people or get them to do things they would not otherwise do. The mobilized cases, in a sense, may represent little more than the occasional failure or

[34] Daintith, "Regulation by Contract: The New Prerogative" (1979) 32 C.L.P. 41. See also Ferguson and Page, "Pay Restraints: The Legal Constraints" (1978) 128 N.L.J. 515, and above p. 17.

[35] Feeley, *op.cit.*, p. 511.

rupture in an otherwise largely invisible or at least self-applying system of control."[36]

Nevertheless, clearly not all claims and disputes are settled without resort, at least to the threat of legal proceedings. A key issue in the selection of one legal form over another is thus whether, where relevant, adequate means exist to enforce the legislation. In this sense the means of enforcement connotes the institutional and procedural arrangements that are available for realising, finally and authoritatively, the legal prescriptions contained in the legislation. These arrangements essentially take the form of the original and appellate jurisdiction of the higher courts or of the specialised jurisdiction of nominate tribunals and administrative agencies, and sometimes of both. Enforcement thus includes an individual suing for damages in the High Court, or seeking a judicial divorce, a decision by the Gaming Board to refuse an application for a consent certificate to manage a casino, an industrial tribunal deciding that an employee was unfairly dismissed, or a local authority prosecuting in a magistrates' court someone who has demolished a listed building.

A distinction which is frequently made in this context is that between private and public enforcement. Private enforcement typically takes the form of an individual seeking a personal remedy, for example, damages, an injunction, or specific performance, while public enforcement takes the form of an individual acting in an official capacity, and on behalf of a public authority. In this latter sense an official is not seeking any remedy for himself or the authority, but is rather concerned to uphold the law in a general way while at the same time enforcing the particular legal norms. To succeed in his action for damages, a private individual also needs to prove that a relevant norm has been departed from, but he is not usually interested in the educative or public impact of a decision.

Private enforcement is, for reasons which we shall discuss below, likely to be idiosyncratic and haphazard. These are qualities that are not conducive to the systematic enforcement of provisions concerning such matters as the disposal of chemical waste, the collection of taxes or the availability of firearms. Partly for this reason, the private enforcement of legislation is substantially confined both in law and in practice to provisions that are facultative in form, such as those concerning family affairs, the disposition of real and personal property or the formation and management of companies. But this is not to say that the public have no interest in these matters. Legislation exists which has a direct impact on the formation,

[36] *Ibid.*, p. 515, original emphasis.

conditions, and performance of such private arrangements; moreover, these features may be directly questioned or enforced by public agencies such as the Commission for Racial Equality or the Office of Fair Trading.[37]

It would be impossible to describe the whole range of public enforcement of legislation, although we have given instances in this and other chapters. As indicated earlier in this section the key issue is whether the means of enforcement are adequate. By this we do not mean *how* the legislation is enforced, for example, vigorously, haphazardly or corruptly, but whether the system of enforcement is apt to control the behaviour in question. This involves such matters as the structure, composition and powers of the enforcing agency, its level of technical or professional expertise, and the nature of the sanctions that it can invoke in the event of non-compliance. A classic example of inadequate means was the failure of the government to establish an appropriate system for enforcing those provisions of the Betting, Gaming and Lotteries Act 1960 which dealt with casinos. Gaming houses had been illegal for centuries, but in response to the recommendations of a Royal Commission which had reported in 1951,[38] the 1960 Act essentially made gaming lawful provided that no charge was made to the participants. The purpose was to prevent commercial exploitation of the casino market, but partly because the provisions were facultative and specified no criteria of eligibility to manage a casino, and partly because no specialised enforcement agency was established, this part of the Act quickly proved to be a failure for the government's policy. Within a few years, there were well over a thousand casino clubs, mostly in London, many of which openly exploited their clientele and some of which were fronts for criminal organisations. The difficulties which were encountered by the police in enforcing the standard criminal prohibitions were considerable:

> "There were inadequate restrictions on advertising. The police had no right of entry to the clubs and such checks as they sought to apply through criminal proceedings were slow and enabled gaming promoters to switch the basis on which they operated—to stay one jump ahead of the law. In the meantime casino proprietors sought to enlarge their clientele through the provision of cabaret, dancing and refreshments, and places of

[37] See Lempert, "Norm-making in Social Exchange" (1972) 7 Law and Society Rev. 1; and Gifford "Communication of Legal Standards" (1970–1971) 56 Cornell L.R. 409.

[38] Report of the Royal Commission on Betting, Lotteries and Gaming, Cmd. 8190 (1951).

> entertainment provided gaming. Special charter flights brought visitors from abroad for what were known as gambling junkets. Large numbers of people, including the young, were introduced by promoters to casino games which were conducted in conditions of minimum supervision with no standardised rules of play. There is little doubt that in a number of clubs gamblers stood to be exploited and there was growing concern that criminals were becoming active in casino operations."[39]

The government's response was to introduce the much more elaborate controls contained in the Gaming Act 1968, enforced by an agency with very wide and virtually unfettered powers. Even so, as recent events have shown, the financial rewards in casino gaming are so vast—the total amount of money exchanged for chips in 126 casinos in 1980–1981 was £930,000,000—and the temptation for corruption and abuse of the law so great, that the Gaming Board has continued to seek further powers to make the means of enforcement adequate in its view to the task of regulating the industry.[40]

In addition to the institutional arrangements that exist, the enforcement of a provision will be influenced by the procedural rules which govern how investigations may be conducted. For example, in the enforcement of the criminal law, the general law of search, seizure, detention and arrest is of importance, as are particular rules contained in the legislation. For example, the Commission for Racial Equality, which is responsible for the implemetation of the Race Relations Acts, has maintained for some time that the offence of publishing material or using threatening, abusive or insulting language in circumstances where "hatred is likely to be stirred up against any racial group in Great Britain" has very little impact because, unlike the offence upon which it is modelled, it is not an arrestable offence.[41] Accordingly the police have no power to take immediate action to terminate a racially inflammatory speech unless they think that a breach of the peace is likely. Similarly, as we saw in connection with the Betting, Gaming and Lotteries Act 1960, the fact that the police had no right of entry to gaming clubs was one reason why the Act failed to curb the commercial exploitation of casinos.

A notorious example of procedural rules specific to a particular statute causing problems for an enforcement agency is the breathalyser provisions relating to the offence of driving with excess alcohol

[39] Report of the Royal Commission on Gambling, Cmnd. 7200 (1978), para. 16.8.

[40] Report of the Gaming Board for Great Britain 1981, (1982; H.C. 324), para. 34; and see Miers, "The Mismanagement of Casino Gaming" (1981) 21 B.J. Crim. 79.

[41] s. 5A (1) of the Public Order Act 1936, as introduced by s. 70 of the Race Relations Act 1976.

in the blood-stream. These provisions are of a technical nature, concerning how, and after what preliminaries the breathalyser is to be inflated. Although the courts take a generally lenient view of the implementation of these procedures by the police, if not complied with, they can still result in the acquittal of a person who was palpably over the limit.[42] The critical issue that is raised by these cases is how such acquittals affect the realisation of the legislation's purposes.

Lastly, the general rules governing the conduct of civil and criminal trials and tribunal hearings, such as those relating to the burden of proof, the admissibility of evidence, the testimony of expert witnesses, or the discovery of documents will have significance for the enforcement of legislation. Particular statutes may modify the effect of these rules to the advantage of one or other party. For example, in section 24 of the Trade Descriptions Act 1968 and section 28 of the Misuse of Drugs Act 1971, the legal burden of proof as distinct from the less onerous evidential burden, is specifically placed upon the defendant who wishes to establish certain defences to criminal charges. Both the Sex Discrimination Act 1975 and the Race Relations Act 1976 provide that their respective enforcement agencies, the Equal Opportunities Commission and the Commission for Racial Equality, may take action to help a person who considers he has been discriminated against to establish his case.[43] One way in which a court or tribunal may conclude that there is a case is if it appears "that the respondent deliberately, and without reasonable cause, omitted to reply within a reasonable period [to questions put to him by the person aggrieved] or that his reply is evasive or equivocal." The court or tribunal may then "draw any inference from that fact that it considers just and equitable to draw, including an inference that he committed an unlawful act."[44] These provisions go some way beyond the normal rules governing the conclusions or inferences that a court may draw from a defendant's testimony.

These modifications may be seen to facilitate enforcement; on the other hand provisions may be included in the legislation which inhibit enforcement. Within the criminal law, there are a number of offences which may be prosecuted only with the consent of the Attorney-General or of the Director of Public Prosecutions. The object is to curb prosecutions that might be contrary to the public

[42] *e.g. Sheridan* v. *Webster* [1980] R.T.R. 349; *Price* v. *Davies* [1979] R.T.R. 204; *Attorney General's Reference (No. 1 of 1978)* [1978] R.T.R. 377; *Kaplan* [1978] R.T.R. 119, and *Parsley* v. *Beard* [1978] R.T.R. 263.

[43] ss. 74 and 65 respectively.

[44] ss. 74(2)(*b*) and 65(2)(*b*) respectively.

interest, spurious or vindictive, such as for the dissemination of official secrets or for taking indecent photographs of children.[45] The offence of inciting racial hatred mentioned earlier may also, for similar reasons, be prosecuted only with the consent of the Attorney-General. It has been argued that the excessively cautious exercise of this power, which has led to only 21 prosecutions since 1976, has seriously weakened the impact of the legislation.[46]

## *THE CHARACTERISTICS OF THOSE ADDRESSED BY THE LEGISLATION*

The Road Traffic Act 1972 defines a range of driving offences and specifies various penalties to be imposed upon those who are convicted of them; the Misrepresentation Act 1967 entitles the victim of an innocent misrepresentation to rescind a contract; the Lotteries and Amusements Act 1976 permits local authorities to promote lotteries; the Licensed Premises (Exclusion of Certain Persons) Act 1980 empowers a court to prohibit a person who has been convicted of an offence committed on licensed premises from entering those premises without the express consent of the licensee. The question which these examples raise, and with which we are concerned in this section, is what disposes the various addressees of legislative provisions—motorists, the police, magistrates and judges, businessmen and others who make contracts, local authorities or publicans—to implement or to comply with them. As these simple examples show, a statute will frequently address a variety of individuals (although the draftsman will usually have one particular audience in mind when preparing a Bill, typically those who will be implementing it in an official capacity), but for the purpose of illustrating the variables which influence their implementation of, or compliance with, its provisions, a distinction may be drawn between individuals acting in a private capacity, whether singly or as a member of a group such as a company, and individuals acting in a public capacity. This distinction mirrors that between private and public enforcement which we made earlier.

### PRIVATE IMPLEMENTATION AND COMPLIANCE

The first and most obvious reason why individuals implement legislation, that is, put it into practice, for example by invoking,

[45] Official Secrets Act 1911, s. 8, (consent of the Attorney-General); and Protection of Children Act 1978, s. 1*(b)*(consent of the D.P.P.).

[46] s. 5A(5) of the Public Order Act 1936, *op.cit.;* and see Runnymede Trust, *Incitement to Racial Hatred* (1982).

enforcing or relying upon it in connection with a claim, dispute or other legal transaction, or comply with legislation, that is, modify or relinquish their behaviour or attitudes in the face of the actual or potential implementation of negative sanctions against them, is a material one: they stand to gain or to lose something of value to them. But it is equally obviously the case that the mere fact of the formal provision of positive or negative sanctions is frequently insufficient to encourage or to discourage the behaviour or attitudes defined in the legislation. Thus, individuals will typically balance the costs of implementing the legislation against the benefits which may formally accrue to them; and conversely, they will balance the costs of non-compliance with the legislation against the benefits of continued disobedience.

A critical issue for the impact of legislation is therefore to identify the individual's perception of what are the costs and benefits relevant to any given action, and of what constitutes an appropriate balance between them. These perceptions will obviously be based upon a wide variety of factors, such as the age, class, race, sex and socio-economic status of the individual; whether he is acting alone or as a member of a group, and if so, the size, composition, legal status, objectives and values of the group and its relationship with others; the nature of the behaviour or attitudes defined by the legislation, in particular whether they are of economic significance, socially acceptable or deeply entrenched within particular groups; and the characteristics of the legislation itself, which, as we have seen, includes such matters as the form of the legal prescription, the kind of incentives and disincentives formally provided, and the means of, and procedures for, enforcement. In addition, the manner of the legislation's enforcement, for example, in the practices of the responsible public agency, is, as we shall see, a significant variable. As we do not have the space to deal with all of these variables in detail, the following paragraphs are confined to giving examples of how some of them may affect the impact of legislation.

Although legislation may formally provide substantial benefits, potential users may settle for less because they perceive that the financial costs of implementation balance or possibly outweigh the chance of realising them to the full. Factors such as the availability of legal aid, the duration, uncertainty and costs of trials and appeals, and the feasibility of enforcing judgments are standard components of this decision, in which the perception and judgment of professional legal advisers is frequently critical.[47] The phenomenon of

[47] See Lempert, "Mobilising Private Law: An Introductory Essay" (1976) 11 Law and Society Rev. 173.

cases being settled out of court is a familiar one.[48] On the other hand, large public companies are better placed than single individuals to sustain the costs of legal action, in particular of enforcement in the courts. This is of significance when individual consumers wish to obtain remedies against manufacturers or retailers for defective goods or services.

The expense of going to law is a principal reason why, as studies by Macaulay in the United States[49] and Beale and Dugdale in England[50] show, not all businessmen routinely rely upon the general law of contract in their commercial dealings, in particular where they have cheaper and more effective ways of accomplishing the goals which might otherwise be secured by the law, such as bringing pressure to bear through the commercial community. The possibility of the chronic non-use of contract law by one segment of the population who might be thought to have reason to use it, raises a more general issue concerning the purposes, and hence the efficacy, of facultative law, including that enacted as legislation. For example, by providing a testator with the knowledge that, properly executed, his will will give effect to his intentions following his death, is it the law's purpose to encourage more testacy? Alternatively, should the law be thought of as being indifferent as between the use and non-use of such legislation? The answer is important, *inter alia*, because non-use may be indicative of inefficacy.[51]

Besides the direct financial costs of implementing the law, other less easily quantifiable factors inhibiting its use may be considered as "costs" by individuals. For example, some of the primary reasons given for the consistent and substantial under-claiming of such benefits as rent and rates rebates and social security payments, are that some individuals are hostile to, or wary of becoming involved in, "the law"; dislike opening up aspects of their lives to official scrutiny and evaluation; find legal and bureaucratic procedures off-putting or incomprehensible; or resent being regarded as objects for "charity" or as being of low income or status.

Thus in so far as the private implementation of legislation is typically motivated by material considerations, the impact of those provisions which primarily serve the interests of individuals and groups, that is, those that are facultative or that confer benefits, is likely to be haphazard, unconcerted, easily compromised or weakened according to a wide variety of variables influencing a

[48] Ross, *Settled out of Court* (2nd ed., 1980) is a classic study of this phenomenon.
[49] "Non-contractual Relations in Business" (1963) 28 American Sociological Rev. 45.
[50] "Contracts between Businessmen: Planning and the Use of Contractual Remedies" (1975) 2 B.J.L.S. 45.
[51] *e.g.* Posner, *Economic Analysis of Law* (2nd ed., 1977) Chap.4.

person's judgment of what is good for him or the group to which he belongs.

Whether acting alone or in concert with others, an individual makes a similar judgment when faced with legislation requiring him to modify or relinquish his behaviour or attitudes, such as that which prescribes the standards that are to be met in the performance of some activity, or which more directly prohibits conduct. Any theory of sanctions is based on the assumption that when the costs of engaging in an activity are increased by legal intervention beyond the benefits that accrue from it, the participants will modify their behaviour or attitudes so as to achieve a balance that is still favourable to them (and which, it is of course hoped, realises the purposes of the legislation). This balance may be expressed in terms of achieving an equivalence between the benefits of compliance (for example, not having one's behaviour subject to official investigation) against the benefits of non-compliance (for example, greater profit margins or reduced losses); or more commonly, and what amounts to the same thing, the costs of compliance (for example, the allocation of resources to meet the law's requirements) against the costs of non-compliance (for example, the imposition of a fine upon conviction for an offence).[52]

Thus, compliance costs may be expressed in terms of the opportunities that are lost to the individual to adopt or maintain alternative forms of behaviour, as a result of his decision to obey the law. These opportunity costs may frequently be expressed in financial terms. For example, many manufacturing companies regard the money that they spend on pollution control as "dead money" as it brings no direct benefits in terms of increased output or more efficient use of plant and labour.[53] They are therefore reluctant to redirect their resources of capital and income from projects designed to yield such benefits, such as research and development, or to acquire additional funds in the form of interest-bearing loans, in order to comply with the law. In addition, compliance will involve administrative costs for the company, for example in keeping up to date with the law's requirements and monitoring their own performance in meeting them.[54] Under this formulation, the benefits

[52] See generally Posner, *Economic Analysis of Law, op.cit.*, and Veljanovski, "The Economic Approach to Law: A Critical Introduction" (1980) 7 B.J.L.S. 158.

[53] Hawkins, "Bargain and Bluff: Compliance Strategy and Deterrence in the Enforcement of Regulation" (October 1982) 4 Law and Policy Q.

[54] It is important in this connection to be clear as to what is involved in compliance. While the statutory provisions formally specify what standards are to be met, or what conduct is prohibited, a typical feature of enforcement practices is the mediation of these norms. In other words, enforcement agents will in many instances settle for action which, though it is not complete compliance with the law,

that accrue to a company from compliance with the law, for example the absence of investigation by enforcement officials and of the possibility of prosecution, may be counted as opportunity costs in that such benefits are achieved at the expense of using resources, for example to instal pollution controls, that were available for alternative investment, for example, research and development. Of course, not all the alternatives which an individual must forgo if he is to comply with the law have direct financial equivalents. For example, a motorist who enjoys speeding incurs an opportunity cost by observing the speed limit, but it is difficult to express that pleasure, although it is valued by the motorist, in quantitative terms.[55]

For many individuals the primary costs of non-compliance are the costs that they incur in attempting to avoid the legal consequences of their behaviour. These too are opportunity costs in the sense that as a result of an individual's decision to disobey the law, the resources consumed by these costs are no longer available for alternative use. The benefits of non-compliance, for example, personal convenience, minimising losses or the maintenance of valued social or individual practices, are thus achieved at the expense of diverting resources away from other uses to such tasks as avoiding detection and prosecution, obtaining legal advice, and paying court costs and fines.[56]

The general deterrent effect of negative sanctions, that is, the likelihood that some or all of the target population will, as a result of hearing about them or seeing them in operation, modify or relinquish their behaviour or attitudes, is in the first instance dependent upon the individuals' perception of the risk of being detected.[57] This perception will obviously vary between different individuals. Professional shoplifters will probably know a good deal more than amateurs, and certainly more than those acting on impulse, of the risks of being caught. Nevertheless, what deters is not the objective risk of being caught, but the perceived risk, which may indeed be based upon uninformed speculation about the rates of

is nevertheless indicative of a willingness to comply. Compliance is an elastic concept in practice, and a company which is polluting a river may be able to reduce its opportunity costs and thus maintain some benefits from continued disobedience by negotiating with the enforcement agency a time-table for the installation of pollution controls in its plant or machinery. See Hawkins, *ibid.*, and below, p.235.

55 *e.g.* Pearce (ed.), *The Valuation of Social Cost* (1978).

56 On the application of economic analysis to criminal law see Becker, "Crime and Punishment: An Economic Approach" (1968) 76 J. Political Economy 169 and Stigler, "The Optimum Enforcement of Laws" (1970) 78 J. Political Economy 526.

57 *e.g.* Andenaes, "The General Preventive Effects of Punishment" (1966) 114 U.Pa.L.R. 949.

detection of particular crimes. Many studies show that, within the range of natural variation, it is the likelihood of detection, rather than the severity of the sanction, which is the more potent inhibitor.[58] This does not mean that the level of response is irrelevant: for corporate bodies, levels of fines for non-compliance, for example, in the case of the Control of Pollution Act 1974, are regarded as derisory.[59] On the other hand, very severe sanctions do not necessarily yield a proportionately greater degree of compliance. There is, in other words, no simple linear relationship between the level of punishments and the incidence of the sanctioned behaviour: a fine of £1000 will not necessarily be twice as effective as one of £500.

> "We expect some sort of curvilinear relationship, a gradual flattening out. At some point, new inputs of fine will produce less and less new compliance, and one may or may not reach a zero effect. This is because, as compliance rises, there are fewer people to affect, and these few are the most difficult cases."[60]

A further variable is the speed with which penalties may be imposed upon offenders. A small penalty imposed after the commission of an offence, may apart from any benefits for the enforcement agency in terms of its enforcement costs arguably be more of a deterrent than a greater, but more distant, penalty.[61]

A great deal of research is focused upon the general deterrent effect of punishments, in particular capital punishment.[62] A point which deserves emphasis is that this effect is achieved so long as *some* people are deterred. To be effective it is not necessary that a punishment should deter all of the target population, nor does the fact that some individuals continue to offend mean that it is ineffective. All that general deterrence implies is that a rise in actual costs will produce more deterred and less forbidden behaviour.[63] However, the fact that individuals may continue to offend raises a further issue, namely how much non-compliance will be tolerable? For example, more non-compliance will be tolerated in the case of traffic offences because they are generally minor deviations that cause little harm, than in the case of murder; but in other instances, determining what constitutes the limits of acceptable deviance will be a very much more complex and potentially controversial social and political decision.

[58] Antunes and Hunt, "The Impact of Certainty and Severity of Punishment on Levels of Crime in American States" (1973) 64 J. Crim. L. and Criminology 486.

[59] Hawkins, *op.cit.*

[60] Friedman, *op.cit.*, p. 76.

[61] Singer, "Psychological Studies of Punishment" (1970) 58 Calif. L.R. 405.

[62] See generally Friedman, *op.cit.*, p. 70, n.6 and pp. 73–75.

[63] Friedman, *ibid.*, p. 75.

Apart from the threat of punishment implicit in general deterrence, deterrence theory assumes that a person who is actually punished will be similarly deterred on subsequent occasions. In Packer's definition, special deterrence means "the asserted propensity [of punishment] to reduce or eliminate the commission of future crimes by the person being punished."[64] As in the case of general deterrence, there is a vast literature which examines the efficacy of punishments according to various criteria, typically rates of recidivism.[65] We cannot begin to summarise even the main conclusions of this research here; but clearly the efficacy of special deterrence will depend on many of the factors we mentioned earlier such as the social variables affecting the individual who is punished, and the degree of his commitment to the prohibited conduct,[66] and more specifically, on the nature of the punishment itself, for example whether it involves the deprivation of property or of liberty, its severity and the conditions under which it was imposed and served. A person whose illegal income far exceeds the occasional fines that he must pay when convicted of an offence will, other things being equal, continue to disobey the law.

Material considerations are not however the only motivation for implementing or complying with the law. In the past, groups such as the London Society for the Reformation of Manners in the late seventeenth century and the London Society for the Suppression of Vice in the late eighteenth and early nineteenth centuries saw it as their duty to prosecute offences relating to gambling, vagrancy, swearing and profaning the Sabbath.[67] Nowadays other moral entrepreneurs such as the National Viewers' and Listeners' Association or the National Association for Freedom actively pursue legal proceedings because they believe the implementation of the statutory norms concerning, for example, blasphemy[68] or aspects of employment law,[69] to be good for everyone. Other groups, for example, the N.S.P.C.C. or R.S.P.C.A. act more concertedly to enforce the law, usually with the co-operation of official agencies

[64] *The Limits of the Criminal Sanction* (1968), p. 45.

[65] *e.g.* Brody, *The Effectiveness of Sentencing: A Review of the Literature* (1976).

[66] Chambliss, "Types of Deviance and the Effectiveness of Legal Sanctions" [1967] Wisconsin L.R. 703.

[67] Radzinowicz aptly called these and similar groups, "evangelical police;" *A History of English Criminal Law and its Administration from 1750*, Vol. I (1948), p. 160.

[68] The N.V.L.A. was active in the prosecution of the editor of *Gay News* for publishing a blasphemous poem; *R.* v. *Lemon* [1979] A.C. 617.

[69] The N.A.F. was active in the unsuccessful attempt by Mr. John Gouriet to obtain an injunction to restrain contemplated breaches of the Post Office Act by postal workers; *Gouriet* v. *Union of Post Office Workers* [1978] A.C. 435.

such as local authorities and the police.[70] Because they are motivated by moral or social, rather than material, aspirations, these organisations will be more inclined to enforce the law than will an individual, for whom the costs may be a disincentive. Although class actions are unknown in this country, the support given by, for example, consumer or tenants' associations to actions against manufacturers, retailers, finance companies or landlords, or by trade unions to actions against employers, may function in a similar way. Even in the absence of a decision in favour of an individual plaintiff creating a precedent for subsequent claims, the actions of committed organisations may eventually benefit other individuals who wish, for more material reasons, to implement the law.

Similarly, we may distinguish from those who comply with the law because they agree with its substance, or because they perceive the costs of non-compliance to outweigh its benefits, those who comply because it *is* the law.[71] "Legitimacy refers to a general attitude toward law, or the rules, or the system. It is not an attitude about the content of rules, nor about their rightness or wrongness in an ethical sense. Judgments about legitimacy are judgments about form, procedure, or source—about the way the rule came about or about the rule-maker and *his* authority."[72]

A deep moral or political conviction in the legitimacy of the law may induce individuals to comply with particular prescriptions notwithstanding their opposition to them; a conviction that may be supported by appeals to values such as political or social stability, wise government or democracy which would be threatened by disobedience.[73] Legitimacy thus expresses an attitude which is learned or unlearned, and which may be reinforced or undermined by the actions of the government, officials, friends and others. But even where an individual generally recognises the legitimacy of the law, this does not mean that he will be compliant on all occasions; as with the decision to balance the costs and benefits of engaging in or continuing some unlawful behaviour, individuals also balance the value they attach to obedience and the authority of the law as a

[70] The N.S.P.C.C. is authorised by the Home Secretary to bring care proceedings under s. 1(1) of the Children and Young Persons Act 1969.

[71] *e.g.* the official reaction of the Freight Transport Association to the compulsory introduction of the tachograph in lorries over 3½ tonnes and some passenger vehicles, following its strenuous objections over a ten-year period: "I don't think our attitudes have changed, apart from the fact that the law is the law." *The Guardian*, December 31, 1981.

[72] Friedman, *op.cit.*, p. 112. See Gerth and Mills, *From Max Weber* (1946), pp. 79, 294–5 and Weber, *On Law and Economy in Society* (Rheinstein ed., 1954), pp. xxxix–xl and 334–336.

[73] Singer, *Democracy and Disobedience* (1973).

general proposition, against the value they attach to the behaviour in question. A particularly well-known instance of non-compliance in circumstances in which many people rejected both the substance *and* the legitimacy of legislation was the opposition of the trade unions to the Industrial Relations Act 1971[74]; an opposition repeated more recently, though so far with less dramatic consequences, in connection with the provisions of the Employment Act 1981.[75]

## PUBLIC IMPLEMENTATION

The primary difference between private and public implementation is that a public body is usually under a duty, which may in particular cases be enforceable, to implement the legislation for which it is responsible. In addition bureaucracies typically generate their own imperatives and values which include the realisation of the purposes for which they were established, although how these are conceived may vary in time and between bodies exercising similar jurisdiction.[76] In some instances an authority will be under a duty to act in response to claims or information supplied by individuals, groups or other public bodies; others, such as the Commission for Racial Equality, have the power to initiate investigations.[77] In both instances, and in the many other permutations of obligation and power which may be defined by statute in the creation of a public body, some element of discretion will exist as to how a claim should be dealt with or in what circumstances investigations ought to be initiated, or indeed as to how many other aspects of its authority should be exercised. The question which is thus prompted is, what motivates the exercise of offical discretion?[78] We cannot attempt a comprehensive answer to this, but as a general proposition, discretion will be exercised by an authority's officials in part according to their conception of its functions both as the means of implementing a particular statutory scheme, and as a bureaucracy,

[74] Anderman "Attempts to Impose Legal Restrictions on Trade Unions in Britain 1968–1974" in *The Imposition of Law* (Burman and Harrell-Bond eds., 1979), p. 237.

[75] *The Guardian,* January 21, 1982.

[76] On the effect that a bureaucracy's own imperatives and values may have on its implementation of a statutory scheme, see generally, Niskanen, *Bureaucracy and Representative Government* (1971).

[77] These alternatives echo the distinction between reactive and proactive enforcement policies; see Black and Reiss, "Patterns of behaviour in police and citizen transactions" in U.S. President's Commission on Law Enforcement and Administration of Justice, *Studies of Crime and Law Enforcement in Major Metropolitan Areas,* Vol. II (1967), p. 1.

[78] *e.g.* Kadish and Kadish, *Discretion to Disobey* (1976).

and in part according to their perception of the costs and benefits of implementing it in individual cases.

Conceptions of how a statutory scheme should be implemented will of course vary. For example, there are significantly different and potentially conflicting ways in which the functions of the distribution of direct financial benefits by the Department of Health and Social Security or of professional time and expertise to such matters as mental health, child care, and other aspects of social work by local authorities, may be conceived: the protection of individuals, of families, or of social interests more generally; the rehabilitation of individuals within either of these two groups; of the correction of undesirable or disabling characteristics; or more radically, as political action.[79] Although necessarily general, such conceptions inform the actions of officials by providing them with criteria for deciding *when* it is appropriate to put a provision into practice, and what constitutes appropriate implementation. In particular, they provide criteria for determining what constitutes *successful* implementation.

Some writers have argued that a function of the distribution and allocation of the benefits of the welfare state is to achieve a degree of compliance on the part of individual recipients.[80] Compliance strategy is however more frequently associated with legislation that imposes duties upon individuals, and may be contrasted with a second style of enforcement, penalty systems.[81]

Compliance systems tend to be dominant in the implementation of regulatory control, in such areas as pollution, health and safety at work, consumer protection and debt collection.[82] Here the responsible authority is concerned to secure conformity to standards; rule breaking is perceived not so much as criminal but as a problem to be solved by the concerted efforts of the authority and the individual concerned. As these problems tend to be both open-ended and continuous, and in some cases to be morally problematic, a central feature of compliance systems in their high degree of exchange of information, consultation, negotiation and bargaining. Accordingly it is quite common for a public authority such as an inspectorate not to enforce the law for every violation that it observes or is reported to it, if it perceives that this would alienate the population with whose conduct it is concerned. Indeed, the invocation of criminal sanctions

[79] *e.g.* Heraud, *Sociology and Social Work* (1971).

[80] *e.g.* Donzelot, *The Policing of Families* (1980), and Garland, "The Welfare Sanction" (1981) 8 B.J.L.S. 29.

[81] Reiss, *The Policing of Organisational Life* (1980), discussed in Hawkins, *Environment and Enforcement: The Social Construction of Pollution* (1982), Chap. 1.

[82] *e.g.* Rock, *Making People Pay* (1973).

may be regarded by the authority not just as a last resort, occasionally threatened but employed only exceptionally, but as indicative of a *failure* on its part to secure compliance with the relevant standards through a process of social mediation. The closeness of such co-operative relationships has led some writers to argue that a regulatory body may become "captured" by those it is supposedly regulating; that is, that it identifies with, and to some extent protects their interests.[83]

The principal objective of a penalty system on the other hand, is retribution; the application of a punishment for harm done. Whereas non-compliance in a regulatory context tends to be perceived as a continuing problem, criminal acts tend to be seen as discrete events, inviting enforcement which is compressed in time and which typically involves the exercise of simple choices—to arrest or not, to charge or not—rather than a choice among options. This is not to say that bargaining and negotiation have no place in penalty systems. For example, police enforcement practices with regard to prostitutes or vagrants may resemble a compliance strategy, and the police may be sensitive to their image with a particular population in one area of their jurisdiction, but these are not standard features of the enforcement of the criminal law.[84] Here prosecution is a standard step in a patterned response; failure occurs when *other* institutions do not perceive the events as disclosing a criminal offence, or they impose punishments that are perceived as too lenient. There are many studies describing and analysing the different conceptions that police authorities have of successful policing, and the consequential costs and benefits of pursuing these various goals.[85]

As in the case of private implementation, costs and benefits can be assessed in both qualitative and quantitative terms. A simple example of quantitative cost is the amount of money it takes to implement the law in any one instance. For example, the DHSS estimated that as a result of the reinterpretation of section 8(2)(*a*) of the Pensions Increase Act 1971 by Treasury Counsel, some 300,000 files would need to be reviewed, involving two years' work for about

[83] *e.g.* Bernstein, *Regulating Business by Independent Commission* (1955) and Bardach, *The Implementation Game: What Happens After a Bill Becomes a Law* (1977).

[84] See also discussions of the enforcement of white-collar crime; *e.g.* Geis (ed.), *White-Collar Criminal* (1968); Packer, *op.cit.*, p. 354; and Carson, "White-collar crime and the enforcement of factory legislation" (1970) 10 B.J. Crim. 383.

[85] *e.g.* Alderson, *Policing Freedom* (1979); Banton, *The Policeman in the Community* (1964); Bittner, "The Police on Skid-Row" (1967) 32 *American Sociological Review* 699; Black, *The Manners and Customs of the Police* (1980); Bordua (ed.), *The Police: Six Sociological Essays* (1967); Mark, *Policing a Perplexed Society* (1977); and Reiss, *The Police and the Public* (1971).

two dozen administrative staff at an approximate cost of £¼million.[86] If a public authority is understaffed and underfinanced, then it will necessarily only be able to enforce or invoke the law on a limited number of occasions. For example, environmental health officers have argued that the effective supervision of the movement of meat intended for human consumption is virtually impossible given the present staffing levels within local authorities. Accordingly it is relatively easy for unscrupulous dealers to introduce unfit meat, thereby making a considerable profit, in contravention of the public health regulations.[87] For some offences effective rates of detection require a considerable allocation of resources, such as where there is a large number of contraventions as in shoplifting or speeding, or where a high level of technical or professional expertise is necessary as in monitoring chemical impurities in food and drugs, detecting the illegal use of broadcasting frequencies or determining whether a bookmaker has returned an accurate account of the bets placed with him. Behaviour may also be difficult to detect because it occurs in private, such as certain sexual offences or drug abuse. Some of the options available to enforcement agencies in these instances, such as "bugging" or the use of *agents provocateurs* may however be regarded as being at least unacceptably intrusive, if not legally impeachable.[88]

The success with which an authority implements the law may be evaluated essentially in one or both of two ways. First, it can be equated with the degree to which the purposes of the legislation are realised; in other words, whether the way in which the authority puts the legislation into practice makes it efficacious. But whether the authority is doing its job depends, as we have seen, on how that job, even in terms of the express or assumed purposes of the Act, is conceived. One police authority may equate success with a high rate of detection, another with a high arrest rate and yet another with good community relations. Similarly, an agency that is responsible

[86] Civil Service Department, *Legal Entitlements and Administrative Practices* (1979), para. 31 and Appendix 2.

[87] *The Guardian*, October 2, 1981.

[88] Detection will also be difficult where behaviour that is explicitly in compliance with the law is indistinguishable from non-compliance; for example, under The Upholstered Furniture (Safety) Regulations 1980 (S.I. 1980 No. 725), made under the Consumer Safety Act 1978, polyurethane foam-filled furniture must undergo cigarette and match tests to assess its propensity to catch fire. Furniture which fails the test must carry sewn-in warning labels, but if it passes, no labels are required. The problem for trading standards officers is that they are unable to tell from simple visual observation whether unlabelled furniture has passed the tests, or whether manufacturers or retailers are simply ignoring the regulations; see *The Sunday Times*, December 6, 1981.

for distributing benefits may equate success with client satisfaction, with a high rate of claim dispositions or with efforts to reach an optimum number of the eligible population.

Secondly, success may be evaluated in terms of allocative efficiency; that is, apart from what the authority conceives its job to be, whether there is an efficient balance between the costs and the results of implementation. Within a limited budget, the allocation of capital and manpower to the implementation of different aspects of the legislation, or to different ways of implementing the same provision is obviously of critical importance. A premium will be placed on routinised patterns of enforcement, on bureaucratic convenience, on the maintenance of agreements encouraging self-regulation or concerning the incidence of enforcement, and on selective enforcement. Sometimes these bureaucratic practices may either be marginally lawful, as in the case of plea-bargaining, or clearly unlawful, as in the case of corruption.

A critical factor in the implementation of legislation by public authorities is the role of the judiciary. In the first place, as we saw in Chapter 7, judicial reactions to an authority's interpretation will in many cases be the acid test of the lawfulness of its actions, and the judicial response to such practices as plea-bargaining or the use of informers and the evidence which they supply, can markedly facilitate or hinder enforcement. But judges also have a key role as the secondary enforcers of legislation, that is, applying the law finally and authoritatively to specific cases brought before them by the enforcement agencies. The judicial perception of the seriousness or importance of a case and of the principles upon which it is appropriate to decide it, and the nature of the decision, will in sum be important influences on the impact of the legislation. For example, in her analysis of the emergence and enforcement of food and drugs legislation, Paulus argues that the ill-informed and prejudiced interpretations held by nineteenth century magistrates frustrated the initial efforts of the primary law-enforcers, the inspectors and public analysts, to realise the law's purposes.[89] Similarly, Marx described how the overt hostility of many of these magistrates, themselves factory owners, frustrated the efforts of the Factory Inspectorate to enforce the legislation designed to curb the worst excesses of contemporary employers' practices.[90]

In addition to the application of statutory provisions to specific sets of facts, the judiciary obviously play a crucial part in influencing the impact of legislation through their enunciation of the principles

89 *The Search for Pure Food* (1974), p. 123.
90 Marx, *Capital* (1957), p. 296.

by which a statute is to be interpreted and implemented. This is exemplified by the interpretation by courts and tribunals of the employment provisions of the Sex Discrimination Act 1975, in particular by the Court of Appeal. The first case to reach this court, *Peake* v. *Automotive Products Ltd.*[91] in fact concerned an allegation by one of the defendant's male employees that the company's practice of allowing female employees to leave work five minutes early, so that they would not be jostled in the rush for the gates, constituted unlawful sexual discrimination against him. In deciding that there was no such discrimination, the Court of Appeal relied on three arguments: first, that "it would be very wrong if this statute were thought to obliterate the differences between men and women or to do away with the chivalry and courtesy which we expect mankind to give womankind;"[92] secondly, that the arrangements made "in the interests of safety or . . . of good administration," even if discriminatory were not unlawful[93]; and thirdly, that the discrimination was in any event harmless or trivial. It should be observed that the Court's reliance on gender-based classifications (chivalry and courtesy) were precisely what was being made unlawful; and that its understanding of the legislation was not that which the draftsman intended can be readily seen in his published reaction.[94] Subsequently, the Court of Appeal decided that the second of these three grounds "should no longer be relied upon," and that "the only sound ground was that the discrimination was de minimis."[95] The judgment that a complaint is trivial involves of course a judgment of the value of the injury being complained of, and as some commentators have noted,

> "a significant part of sex discrimination in practice does consist of trivialities: these however, can have a great symbolic importance, not least in terms of human dignity, and it could be argued that there should be some method of requiring the cessation of such practices."[96]

[91] [1977] 3 W.L.R. 853. The final appellate court in this context is the House of Lords, but no appeals have been heard there as yet.

[92] *Per* Lord Denning, *ibid.*, 856. His Lordship also remarked that "The natural differences of sex must be regarded even in the interpretation of an Act of Parliament," *ibid.;* the point of course is that chivalry and courtesy are not based upon natural differences of sex, but upon social conventions.

[93] *Ibid.*, 857.

[94] *The Times*, letters, July 15, 1977.

[95] *Ministry of Defence* v. *Jeremiah* [1979] 3 W.L.R. 857, 862, *per* Lord Denning M.R.

[96] Byrne and Lovenduski, "Sex Equality and the Law" (1975) 5 B.J.L.S. 148, 154.

Moreover, it may be argued that judges "should be hesitant to dismiss as of minimal importance a right otherwise guaranteed by Parliament."[97]

The impact of a statutory provision obviously depends upon what it says, and thus one precondition of the consequences that are brought about realising *in practice* what government's intentions are, is that the legislation should realise *in law* what its intentions are; and this in turn is dependent on how it is interpreted and applied by those responsible for its implementation.

[97] Pannick, "Sitting it out at El Vino" *The Guardian*, September 21, 1981. There are other important decisions of the Employment Appeal Tribunal concerning the interpretation and implementation of the Act; *e.g.*, *Oxford* v. *DHSS* [1977] I.L.R. 884 (burden of proof); *University of Reading* v. *MacCormack* [1978] I.R.C.R. 491 (discovery of documents); *Price* v. *Civil Service Commission* [1977] 1 W.L.R. 1417 (age limits) and *Skyrail Oceanic* v. *Coleman* [1980] I.L.R. 596 (dismissal). The decisions of industrial tribunals are also of importance to the implementation of the Act; see Byrne and Lovenduski, *ibid.*

Appendix

# THE INTERPRETATION OF LEGISLATION BILL 1981

BILL
Intituled

An Act to make provision for certain additional matters to be considered and principles to be applied in interpreting Acts of Parliament and other instruments. A.D. 1981

Be it enacted by the Queen's most Excellent Majesty, by and with the advice and consent of the Lords Spiritual and Temporal, and Commons, in this present Parliament assembled, and by the authority of the same, as follows:—

## Aids to interpretation

**1.**—(1) In ascertaining the meaning of any provision of an Act, the matters which may be considered shall, in addition to those which may be considered for that purpose apart from this section, include the following, that is to say—

(a) all indications provided by the Act as printed by authority, including cross-headings, punctuation and side-notes, and the short title of the Act;

(b) any relevant treaty or other international agreement which is referred to in the Act or of which copies had been presented to Parliament by command of Her Majesty before that time,[1] whether or not the United Kingdom were bound by it at that time;

(c) any relevant report of a Royal Commission, committee or other body which had been presented or made to or laid before Parliament or either House before the time the Act was passed[2];

(d) any provision of the European Communities Treaties and any Community instrument issued under any of the Treaties to which the Act is intended to give effect.

[1] The words "that time" were amended in Committee to read "the time when the Act was passed"; H.L.Deb., Vol. 418, ser. 5, col. 1341 (March 26, 1981).
[2] This clause was withdrawn in Committee; *ibid.*

(2) The weight to be given for the purposes of this section to any such matter as is mentioned in subsection (1) shall be no more than is appropriate in the circumstances.

(3) Nothing in this section shall be construed as authorising the consideration of reports of proceedings in Parliament for any purpose for which they could not be considered apart from this section.

### Principles of interpretation

**2.** The following shall be included among the principles to be applied in the interpretation of Acts where more than one construction of the provision in question is reasonably possible, namely—

(a) that a construction which would promote the general legislative purpose underlying the provision is to be preferred to a construction which would not; and

(b) that a construction which is consistent with the international obligations of Her Majesty's Government is to be preferred to a construction which is not; and

(c) that, in the absence of any express indication to the contrary, a construction which would exclude retrospective effect is to be preferred to a construction which would not.

### Application to subordinate legislation

**3.** Sections 1 and 2 above shall apply to Measures and with the necessary modifications to Orders in Council (whether made by virtue of any Act or by virtue of Her Majesty's prerogative) and to orders, rules, regulations and other legislative instruments made by virtue of any Act (whether passed before or after this Act), as they apply in relation to Acts.

### Citation and extent

**4.**—(1) This Act may be cited as the Interpretation of Legislation Act 1981.

(2) This Act shall extend to Scotland and Northern Ireland.

# INDEX OF BOOKS AND ARTICLES

# INDEX

[*See p. 247 for Index of Books and Articles.*]